Demystifying Big Data Analytics for Industries and Smart Societies

This book aims to provide readers with a comprehensive guide to the fundamentals of big data analytics and its applications in various industries and smart societies.

What sets this book apart is its in-depth coverage of different aspects of big data analytics, including machine learning algorithms, spatial data analytics, and Internet of Things (IoT)-based smart systems for precision agriculture. This book also delves into the use of big data analytics in healthcare, energy management, and agricultural development, among others. The authors have used clear and concise language, along with relevant examples and case studies, to help readers understand the complex concepts involved in big data analytics.

Key Features:

- Comprehensive coverage of the fundamentals of big data analytics.
- In-depth discussion of different aspects of big data analytics, including machine learning algorithms, spatial data analytics, and IoT-based smart systems.
- Practical examples and case studies to help readers understand complex concepts.
- Coverage of the use of big data analytics in various industries, including healthcare, energy management, and agriculture.
- Discussion of challenges and legal frameworks involved in big data analytics.
- Clear and concise language that is easy to understand.

This book is a valuable resource for business owners, data analysts, students, and anyone interested in the field of big data analytics. It provides readers with the tools they need to leverage the power of big data and make informed decisions that can help their organizations succeed. Whether you are new to the field or an experienced practitioner, *Demystifying Big Data Analytics for Industries and Smart Societies* is a must-read.

Demystifying Big Data Analytics for Industries and Smart Societies

Edited by
Keshav Kaushik
Mamta Dahiya
Ashutosh Dhar Dwivedi

CRC Press
Taylor & Francis Group
Boca Raton London New York

CRC Press is an imprint of the
Taylor & Francis Group, an **informa** business
A CHAPMAN & HALL BOOK

Designed cover image: © Shutterstock

First edition published 2024
by CRC Press
2385 NW Executive Center Drive, Suite 320, Boca Raton, FL 33431

and by CRC Press
4 Park Square, Milton Park, Abingdon, Oxon, OX14 4RN

CRC Press is an imprint of Taylor & Francis Group, LLC

Library of Congress Cataloging-in-Publication Data
Names: Kaushik, Keshav, editor. | Dahiya, Mamta, editor. | Dwivedi,
Ashutosh, 1988- editor.
Title: Demystifying big data analytics for industries and smart societies /
edited by Keshav Kaushik, Mamta Dahiya, Ashutosh Dhar Dwivedi.
Description: First edition. | Boca Raton, FL : CRC Press, 2024. |
Includes bibliographical references and index.
Identifiers: LCCN 2023011473 (print) | LCCN 2023011474 (ebook) |
ISBN 9781032361529 (hbk) | ISBN 9781032362304 (pbk) |
ISBN 9781003330875 (ebk)
Subjects: LCSH: Big data–Industrial applications. | Machine learning. |
Society 5.0.
Classification: LCC QA76.9.B45 D46 2024 (print) | LCC QA76.9.B45 (ebook) |
DDC 005.7–dc23/eng/20230519
LC record available at https://lccn.loc.gov/2023011473
LC ebook record available at https://lccn.loc.gov/2023011474

ISBN: 9781032361529 (hbk)
ISBN: 9781032362304 (pbk)
ISBN: 9781003330875 (ebk)

DOI: 10.1201/9781003330875

Typeset in Times
by codeMantra

Contents

Preface

In today's digital age, data has become the most valuable asset for businesses and societies. The increasing digitization of processes and the rise of the Internet of Things (IoT) have led to an exponential growth in the amount of data being generated. This data holds valuable insights that can help businesses make better decisions, optimize processes, and improve customer experiences. However, managing and analyzing this massive amount of data can be overwhelming, especially for those who are new to the field of big data analytics.

This book, *Demystifying Big Data Analytics for Industries and Smart Societies*, is a comprehensive guide that explains the fundamentals of big data analytics, and its applications in various industries and societies. This book is divided into several parts, each covering a specific aspect of big data analytics.

The first part of this book discusses the challenges faced by librarians in Nigeria in collecting big data for research purposes. It also explores the role of EDM and LA techniques in analyzing big data in the education system. The second part of this book focuses on spatial data analytics and its use in studying the pattern of water bodies over time. It also looks at the possibilities of their revival, using a case study of Sohna MC Water Bodies in Gurugram, India. The third part of this book delves into machine learning algorithms and their use in big data analytics. It discusses the various methods and tools used in sentiment analysis in big data and the open challenges involved. The fourth part of this book examines the use of big data analytics, Internet of Things (IoT), and biorobotics in the prevention of plant-related emerging disease distribution, monitoring, and management.

The fifth part of this book explores the use of big data analytics in the healthcare industry in India. It analyzes the utility, challenges, and legal framework involved. The sixth part of this book focuses on big data analytics in energy management, from energy generation to consumption. The seventh part of this book looks at the use of artificial intelligence (AI) at the edge for smart societies' applications with big data. It also discusses a power system load research tool for the energy supply industry, with data analytics and visualizations. The eighth part of this book examines data analytics in the context of agricultural development, including the international scenario and Indian potentialities. The final part of this book discusses IoT- and data analytics-based smart systems for precision agriculture. It provides practical examples and case studies to help readers understand the complex concepts involved in big data analytics.

Throughout this book, we have used clear and concise language, along with relevant examples and case studies, to help readers understand the complex concepts involved in big data analytics. Whether you are a business owner looking to leverage the power of big data, a data analyst looking to enhance your skills, or a student interested in the field of big data analytics, this book is an essential resource that will help you demystify the world of big data analytics, and its applications in industries and smart societies. We hope you find this book informative and useful, and we welcome your feedback and comments.

Editor Biographies

Keshav Kaushik is an experienced educator with over eight years of teaching and research experience in Cybersecurity, Digital Forensics, and the Internet of Things. He is working as an Assistant Professor (Senior Scale) in the systemic cluster under the School of Computer Science at the University of Petroleum and Energy Studies, Dehradun, India. He has published 80+ research papers in international journals and has presented at reputed international conferences. He is a Certified Ethical Hacker (CEH) v11, CQI and IRCA Certified ISO/IEC 27001:2013 Lead Auditor, Quick Heal Academy Certified Cyber Security Professional (QCSP), and IBM Cybersecurity Analyst. He acted as a keynote speaker and delivered 50+ professional talks on various national and international platforms. He has edited over ten books with reputed international publishers like Springer, Taylor and Francis, IGI Global, Bentham Science, etc. He has chaired various special sessions at international conferences and also served as a reviewer in peer-reviewed journals and conferences.

Prof (Dr.) Mamta Dahiya has over 21 years of experience in the academia, industry, and research. She is a Professor, Department of Computer Science & Engineering at Manav Rachna International Institute of Research & Studies, Faridabad, India. She was closely associated with research and development in the field of spatial data retrieval and related security. Building her research in Pattern Recognition, Data Science, and Information Security focusing on multiple aspects of societal problems, she has almost 85 research publications in various international and national journals of repute and conferences. She has multiple Indian and international patents granted and published. She chaired technical sessions in multiple conferences under the umbrella of Elsevier, IEEE, and TQP. She has completed multiple research projects funded by national and international agencies. She has recently completed the Consultancy on "Asian Metropolis" services to carry out the full process of research, analysis, and elaboration of the contents of the publication "Asian metropolitan report" with Metropolis, World Association of the Major Metropolises, Barcelona, Spain.

Dr. Ashutosh Dhar Dwivedi is a Postdoctoral Researcher in Cybersecurity Group, Aalborg University, Copenhagen, Denmark. His research field includes Machine Learning, Cryptography, Security, and Blockchain. He completed his PhD from the Polish Academy of Sciences, Poland in March 2020. He received the B.Sc. (Maths) degree from Ewing Christian College (an autonomous college of the University of Allahabad), Allahabad, India, and the MCA degree from the Amity School of Computer Sciences, Noida, India. Prior to joining Aalborg University, he worked as Postdoctoral Researcher at the Department of Digitalization, Copenhagen Business School, Denmark, DTU Compute (Cyber Security Section), Technical University of Denmark, full-time Visiting Researcher at the University of Waterloo, Ontario, Canada, Research Associate at the Brandon University, Manitoba, Canada, Research Employee and PhD at Polish Academy of Sciences, Warsaw, Poland, and Research Scholar at the Military University of Technology, Warsaw, Poland. He has a rich industry experience as well. He was an Intern (under his master's project) with the prestigious organization "Center for Railway Information Systems, New Delhi," governed by the Ministry of Railways, India. He was with organizations related to software development projects for two years. In 2015, he moved to Poland and started a career in cryptography research.

List of Contributors

Ahatsham Hayat
Indian Institute of Technology, India
(University of Madeira & ITI/Larsys/
    ARDITI, Funchal, Portugal)

C. O. Alabi
Federal University Lokoja,
Nigeria

Nitin Arora
Indian Institute of Technology
India

Latika Choudhary
School of Law
University of Petroleum & Energy
    Studies
Dehradun, India

Hardik Daga
School of Law
University of Petroleum & Energy
    Studies
Dehradun, India

Mamta Dahiya
MRIIRS
India

Armaan Dhanda
Department of Information Technology
Delhi Technological University
New Delhi, India

Amita Dhankhar
Maharshi Dayanand University,
    Department of Computer Science
India

Temitope C. Ekundayoc
Department of Biotechnology and Food
    Science
Durban University of Technology
Durban, Nigeria
and
Department of Biological Sciences
University of Medical Sciences
Ondo City, Nigeria

Shelly Garg
University of Petroleum & Energy
    Studies
India

Gökçen Bayram
Faculty of Engineering
Marmara University
Maltepe, Turkey

Bright E. Igere
Department of Microbiology and
    Biotechnology
Western Delta University
Oghara, Nigeria
and
Biotechnology and Emerging
    Environmental Infections Pathogens
    Research Group, Department of
    Microbiology and Biotechnology
Western Delta University
Oghara, Nigeria

Mercy A. Igere
Department of Library and Information
    Science
Delta State University
Abraka, Nigeria

Oluwatosin A. Ijabadeniyi
Department of Biotechnology and Food
    Science
Durban University of Technology
Durban, South Africa

S. Indu
Department of Electronics and
    Communication Engineering
Delhi Technological University
New Delhi, India

Uzezi E. Isiosio
Department of Biochemistry and Cell
    Biology
Western Delta University
Oghara, Nigeria

Anukriti Kumar
Department of Information Technology
Delhi Technological University
New Delhi, India

Rajesh Kumar
School of Law
University of Petroleum & Energy
    Studies
Dehradun, India

Khushpal
Department of Civil Engineering
SGT University
India

Er Merve
Faculty of Engineering, Department of
    Industrial Engineering
Marmara University
Maltepe, Turkey

Sangini Miharia
University of Petroleum & Energy
    Studies
India

Nidhi Mouje
Indian Institute of Technology
India

Anurag Mudgil
Department of Information Technology
Delhi Technological University
New Delhi, India

K. S. Sastry Musti
Namibia University of Science and
    Technology
Namibia

Julius Namwandi
Namibia University of Science and
    Technology, Windhoek
Namibia

Anvit Negi
Department of Electronics and
    Communication Engineering
Delhi Technological University
New Delhi, India

N. A. Oseji
Federal University
Nigeria

P. K. Paul
Department of CIS, Information
    Scientist (Offg.)
Raiganj University, Raiganj, India

S. Santhiya
Kongu Engineering College,
    Perundurai, Erode, Tamilnadu
India

Vivek Shahare
Indian Institute of Technology
India

M. Shalini
Kongu Engineering College,
Perundurai, Erode, Tamilnadu
India

C. Sharmila
Kongu Engineering College,
Perundurai, Erode, Tamilnadu
India

Kamna Solanki
Maharshi Dayanand University
Rohtak, India

Sudhanshu Srivastava
University of Petroleum & Energy
Studies
India

Surendrabikram Thapa
Department of Computer Science
Virginia Tech
Blacksburg, Virginia

1 Big Data Collection in Library for Research Purpose
Issues with Librarians in Nigeria

N A Oseji and C O Alabi
Federal University Lokoja, Nigeria

CONTENTS

1.1 INTRODUCTION

With the introduction of new cutting-edge technology as they become available, libraries and librarians will continue to thrive; this is simply because librarians have always functioned and played a pivotal role as information managers and organisers. Contemporary libraries provided wealth of information through the internet by inter-acting with the library catalogue (OPAC), granting access to electronic resources, accessing library database, and engaging in virtual reference and gaming activities. Librarians trained in searching, retrieving and analysing data are uniquely positioned to work with big data. Big data gives research a competitive edge, and librarians can make big data visible, accessible, and useable by creating systemic retrieval techniques and designing metadata. The library can evaluate data sets using big data methods to make them easy to understand, searchable and useful for researchers. The massive amount of data generated from sciences, private and public sectors, government, social sciences and daily activities birthed the concept of big data, thus creating a data-driven society. This development has ignited a new perspective of research in big data, by extension creating opportunities for the libraries. This chapter delves into the potential of big data and addresses the challenges faced by librarians in gathering and overseeing large datasets for research objectives.

1.2   CONCEPTUAL DEFINITIONS

1.2.1   LIBRARIES

The Latin word "Liber," which means "book," is where the word "library" first appeared. Achebe [1] describes a library in accordance with this as a collection of books and non-book items that are kept, arranged and interpreted to satisfy people's need for information, knowledge, recreation, aesthetics, research and enjoyment. Hence, irrespective of types, libraries are regarded as collective memory of the society, and it comprises all the thoughts and wisdom of man, and has the ability to communicate in time and space. Big data management and organisation involve the library as a partner. It can offer a range of services and a repository to aid researchers at all stages of the lifetime of research data, including planning, development, organisation, sharing and preservation. The core of the library is the management of information resources from various sources in different types and formats to satisfy the varying needs of users. Okube et al. [2] noted that the provision of continuous access to the right information to every individual, households, community and state to enable them make informed decision is the utmost responsibility of libraries and librarians. Libraries through information services have provided opportunity for the users to interact and share ideas with others, and foster a sense of belongingness to the community.

   In order to facilitate the creation, organisation, and sharing of big data contents through seamless collaboration between researchers and the librarians, libraries are currently engaged in big data collections and deploying emerging technologies like the semantic web, cloud computing, mobile devices and established tools like federated search systems, which are such appealing and inspiring services to the patrons. For libraries to use big data, librarians will need to be familiar with integrated software tools that can be used to repackage library services to better serve her patrons.

1.2.1.1   Librarians

The search, selection, acquisition, organisation, preservation, repackaging and dissemination of information are the areas in which librarians receive specialised training. Thus, one of the most important tasks performed by librarians is information management as a foundation for further specialised work. The position of gatekeeper is given to librarians by information management. They have good relationships with both internal and external clients as formal gatekeepers, and they are able to translate organisational information across different fields of expertise [3]. Librarians are expected to **collect** data from a variety of sources, which can be in form of semi-structured, unstructured data and structured data, and harmonised for research purposes. This will facilitate access to relevant information resource for research [4]. It is observed that scholars from various fields are progressively embracing big data analysis in their research and educational practices. Engaging in research data services will give the libraries in Nigeria new faces.

By supporting researchers in conceptualising how data is searched, libraries can act as a research resource and support them as they advance their data analytics skills (e.g., by utilising various search keywords to achieve the most efficient result). For the organisation of big data and data mining processes, librarians' expertise in database design and development may be useful [5].

1.2.2 RESEARCH

Research is characterised as human activity focused on intellectual application in the investigation of matter with the goal of gaining new information to address the primary issue. The main goal of research is to advance human knowledge on a wide range of scientific topics related to our world and the universe by discovering, interpreting, and developing new methods, theories, and systems [5,6]. Research is a scientific way of finding solutions to problems, improving a worrisome or unacceptable state of affairs, and generating knowledge in order to have more information on a given phenomenon through data collection and data analysis.

It is a process of rigorous, systematic, validating, verifiable, empirical, critical, analysing and interpreting data to answer questions. Research occupies a critical position in promoting the prosperity of a nation and its citizens' well-being [5,6]. Research is essential for evidence-based decision making and for economic development. Al-Barashdi and Al-Karousi [7] posit that big data can be used as information resource in research and when analysed, used for decision making. To further enhance quality research for effective decision making, the library is in charge of offering a network of services called the Research Data Service, which helps users at every stage of the research data lifecycle. Recent years have seen a rise in the use of big data as a significant resource for study, notably due to its usage in educational analysis and data-driven decision making.

1.2.3 BIG DATA

Data literarily means raw facts that can be structured, unstructured or semi-structured. Data must be collected, organised and processed with various tools for it to have any significant use and application in any area of endeavour, specifically for libraries that are the hub of information centres that provide resources for research advancement toward national and economic development. In the field of information technology and computer science, data is primarily understood as the amounts, characters or symbols on which a computer performs operations. Data is also stored and transmitted in electrical machines, like signals and waves, and recorded on magnetic, optical or mechanical recording media for dissemination and use in resolving human puzzles. The idea of big data refers to an accumulation of data gathered from numerous areas.

The term "Big Data," which stands for volume, variety and velocity, was coined as a result of the Internet's impact on the amount of organised, semi-structured and unstructured data. To process large amounts of data with a wide variety (text, number, audio, video, etc.), generated at a fast velocity, specialised tools and systems are needed. Big data is a term used to describe an enormous amount of structured and unstructured data that cannot be managed using conventional database and hardware/software solutions. Due to the amount, pace, diversity, validity and range of data that must be processed in order to obtain produce useful information and visualisation, it can be said that there is an information overload [8]. In the words of Mayer-Schonberg and Cukier [9], big data is the capacity to quickly evaluate enormous amounts of information and come to sometimes astounding conclusions. As the name implies, big data can be extremely large, but its size is less significant than what we can do with it. Big data is extremely large and can only be quantified in terabytes, petabytes, exabytes or zettabytes, rather than megabytes or gigabytes. Jim [10] emphasised that big data is made up of expensive, high-velocity, high-variety and high-volume information that may be leveraged for innovation to improve perception and decision making. Big data is all about making predictions; it can be used to diagnose illnesses, suggest therapies and even catch criminals in the act. Big data is being used by certain companies to track client's buying preferences in order to provide highly targeted offers that boost sales while fostering customer loyalty. Petabytes of data in a variety of file formats, media types and licence conditions make up big data. It also includes processed and interpreted data as well as raw data.

Big data analytics is a challenging process that involves sifting through large amounts of data to find information that might assist businesses in making wise decisions about their operations, such as hidden patterns, correlations, market trends and customer preferences. In order to find relevant information, provide recommendations and aid in decision making, it involves evaluating, cleaning, transforming and modelling data. This is sometimes referred to as "business analytics," and it is widely utilised in many industries to enable businesses and organisations to employ the science of analysing raw data with the aim of coming to informed judgements and bettering their operations.

1.3 CHARACTERISTICS OF BIG DATA

Olendorf and Wang [11] initially stated that big data has three dimensions, also known as three V's (**V**olume, **V**elocity and **V**ariety). Later, with Value as a lower entry, Veracity/Validity became an important attribute of big data [11–13]. Big data also includes variation and visualisation as extra qualities. Below are the general characteristics of big data:

1. **Volume:** Every human action, speech and conservation create more data, resulting in overwhelming amount of data, which is made possible with

the application of Internet of Things. With ever-increasing user base and increased demand, evaluating and forecasting of extra attention is needed while dealing with this much information.

2. **Velocity:** Is the rate at which data is analysed and made accessible. More rapid than real-time information transfer is made possible by big data.

3. **Variety:** A wide range of data obtained from various sources in various kinds and formats. With libraries servicing a varied population with a variety of disciplines and interdisciplinary study, researchers' needs are also expanding.

4. **Veracity:** Authentic, trustworthy and accurate information to lessen ambiguity and discrepancies.

5. **Value:** Giving users the tools and confidence they need to transform information into something worthwhile.

6. **Variability:** It is distinct from variety; data homogenisation is significantly impacted by changes in meaning, value, validity and presentation across time that occur in a same big data file.

7. **Visualisation:** The right visualisation is essential for understanding vast amounts of information.

Spreadsheets and reports perform far worse than charts and graphs at conveying meaning when displaying large amounts of complex data.

1.4 RELEVANCE OF BIG DATA IN RESEARCH

It is relevant to all disciplines, sectors and organisations, and can be used in various research areas. Big data's importance can be used by various businesses, organisations and establishments to their advantage, particularly in the fields of data management, curation and archiving, as well as information search and retrieval [14]. Research provided additional evidence that since 2012, each industry has been fascinated by the purportedly recent discovery of big data and its exceptional potential to spark analytic discoveries.

In order to make precise and informed decisions, big data is used to examine a large amount of data. It offers answers to a number of crucial queries on the patterns, trends and connections of user behaviour.

It aids libraries in understanding the changing needs of their users accurately, and reshaping and restructuring their services and procedures as a result. Although a good data processing tool and data storage are needed to handle the enormous volume of data, it also combines the answers to many worthwhile queries [11]. It improves the services in organisational level [13]. The use of big data for research data services may be advantageous for libraries. Since researchers might not have the skills or resources needed to maintain the data during their projects, libraries have traditionally served as the repository for society's academic and research output. These services now include big data analytics. Currently, many libraries offer research data services including collecting data, curating data, planning data management and conserving data.

1.5   STEPS TO INTRODUCE BIG DATA IN LIBRARIES

Big data analytics is influenced by two major issues. Firstly, the issue of massive volume of information, its management and exponential growth overwhelmed the traditional management, processing and storage system. Secondly, the complexity and extensiveness of analytical methods and tools used to analyse the big data. [7]. A way of solving these challenges is for the library to go through the steps listed below before big data can function successfully in the library.

1. **Identify the framework:** Clear-cut understanding of the framework through in-depth study of the big data characteristics (7 V's framework, which includes Volume, Velocity, Variety, Veracity, Value, Variability and Visualisation) guides the library to know the area for implementation of big data in the library environment.
2. **Need analysis:** Big data can be used by libraries to enhance their holdings, make better use of their space, evaluate their instruction, give information to their patrons and provide services in the field of research data. The implementation of big data in libraries will be prompted by an understanding of these potential advantages and the current requirements of the users. It is necessary for libraries to estimate the cost of the implementation and identify the resources library already have that fit well with it before introducing big data into library services. Needs analysis is very important to consider the necessary infrastructures and staff strength that must be put in place to enhance effective implementation of big data services in the library.
3. **Solutions identification:** Having conducted need analysis and have identified the essential needs, libraries need to find solutions to fill the gap between the availability and the minimum requirement to implement big data analytics. Libraries should focus their attention on data stores that can assess how sufficient a particular dataset is for a given project, such as CSV or excel files, SQL databases, or document-based databases like Mongo DB or Hadoop. In order to provide a low-level interface to the data, libraries are required to provide an administrative layer, policies of use and access, analysis and visualisation, and query access.
4. **Implementation:** Final implementation is completed after due consideration of the above requirements, and in case of any insufficiency, the library has the option of collaborating with other institutional departments such as Management Information System (MIS) ICT or high-performance computing, advanced cyber infrastructure or similar units.

1.6   BIG DATA COLLECTIONS IN THE LIBRARY

It is increasingly essential for libraries to grasp the necessity for and significance of using big data in their operations, and to have a basic understanding of how to use such specialised tools. Due to the complexity of big data analytical tools and the overwhelming nature of big data, librarians planning to build big data collection must be familiar with the specifics of data techniques, as well as understanding the data structure and the possible advantages and existing needs of their users. Data structure is a way to store and organise data to facilitate access and medications.

The creation of collections and the preservation of data sets are two ways that librarians might participate in big data. Researchers will require direction and resources, as they develop an interest in working with big data. They are in the best position to guide researchers in learning where and how to find these data sets, as well as to conserve them for use by others in the future. The creation of Worldcat by OCLC and the automation of library circulation systems can be regarded as the first big data applications in libraries. Anil [15], they merely need to shift their attention to fresh problems and demands. The ability to conceptualise links between data is a skill that librarians with experience in cataloguing and metadata generation possess. In order to make it simpler to gather, organise and protect the data that will be generated, they can therefore be the best people to advise researchers on the data management techniques to be used from the outset of a research project. A frequently provided service by academic libraries is assistance in Data Management Plans (DMPs). Even though the collection of big data would seem to be outside the purview of typical library services, there are still two ways that libraries might help scholars. To start, some libraries may already have access to popular big data sources, such as social media feeds, or they may choose to purchase commercially available big data sources and treat them as if they were a part of their library collection. Second, compiling and utilising big data can use a lot of processing resources. Libraries can build synergies with other departments, performing computing, to offer computational support as well as the technical infrastructure needed to handle big data. Here, the library's main responsibility may be to see to it that the information gathered is well-documented and arranged, so that it may be archived afterwards.

Quality assurance (QA) is mandatory to validate the acceptance of the collected data for the research. After assuring the quality of the collected data, it is analysed with the help of relevant tools and techniques to organise, classify and summarise the data being collected for better comprehension and interpretation, leading to understanding and exploring answers or solutions to the research problem that originally triggered the research. The researcher is often in charge of data integration, analysis and quality assurance (QA). However, there might be some obligations for librarians to assure quality on the data and give sufficient assistance for researchers to conduct their own QA procedures when they are providing data as part of their collection. Collaborating with researchers to identify pertinent valuable datasets is a beneficial task for librarians engaged in research data support. As information scientists, librarians should be knowledgeable about methods for quickly gathering, storing and processing data in addition to knowing where to find datasets.

The handling of research data has changed in the twenty-first century. The idea of big data, which was brought about by the pervasiveness and data power of computation and networks, is starting to supplant conventional methods of data storage and management, forcing libraries to reframe their position in the ecosystem of digital scholarly communication. It has become a necessity given the shortage of data scientists that businesses of all sizes find ways to pool their big data skills in order to improve their services.

However, libraries have a significant edge when it comes to any applications for big data analytics, since they are familiar with the ontology work involved in developing the metadata that powers those applications. Libraries can take the advantage of big data to facilitate various library operations for users' benefit, such as data repository, metadata services, cloud-based library services, etc. For instance, the library at Purdue University worked with the IT research department to build a data repository called the Purdue University Research Repository, which was at the vanguard of data teaching and reference while also guiding metadata standards. The cloud-based library services platform Alma from Ex Libris, which is tackling the difficulties that have evolved from the dramatically increased academic research and scholarly communication, has also been heavily embraced by Boston University Libraries.

By developing metadata schemes and taxonomies as well as providing common retrieval techniques, librarians can increase the visibility, usability and accessibility of massive data collections. Since the beginning of time, librarians have dealt with information sources; one can examine data in various ways with the aid of new big data analysis tools. Tools for information visualisation make it possible to mine raw data for new information that isn't related to the original usage of the data.

1.7 BIG DATA TOOLS AND USAGE

For effective data service in library operations, big data tools are a necessity. Computer Business Review [16] has made available a list of the most popular big data tools, which include:

1. **Cambridge semantics:** This is an open platform that helps librarians to collect, integrate and analyse big data using Anzo Software Suite to build Unified Access solutions. This software has a data integration machine that streamlines data collection and assists with analytics. It also has the ability to combine data from multiple sources and customised dashboards for easy analysis.
2. **Splice machine:** For individuals hoping to advance quickly, this real-time SQL-on-Hadoop database assists libraries in obtaining real-time actionable information. It can scale from gigabytes to petabytes and complies with ANSI and SQL 99 standards. It offers support for programs written in JavaScript, Python, Java and .NET.
3. **MarkLogic:** It is a veritable instrument in the hands of librarians that deals with heavy data loads, and allows users to access it through real-time updates and alerts. It provides geographical data that is combined with content and location relevance along with data filtering tools.
4. **Google charts:** It enables librarians to seek and connect to database or pull data from websites. It is free and comes with diverse proficiencies for visualising data from a website such as hierarchical tree maps or simple charts. It works well with Java Script code and also offers support for popular languages, knowing that Google will likely keep on improving its offering.

5. **SAP in memory:** SAP's HANA platform has the ability to integrate and analyse large workloads of data to be analysed in real time. This has immense benefit for librarians whose interest is to harmonise information sources from various sites in order to provide maximum satisfaction to their users through quick access to the organised information resources.

6. **MongoDB:** For librarians who are interested in having precise control over the final big data results, this open-source documental database is perfect. Additionally scalable, MongoDB offers third-party log tools like Edda and Fluentd.

7. **Pentaho:** This combines data integration and business analytics for visualisation, analytics and blending of big data. It is an open platform with extensive analytics capabilities in data mining and predictive analysis. The data integration tools mean that users do not require becoming programmers before getting the available information.

8. **Talend:** Open Studio from Talend is a free software that includes tools for creating, testing and implementing data management and application integration products.

9. **Tableau:** Tableau is useful for data visualisation, and its in-memory analytics database and powerful query language are its standout features. It works with a variety of browsers and supports API, XML, User Scripts, Python and JavaScript.

10. **Splunk:** This tool specialises in utilising machine data that is generated from numerous sources, including websites, applications and sensors. Developers can use any technology platform, language or framework to write codes.

11. **Hadoop:** Hadoop is an open-source software developed by Apache Software Foundation. It is written in Java language. It has Apache License 2.0. The apache Hadoop project develops open-source software for reliable, scalable, distributed computing. The apache Hadoop software library is a frame work that allows for the distributed processing of large data sets across clusters of computers using simple programming models. It is designed to scale up from single services to thousands of machines, each offering local computation and storage.

1.8 CHALLENGES OF BIG DATA COLLECTIONS IN THE LIBRARY

Data processing is necessary to turn gathered data into more relevant information that can be used, and is often carried out by a data analyst or group of data scientists [17]. In order to use such specialised tools for information organisation, librarians must be fully aware of the need and significance of big data in libraries as well as the fundamentals of how to use them. Considering the complexity and extensiveness of the analytical methods and tools of big data [7], training and retraining is needed.

Libraries have been impacted by big data analytics in two ways. First, the system's storage and processing requirements are quite demanding because of the enormous amount, variety and speed of the knowledge in question. big data analytics requires a lot of computer power due to the complexity of the analytics methods and algorithms. The underlying issue is that even after finding such big data analytics resources, it takes time to make sense of all the data [18].

Big data enables the creation of intricate visualisations that reveal patterns and trends in human interaction and behaviour. Big data can also exaggerate and skew valid patterns, making them seem more significant than they actually are.

Based on the abundance of data on the Internet and World Wide Web (www), librarians worldwide are beginning to face challenges handling massive data sets, handling real-time information, processing and moving information that was previously in the university's domain or library's community server to known and unknown servers.

The topic of knowledge, along with data storage, analysis and sharing, is another difficulty that the librarians are facing at the moment. Furthermore, huge data storage and analysis require both physical and digital infrastructures [19].

In summary, the challenges associated with big data are as follows:

- **Errors in analysis and prediction:** When people are unable to comprehend the analysis and there are mistakes in the data's interpretation, big data faces significant challenges. Users should be able to comprehend why they are seeing certain results in addition to the findings themselves.
- **Volume and transfer speed:** It is difficult to deal with the sheer volume and transfer speed of enormous volumes of data. Big data is enormous, and the transfer rate did not keep up with it.
- **More robust processing power:** There are larger processors available but not as large as the volume of data that they need to process. Trying to compress huge volumes of data and then analyse it is a tedious process which might ultimately prove to be ineffective.
- **Speed of data transfer rate:** Because requests can be made at a limitless pace, but the transfer rate is constrained, it is difficult to stream data in real time.
- **Relevancy and redundancy:** Data are received by big data systems in a variety of unsorted formats. It is difficult to sort through these massive amounts of data files for relevance and "readability," analyse the information and come to wise decisions.
- **Data privacy and security:** Amidst the numerous promises inherent in the big data revolution, the problem of privacy and data ownership is of great concern. Big data raises serious issues with regard to data security and privacy. People who must give their personal information experience significant anxiety and reluctance, especially when data from various sources are linked together.
- **Inadequate infrastructure:** Before big data can truly be used as a tool in the library profession, infrastructure issues must be fixed. Big data entails large amounts of physical and digital information.

1.9   ISSUES WITH LIBRARIANS ON COLLECTION OF BIG DATA IN LIBRARIES

Issue of awareness: Most librarians, especially in developing countries, are yet to notice the big data revolution of our time; thus, they are not aware of the changes brought about by data science. They do not comprehend the potential of big data in the field of libraries and information.

Limited expertise: When it comes to data science, there is an unfortunate talent divide. Even though it can be frustrating, it shouldn't come as much of a surprise, given that data science calls for a desirable and adaptable skill set. Most libraries in developing economies have few technical staff for the deployment of big data tools. Hence, inadequately trained librarians pose a serious challenge to the effective deployment of big data in libraries.

Lack of documented big data collection policy: Successful deployment of big data is dependent on the availability of well-documented policy, which will determine the procedures, facilities specifications, personnel, training, etc.

Issues with inadequate funding: In the midst of poor budget allocation to libraries irrespective of various types especially in developing countries, it will be difficult for librarians to successfully implement and sustain big data, because it is a capital-intensive project.

Issues with training opportunities: Availability of training opportunities in the area of machine learning seems to be scarce in developing economies like Nigeria. This is due to lack of experts in such area. Only few librarians could afford to travel abroad to update their skills.

Technophobia: Most of the librarians do not have any computer education background; hence, they are afraid of deploying the available big data analytics tools having heard of their complexities. In this age of vast amounts of data, often measured in petabytes, data has emerged as the invaluable resource akin to oil. Just as oil has been a driving force in various industries, data now holds immense potential to revolutionize the way we operate and make informed decisions. Therefore, it is imperative to prioritize and invest significant attention in harnessing the power of data, as it has the capability to shape our future and drive innovation across diverse domains.

1.10   AMELIORATING BIG DATA CHALLENGES IN LIBRARIES

Gazetted big data policy: As a starting point, there is a need to deliberately articulate a policy to integrate big data analytics into the mainstream of librarianship in Nigeria.

Funding: Successful adoption of big data analytics in libraries is capital intensive; thus, librarian, professional bodies, library schools and government should contribute their quota to see that the required infrastructures and personnel are put in place.

Training: Following the trends in machine learning, librarians in Nigeria should make every effort both personal and collaborative to become data scientists in combination with their conventional library skill.

Finding skilled workers: Wherever possible, libraries should look for talent, as opposed to cutting corners and hiring unskilled workers. They should think about working with companies that have a good track record and partnering with smart people that can.

1.11   CONCLUSION

We live in a 'petabytes and zetabytes age', when data is generated and transferred in a very high speed rate. It is finding application in various areas, majorly where information is the only commodity for exchange. Librarians are expected to keep abreast with the trends, especially in data science, work closely with other informa-tion providers, build synergies and improve performance with the available big data analytically tools. Introducing big data into the library for research purpose has both opportunities and challenges. Librarians need to understand types of scientific data, characteristics of big data, potentials of big data, big data analytical tools so as to contribute meaningfully to its storage, use and reuse. Big data has great potential for libraries and librarians but requires combination of competencies that harness their services resulting to innovation and invention.

REFERENCES

1. Achebe, N. E. Concept of library. In N. Achebe (ed.), *Library and information for higher education* (pp. 1–5). Enugu: The Nigeria Library Association, 2008.
2. Okube, N. O., Nneka, A. S, Job, O. & Abdulmalik, M. *Leveraging on library and infor-mation services for enhancing food security in Nigeria in the era of crisis.* Ayingba: Kogi State University, 2021.
3. Achor, P. N. Assessing the impact of ICT education and knowledge on public relation mangers in their information management functions, PhD seminar paper presented to department of marketing, University of Nigeria, Enugu campus, 2011.
4. Gbaje E. S., Yani S. D., and Odigie I. O. Digital scholarship practices in Nigeria univer-sity libraries. In A. O. Issa, A. A. Salman, T. K. Omopupa, L. Kayode Mustapha, and S. Agboola Olarongbe (eds.), *Management of library and information centres in the era of global insecurity.* 2020. Tim-sal & Bim publishing Ltd.
5. DDS. The importance of libraries (and librarians) to the data science movement. https://www.discoverdatascience.org/resources/data-science-andlibrarians/#:~:text= Libraries%20can%20support%20data%20scientis, 2021.
6. Inuwa, I. I. Concept of research methodology in academic research report writing. *A Paper Presented at a Research Seminar Organized by Research Committee.* Bauchi, Nigeria: Federal Polytechnic, 2016.
7. Al-Barashdi, H., & Al-Karousi, R. Big Data in academic libraries: Literature review and future research directions. *Journal of Information Studies & Technology (JIS&T)*, 2 (2019): 1–16.
8. Panda, S. Usefulness and impact of big data in libraries: An opportunity to implement embedded librarianship. In *Technological innovations and environmental changes in modern libraries* (pp. 45–60). (2021). Delhi: Shree Publishers & Distributors.
9. Mayer-Schonberg, V., and Cukier, K. *Big data: A revolution that will transform how we live, work and think.* Boston: Houghton-Mifflin Harcourt, 2013.
10. Jim, L. Analytics and big data for accountants. In *What are big data and analytics?* (pp. 1-1-1-13). 2018. John Wiley & Sons, Ltd. https://doi.org/10.1002/9781119512356.ch1

11. Olendorf, R., & Wang, Y. Big data in libraries. In S. C. Suh & T. Anthony (Eds.), *Big data and visual analytics* (pp. 191–202). Springer International Publishing, 2017.
12. Jain, A. *The 5 V's of Big Data.* Watson Health Perspectives, 2016. https://www.ibm.com/blogs/watson-health/the-5-vs-of-big-data
13. Kiran, R. *What Are the Characteristics of Big Data? 5V's, Types, Benefits,* 2019. https://www.edureka.co/blog/big-data-characteristics/
14. Reinhalter, L. & Wittmann, R. J. The library: Big data's boomtown. *Serials Librarian* 67, No. 4 (2014): 363–372.
15. Anil, K. J. *Big data technology: Big opportunity for librarians.* Delhi, India: Tecnia Institute of Advanced Studies, GGSIP University. 2019.
16. CBR. *Ten of the most popular big data tools for developers.* Retrieved 07/07/2022, from http://www.cbronline.com/news/bigdata/analytics/10-of-the-most-popular-big-data-tools-for-developers-4570483, 2015.
17. Pearlman, S. *What is data processing? Definition and stages.* Talend Cloud Integration, 2018. https://www.talend.com/resources/what-is-data-processing/
18. Sengupta, S. Big data: The next big opportunity for librarians. *International Conference on Contemporary Innovations in Library Information Science, Social Science & Technology for Virtual World,* (2016). pp. 89–91.
19. Hodonu-Wusu, J. O., Lazarus, N. G. Otun, M. O. Arekemase, O. B. & Olayiwola, T.T. Big data and openness: a big issue with librarians. *Library Philosophy and Practice,* 4279 (2020).

2 Role of EDM and LA Techniques in Analyzing Big Data in Education System

Amita Dhankhar and Kamna Solanki
Maharshi Dayanand University, Department
of Computer Science, India
Maharshi Dayanand University, Rohtak, India

CONTENTS

Big data has been more accessible in the recent years, opening up new possibilities for monitoring, interpreting, and assessing educational processes. This has helped to inform decision making and efforts to increase educational efficiency. The recent technological advancement is the main root cause of the generation of tremendous amounts of big data generation in the educational sector. The widespread use of digital instruments in daily life generates an extraordinary amount of data (volume), at an increasing speed (velocity), and from various modalities and time ranges, compared to past generations of data obtained by significant human effort (variety). Thus, this big data requires considerable computing resources and alternative analytical methodologies to process and interpret. Over the past few years, higher education institutes are facing two major challenges, namely, enormous generation of big data in the field of education along with the exploration and analysis of this enormous amount of educational data so that significant patterns, useful information, and relationship can be discovered for the educational use and decision making. The biggest challenge for educational institutes is how to transform an enormous amount of potential data collected from multiple sources into information that can help learners, educators, course designers, and administrators in multiple ways.

DOI: 10.1201/9781003330875-2

The advancement of technology has greatly affected the world of higher education. Online and blended learning is changing the way of learning and teaching. At all educational levels, emerging technologies like interactive learning environments, learning management systems (LMS), student information systems (SIS), intelligent tutoring systems, and online learning enable access to enormous amounts of student data. This diversity leads to heterogeneous and multimodal student data generation in large volumes. Automatically gathered student information from online learning environments is typically not turned into relevant teaching information. It is challenging to handle this enormous educational data and extract the knowledge embedded in it. Also, the main concern of higher education institutes and educators is to predict the student's performance with high accuracy and to identify the factors that influence student performance. Efficient analysis of this big data may help administrators to take organizational decisions for enhanced teaching and learning. This chapter attempts to analyze the role of EDM and LA in analyzing big data in the education system.

2.1 INTRODUCTION

With the latest upcoming technologies every day, it becomes technically feasible to extract knowledge and hidden patterns through the application of data mining and learning analytics (Dietz-Uhler and Hurn, 2013). In the last couple of years, the analysis of student performance becomes one of the most significant topics in the field of Educational Data Mining (EDM) and Learning Analytics (LA). Educational institutions are using EDM and LA approaches to forecast student performance, which enables instructors and decision-makers to monitor individual students, detect students at risk, and take prompt corrective action. Researchers have used EDM and LA to forecast students' performance, engagements, or likelihood of dropping out or retention during the past few years (Ferguson, 2012). The study of forecasting models that can properly and effectively anticipate student's performance is motivated by the significance that the prediction of students' performance plays an important role in the field of education today. The greatest challenge faced by educational institutes lies in harnessing the vast amount of potential data gathered from various sources and effectively transforming it into actionable information that can benefit learners, educators, administrators, and course designers. To address this challenging task, there is a field of research that is devoted to analyzing educational data, namely, Academic Analysis (AA), Learning Analytics (LA), and Educational Data Mining (EDM). Even though AA, LA, and EDM share the common interest of enhancing the educational process, these three fields focus on different stakeholders in the education system. Figure 2.1a and b shows the educational data analysis and their stakeholders (Adejo and Connolly, 2017).

2.2 EDUCATIONAL DATA MINING (EDM) AND LEARNING ANALYTICS (LA)

The multidisciplinary and rapidly growing subject of educational data mining (EDM) has seen increasing interest over the past few years. This interest is sparked

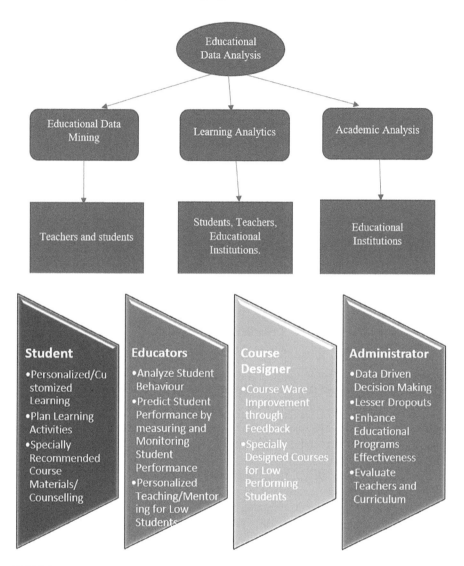

FIGURE 2.1 (a) Educational Data Analysis and Stakeholders (Adejo and Connolly, 2017); (b) Big data scopes for four Stakeholders in higher education (Romero and Ventura, 2013).

by digitalization and the swift technological progress that makes a vast amount of educational data available. The first conference on EDM was organized in 2008 in Montreal, Canada by the International Educational Data Mining Society. Data mining techniques applied to educational data are known as EDM. EDM has been defined by Romero et al. (2010) as 'developing, researching, and computerized techniques to identify patterns in a huge gathering of academic data that would not be possible to explore because of massive data in which they exist'. The goal of EDM is to adapt and develop data mining methods, machine learning, and statistics to analyze educational data generated by teachers and students. Romero has given four

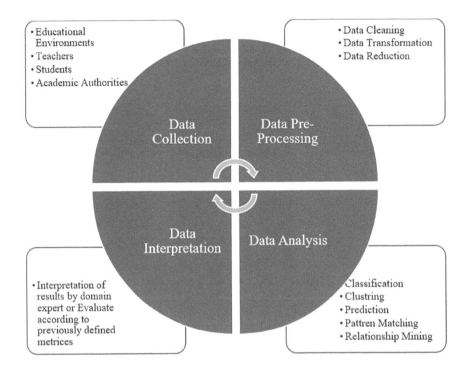

FIGURE 2.2   Educational Data Mining Process (Romero et al., 2008).

main steps for the EDM process, namely, data collection, data preprocessing, data analysis, and data interpretation (Romero et al., 2008). Figure 2.2 shows the stepwise EDM process.

First and foremost, define the educational problem that needs to be resolved; then accordingly data collection can be performed from different educational environments (blended education, computer-based, traditional classroom) and information systems, namely, MOOC, LMS, and ITS. The preprocessing of data is needed as it may be collected in different formats from multiple sources and different levels of hierarchy (Romero et al., 2014). Afterward, data analysis is performed using different methods and techniques such as classification, clustering, prediction, relationship mining, and pattern matching. Once the data analysis has been completed, data interpretation is performed by stakeholders to make decisions and interventions to enhance students' learning process. Romero and Ventura (2013) discussed applications of EDM, namely, student's performance prediction for providing feedback, personalization, and recommendations to students for providing alerts to stakeholders.

2.2.1 Educational Data Mining (EDM)

The use of data mining (DM) in the educational domain is known as EDM, which emphasizes mining patterns and recognizing beneficial information from the learning data systems, like registration, course management, admission, and other systems working with learners at various learning levels from schools to colleges and universities (Saa, 2016).

- **The basic concept of EDM:** The main motive of extracting useful knowledge is to provide help to educational organizations in managing their students in a better way, and to help students in managing their education and achievements, which improves their performance. Estimating students' data for categorizing students for building better results or for enhancing the performance of students is an interesting domain of research that uses students' educational information, which shows their educational performance and identifies poorly performing students thereby helping teachers to intervene timely. Such a study aims to recognize the associations between students' personal and social aspects and their educational presentation. Such information is useful for students and instructors in executing educational quality by discovering at-risk students. It is useful in paying more attention to these students for helping them in their academic processes and attaining good marks. Apart from the underperforming students, the students who perform well can also be benefited and put more effort into conducting enhanced projects and research with the help and assistance of their teachers.
- **Process of EDM:** EDM is a growing domain. An enormous amount of data produced in Educational Systems (ESs) can be used for making decisions that could help stakeholders at all levels of the educational system. This process works on creating methods for evaluating different kinds of information in an educational environment and examining the students and the environment in which they study by utilizing such methods (Anjum and Badugu, 2020). The transformation of raw information from educational institutes into useful data can be utilized by teachers, researchers, management, etc. The information should either be made accessible by public warehouses or can be created in an educational environment. This information is used for executing the following three phases:
  - **Preprocessing:** In this stage, the information from the ES is preprocessed and converted to the desired format so that the data mining methods could be implemented. Several preprocessing methods include noise reduction, information cleaning, choosing attributes, etc.
  - **Data mining:** The next stage in the education data mining procedure is an intermediate phase in which the DM methods are developed for the preprocessed information. The use of grouping, analysis, visualization, regression, classification, and other data mining techniques is widespread.
  - **Post-processing:** This is the last stage in which the outputs collected are explained and utilized for decision making concerning the educational environment. Once these phases are executed, the model is created and could be utilized in the educational environment to enhance the performance of the students and help teachers to better understand their students.

2.2.2 LEARNING ANALYTICS (LA)

The use of information for predicting the performance of students, and for teachers and management to make decisions regarding educational policies, is the state of the art. Businesses have been utilizing smart methods and designs for predicting patterns and trends. In schools, colleges, and universities, the term LA is widely utilized in predictive analysis (Javidi et al., 2017). LA empowers educational organizations for better usage of resources and to handle student results by identifying unknown patterns in huge datasets. It could help educational institutes in developing analytical prototypes that can address problems like recruitment, retention, and attrition. This data may help K-12 and Higher Education (HE) in making better results by providing them with figures that could talk about the main reasons for the issues faced in academics. Hence, teachers and administrators must create a culture of using information for making the best educational decisions.

- **Basic concept of LA:** LA is the gathering, measurement, evaluation, and recording of information regarding students and their situations, with the aim of understanding and optimizing knowledge and the surroundings where it happens. The definition of LA involves three major elements, as shown in Figure 2.3 (Omedes, 2018).
    - **Data:** The data in LA are the primary asset. It is containing the information of students collected from different learning environments (such as LMS, MOOC, and SIS) and interactions that provide data like demographic, academic, social networking, etc.
    - **Analysis:** By use of different EDM/LA methods or techniques, intelligence is added to data.
    - **Action:** The most facet of LA definition in action. The ultimate purpose of the LA process is to take action, like what action needs to be taken for those students who are identified as "at-risk" by the analysis process.
- **Process of LA:** The foundation of the LA process is the educational data. The data collection can be performed from different educational environments (blended education, computer-based, traditional classroom) and information systems, namely, MOOC, LMS, and ITS. The data collected may contain many irrelevant attributes. Therefore, the preprocessing of data

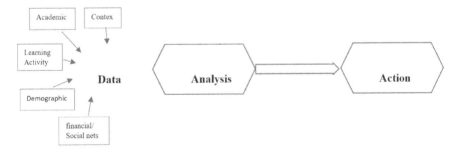

FIGURE 2.3 Three major elements of LA.

is needed, as it may be collected in different formats from multiple sources and different levels of hierarchy. It includes "data cleaning, data integration, data transformation, data reduction" (Romero et al., 2014). Afterward, data analysis is performed on the preprocessed data to find the hidden patterns using different methods and techniques, such as classification, clustering, prediction, relationship mining, and pattern matching. Once the data analysis has been completed, actions need to be performed on the information. The main aim of the analytic process is to take action and include "monitoring, analysis, prediction, intervention, assessment, adaptation, personalization, recommendation, and reflection." The next step in the LA process is post-processing, which includes "compiling new data from additional data sources, refining the data set, determining new attributes required for the new iteration, identifying new indicators/metrics, modifying the variables of analysis, or choosing a new analytics method" to enhance students learning process (Chatti et al., 2012).

2.2.3 COMPARISON AND CONTRAST: EDM AND LA

The similarities between EDM and LA suggest large fields of research overlap. Moreover, the structural arrangement of EDM and LA needs the same information and skills. But both have different foundations, types of analysis, and areas of importance. It is vital to note that such differences represent broader trends in EDM and LA. Various EDM researchers conduct research that could be placed on the difference of the LA side, and many LA researchers conduct research that could be placed on the EDM side of such LA differences. By recognizing such differences, there is a chance of identifying places in which EDM and LA can learn from one another (Siemens and Baker, 2012). Figure 2.4 shows the comparison and contrast between EDM and LA.

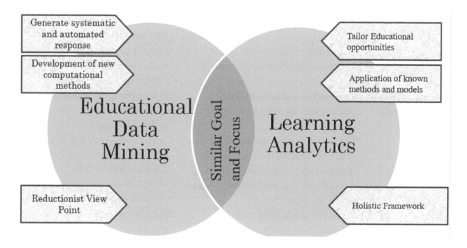

FIGURE 2.4 Comparison and contrast between EDM/LA (Siemens and Baker, 2012).

The first and foremost difference is the kind of detection in EDM and LA. EDM mainly focuses on automatic identification, whereas, LA mostly focuses on supporting human judgment. Secondly, the format and personalization are maintained by them. As there is more emphasis on automatic identification in EDM, the prototypes are mostly utilized as the basis of automated adaptation like an Intelligent Tutoring System (ITS), whereas, models are mostly created for updating and empowering learners, and instructors in LA. A third difference is between holistic and reductionist structures. EDM researchers emphasize the researches that analyze every component and all the links between them. In comparison, LA researchers mostly emphasize and attempt for understanding systems with their complete complexity. The fourth difference is the origins and approaches of researchers in EDM and LA. More details on such problems that are provided in Table 2.1 depict a comparison between various techniques used for EDM and LA using different characteristics.

2.3 EDM/LA: METHODS/TECHNIQUES

This section explains EDM and LA methods/techniques in detail. EDM/LA techniques are analyzed from the literature that includes data mining, machine learning (ML), and other computation models (Algarni, 2016). The different categories of practical methods are explained below (Baker and Inventado, 2014):

TABLE 2.1

The Detailed Comparison of the EDM and LA (Siemens and Baker, 2012)

Techniques	Learning Analytics	Educational Data Mining
Discovery	Supports human decisions. Automated discovery is used to achieve this aim.	Supports automated discovery. The human decision is used to achieve this aim.
Reduction	Emphasis on systems completely along with the complexities.	Emphasis on managing components, and evaluating every component and links between them.
Origins	Origins in the semantic web, output estimation, and systemic interventions.	Origins in academic software and student modeling along with estimating course outcomes.
Adaptation and personalization	More emphasis on informing and empowering teachers and students.	More emphasis on automatic adaptation like by the computer with no human intervention.
Techniques	Social network (SN) analysis, sentiment analysis, influence analytics, discourse analysis, learner success estimation, concept analysis, sense-making designs.	Classification, clustering, Bayesian modeling, relationship mining, discovery with models, visualization.
Approach	Bottom-up approaches.	Top-down approach.
Models	Applied to already build methods. Learning by the test process.	Find new pattern. Develop new algorithms.
Structure	A holistic structure was capable to determine the complexity.	The new computational methods are developed.

- **Prediction:** This method aimed to predict the unidentified variable that depends on the previous information for similar variables. The efficiency of the Predictive Model (PM) is based on the kind of input variables. Therefore, the PM is necessary to get limited labeled data for the output variables (Bienkowski et al., 2012). Thus, the labeled data provides current knowledge about the variables that are required to predict. Hence, it is necessary to deliberate the impact of the feature of trained information on the prediction model. The different types of predictions are classification, regression, and density approximation.

- **Clustering:** It refers to the separation of data in various groups that depends on definitely shared features. A clustering technique provides the user with a broad view of what happened in that data set. The clustering is called an unsupervised classification due to unknown class labels. The data points are searched that naturally group or cluster together to separate the database into different clusters (Fayyad et al., 1996). The groups may be predefined in the clustering technique. Clustering is done when the common group in the dataset is not known. It is used to decrease the dimension of the learning region. For instance, various institutes may be grouped depending on the similarities or differences between them.

- **Relation mining:** It includes the learning relations among the variables in the data set and encoding them as rules for later use. This method aims to find the relation among different variables in a data set with large variables. This involves searching the type of the most significant variable with specific concern. Relation mining measures the power of relationships among several variables. Relation mining methods are categorized as (i) Association Rule Mining (ARM) and (ii) Sequential Pattern Mining (SPM).

- **Refinement for human judgment:** This method aims at data refinement for human judgment which creates logical data. The demonstration of the information in various aspects guides the brain of humans to discover innovative data (Kay et al., 2006). Different techniques are required to visualize diverse kinds of data. Hence, the techniques used in EDM are varied from visualization to data sets. Thus, the data refinement for social judgment functioned in education information for two different aspects: Classification and Detection.

- **Detection with models:** This is the method that includes the use of an authenticated model of prediction or clustering approach as a component in future assessment. The models depend on clustering and prediction using human reasoning instead of automatic techniques. However, the build model is used as a segment of other complete approaches like relation mining. For instance (Jeong and Biswas, 2008), construct methods that classified student activities from main behavior data: students' interface with learning situations that use learning through teaching. An analytical map model was used within subsequent models of learning aspects and helped the investigators identify the different models. The innovation with models maintains the relationship between the behavior of the student and student features, and analyzes research inquiries over a range of backgrounds and assimilation of psychometric modeling frameworks in machine learning models.

- **Content exploration:** In learning assessment, the content analysis denotes the assessment of the text content linked to the individual research that is built through students (Mao et al., 2014). LMS scheme is used in updating research to explore the conduct of the students and interface in education (Macfadyen and Dawson, 2010), which comprises the content as well as deposition data. For instance, digital speech is executed by direct response, which is a significant element of the MOOC method, where learning analytics may enhance accuracy by analysis of quantitative records. This method aims to evaluate the content developed by learners.

- **Social education analytics:** In communication networks containing persons and situations, developing a system linked with the education internet is known as Social Education (SE) (Ferguson and Shum, 2012). Social knowledge analytics motivated exploring students' conduct on constructing education collectively in social media. This method aimed to search the social network relations (SNR) in knowledge and recognize the significance of SE networks.

- **Discourse analytics:** It is the method of learning analytics that helps in acquiring valuable information under administrative and language characteristics of the learner's interface. This technique explores and understands the semantics of language open function, and the intellectual features of the user (Su et al., 2017). This method was established in the year 2011, and about 15 articles have been published.

- **Disposition analytics:** It denotes the acquisition of information that represents a learner's abilities, and relations among these records and learning. Based on this method, various investigators have surveyed and experimented with data that aims to encourage educational performance. Few research studies have been done on this method. This method was considered in social analytics (Shum and Ferguson, 2012). Through social learning and perception, the disposition analysis provides methods of inspiring theoretical modification, distributed knowledge, teamwork, and innovation. Analytics link a cumulative emphasis on educational skills, and it may be used to inspire students to reproduce their paths of recognizing, treating, and responding to knowledge interface. From the viewpoint of instructors, the consciousness of these components supports their skills to employ a group of students in fetching knowledge. Table 2.2 shows the different methods/techniques used for EDM and LA.

2.4 APPLICATIONS OF EDM/LA

Educational data mining uses emerging new techniques to discover knowledge from the education data set to examine students' learning and activities (Bhise et al., 2013). Romero and Ventura discussed applications of EDM, namely, student performance prediction, feedback, personalization, recommendations to students, alerts to stakeholders, student modeling, and creation of courses (Romero and Ventura, 2013). EDM/LA are

TABLE 2.2

Different Techniques used for EDM and LA (Romero & Ventura 2013; Ashraf and Khan, 2017)

Techniques	Objectives	Usage	References
Prediction	This prediction can help to verify the performance of the weak students and evaluate the better marks.	Classification of the student's performance and identifies the student's behaviors.	Kumar and Pal, 2012
Clustering	Analyze learning behavior (LB) features while students are involved in problem-solving events in online learning environment (OLE).	Use of cluster analysis (CA) to parse click-stream (CS) information, and verify the feature sets of successful and unsuccessful learning systems in an online learning environment.	Antonenko et al., 2012
Sequence mining (SM)	This research work incorporates iterative refinement of the action abstraction step, and focuses the study on several learning events and activities.	The main focus of this examination is the efficiency and change in the reading behavior of high- and low-performing learners.	Kinnebrew and Biswas, 2012
Process mining	To get the process data from event logs.	Reflect on the student's conduct in terms of assessment and examine the students' events.	Calders & Pechenizkiy, 2012
Text mining	Extract the high-value data from the online dataset.	Explore the substance of web pages and documents.	Tane et al., 2004

also used to enhance the capability to make organizational decisions, impact student outputs, allow students to change their behavior that has a positive effect on their learning, allow faculty to help students and make changes to their courses based on the information, support faculty teaching and pedagogy, predict the learner's performance (Abdous et al., 2012), educate the students using big data (Romero-Zaldivar et al., 2012), analysis of the learners' education (Pechenizkiy et al., 2008), training and research, identify the drop-outs and provide feedback. The applications of EDM/LA are shown in Figure 2.5.

2.5 EDM/LA: SIGNIFICANCE AND CHALLENGES

This section explains the significance and challenges of Educational Data Mining and Learning Analytics. Generally, researchers are motivated on discovering valuable data to support education institutes for the better performance of the students; for instance, mining program content, assessment of students, admission procedure, selection of courses, and performance of the student (Javidi et al., 2017). Educational data mining is motivated by different methods to explore specific kinds of information, recognizing the previously unidentified patterns from data created by education

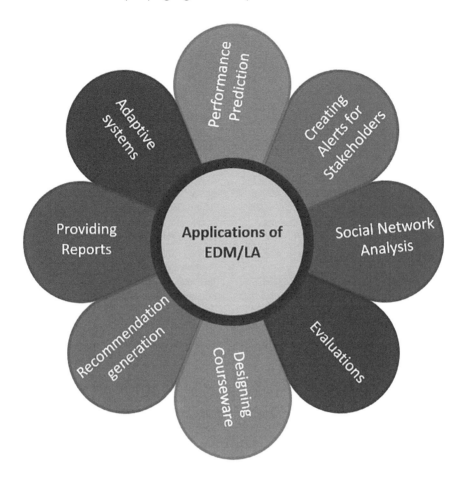

FIGURE 2.5   Applications of EDM/LA (Bakhshinategh et al., 2018).

procedures. According to Baker, in his research, DM in education is built to 'predict the future and change the future' (Baker and Inventado, 2014).

Educational data mining and Learning Analytics have main significance in various areas, which are listed below as:

- **User knowledge modeling:** This area is aimed at finding the known content that encloses specific conception and practical understanding—time devoted by the student to the study, the time when the student asked the hints, the number of accurate responses, the repetition of errors by the student.
- **User behavior modeling:** The modeling of the specific changes among the students is significant in EDM and LA. The student's behavior identifies the level of learning and helps in the prediction of the student's knowledge and future performance. Generally, EDM and LA techniques have the main significance in user behavior modeling, because it enables instructors to

analyze the factors that are more significant, which may result in controlling the learning procedure between the students.

- **Domain model:** The domain modeling defined the real-time objects. Rule induction algorithms are used to handle categorical outcomes. Learning may be better if the idea is more generalized.

Currently, the main concern of EDM and LA is data gathering and assessment (student data and progress report, lectures), data extraction, and making the right decisions in the education system. It is a complicated and multiaspect procedure. Thus, educational institutes' future growth is impossible without the growth and application of specific models and techniques aimed at recognizing data and searching for hidden patterns in education procedures (Kovalev et al., 2020).

The challenges of EDM/LA are explained below:

- Based on the global competitive index report in 2016, it is reported that 24 million families may not have educational skills. Authorized data of education systems are unpredictable. There is an administrative interface in the education structure. Besides, each governmental administration conveys to develop new policies that result in poor results (Ullah et al., 2019).
- The low economic share of education is an issue, and having less ability to use the existing budget correctly is another issue. Insufficient capital with poor maintenance results in less growth in the educational sector.
- Unavailability of instructors is the other issue, which results in obstacles to the growth of the institutes. About 15%–20% of the available instructors were not included in educational development (Chughati and Perveen, 2013).
- Coaching becomes common among people. The instructors put less effort into classes and inspire beginners to get tuition classes. It increases pseudo-intelligence and shows fake education results (Sahito et al., 2017).

REFERENCES

Abdous, M. H., Wu, H., & Yen, C. J. (2012). Using data mining for predicting relationships between online question theme and final grade. *Journal of Educational Technology & Society,* 15(3), pp. 77–88.

Adejo, O. W., & Connolly, T. (2017). Learning analytics in higher education development: A roadmap. *Journal of Education and Practice*, 8, pp. 156–163.

Algarni, A. (2016, June). Data mining in education. *International Journal of Advanced Computer Science and Applications*, 7(6), pp. 456–461.

Anjum, N., & Badugu, S. (2020). A study of different techniques in educational data mining. *Advances in Decision Sciences, Image Processing, Security and Computer Vision*, 1, pp. 562–571.

Antonenko, P. D., Toy, S., & Niederhauser, D. (2012). Using cluster analysis for data mining in educational technology research. *Educational Technology Research and Development*, 60, pp. 383–398. Doi: 10.1007/s11423-012-9235-8.

Ashraf, A. & Khan, M. G. (2018). *A Comparative Study of Predicting Student's Performance by use of Data Mining Techniques*. Doi:10.13140/RG.2.2.28495.12960.

Baker, R. S., & Inventado, P. S. (2014). Educational data mining and learning analytics. *Learning Analytics,* Springer, pp. 61–75.

Bakhshinategh, B., Zaiane, O.R., ElAtia, S., et al. (2018). Educational data mining applications and tasks: A survey of the last 10 years. *Education and Information Technologies,* 23, pp. 537–553. https://doi.org/10.1007/s10639-017-9616-z

Bhise, R. B., Thorat, S. S., & Supekar, A. K. (2013). Importance of data mining in the higher education system. *Journal of Humanities and Social Science,* 6(6), pp. 18–21.

Bienkowski, M., Feng, M., & Means, B. (2012). Enhancing teaching and learning through educational data mining and learning analytics: An issue brief. *US Department of Education, Office of Educational Technology,* 1, pp. 1–57.

Calders, T., & Pechenizkiy, M. (2012). Introduction to the special section on educational data mining. *Sigkdd Explorations*, 13, 3–6. Doi: 10.1145/2207243.2207245.

Chatti, M. A., Dyckhoff, A. L., Schroeder, U., & Thüs, H. (2012). A reference model for learning analytics. *International Journal of Technology Enhanced Learning*, 4(5–6), pp. 318–331.

Chughati, F. D., & Perveen, U. (2013). A study of teachers workload and job satisfaction in public And private schools at secondary level in Lahore city Pakistan. *Asian Journal of Social Sciences & Humanities*, 2(1), pp. 202–214.

Dietz-Uhler, B. and Hurn, J. E. (2013). Using learning analytics to predict (and improve) student success: A faculty perspective. *Journal of Interactive Online Learning*, 12(1), pp. 17–26.

Fayyad, U., Piatetsky-Shapiro, G., & Smyth, P. (1996). The KDD process for extracting useful knowledge from volumes of data. *Communications of the ACM,* 39(11), pp. 27–34.

Ferguson, R. (2012). Learning analytics: Drivers, developments and challenges. *International Journal of Technology Enhanced Learning*, 4(5–6), pp. 304–317.

Ferguson, R., & Shum, S. B. (2012). Social learning analytics: Five approaches. *2nd International Conference on Learning Analytics and Knowledge*, Association for Computing Machinery, pp. 2333

Javidi, G., Rajabion, L., & Sheybani, E. (2017). Educational data mining and learning analytics: Overview of benefits and challenges. *International Conference on Computational Science and Computational Intelligence,* IEEE, pp. 1102–1107.

Jeong, H., & Biswas, G. (2008). Mining student behavior models in learning-by teaching environments. *Educational Data Mining,* pp. 127–136. www.educationaldatamining.org

Kay, J., Maisonneuve, N., Yacef, K., & Reimann, P. (2006). The big five and visualizations of teamwork activity. *International Conference on Intelligent Tutoring Systems*, Springer, pp. 197–206.

Kinnebrew, J., & Biswas, G. (2012). Identifying learning behaviors by contextualizing differential sequence mining with action features and performance evolution. *Proceedings of the 5th International Conference on Educational Data Mining* Chania, Greece.

Kovalev, S., Kolodenkova, A., & Muntyan, E. (2020). Educational data mining: Current problems and solutions. *International Conference on Information Technologies in Engineering Education*, IEEE, pp. 1–5.

Kumar, S. & Pal, S. (2012). Data mining: A prediction for performance improvement of engineering students using classification. *World of Computer Science and Information Technology Journal*, 2, pp. 51–56.

Macfadyen, L. P., & Dawson, S. (2010). Mining LMS data to develop an "early warning system" for educators: A proof of concept. *Computers & Education,* 54(2), pp. 588–599.

Mao, J., Ifenthaler, D., Fujimoto, T., Garavaglia, A., & Rossi, P. G. (2019). National policies and educational technology: A synopsis of trends and perspectives from five countries. *TechTrends,* 63(3), pp. 284–293.

Omedes, J. (2018). *Learning Analytics 2018: An Updated Perspective*. SNOLA.

Pechenizkiy, M., Calders, T., Vasilyeva, E., & De Bra, P. (2008). Mining the student assessment data: Lessons drawn from a small-scale case study. *Educational Data Mining*, 1, pp. 187–191.

Romero, C., and Ventura, S. (2013). Data mining in education. *WIREs Data Mining and Knowledge Discovery,* 3, pp. 12–27.

Romero, C., Romero, J. R., & Ventura, S. (2014). A survey on pre-processing educational data. *Educational Data Mining,* Springer. pp. 29–64.

Romero, C., Ventura, S., Garcia, E. (2008). Data mining in course management systems: Moodle case study and tutorial. *Computer & Education,* 51, pp. 368–384

Romero, C., Ventura, S., Pechenizkiy, M., & Baker, R. S. (Eds.). (2010). *Handbook of Educational Data Mining.* CRC press.

Romero-Zaldivar, V. A., Pardo, A., Burgos, D., & Kloos, C. D. (2012). Monitoring student progress using virtual appliances: A case study. *Computers & Education,* 58(4), pp. 1058–1067.

Saa, A. A. (2016). Educational data mining & students' performance prediction. *International Journal of Advanced Computer Science and Applications,* 7(5), pp. 212–220.

Sahito, Z., Khawaja, M., Siddiqui, A., Shaheen, A., & Saeed, H. (2017). Role of tuition centers in the performance and achievement of students: A case of Hyderabad District, Sindh, Pakistan. *Journal of Education and Training Studies,* 5(4), pp. 90–102.

Shum, S. B., & Ferguson, R. (2012). Social learning analytics. *Journal of educational technology & society,* 15(3), pp. 3–26.

Siemens, G., & Baker, R. S. D. (2012). Learning analytics and educational data mining: Towards communication and collaboration. *2nd International Conference on Learning Analytics and Knowledge,* Association for Computing Machinery, pp. 252–254.

Su, J., Yi, D., Liu, C., Guo, L., & Chen, W. H. (2017). Dimension reduction aided hyperspectral image classification with a small-sized training dataset: Experimental comparisons. *Sensors,* 17(12), pp. 2726.

Tane, J., Schmitz, C., & Stumme, G. (2004, May). Semantic resource management for the web: an e-learning application. In Proceedings of the 13th international World Wide Web conference on Alternate track papers & posters (pp. 1–10).

Ullah, M. R., Shahzad, S. K., & Naqvi, M. R. (2019). Challenges and opportunities for educational data mining in Pakistan. *International Conference on Engineering and Emerging Technologies,* IEEE, pp. 1–6.

3 Spatial Data Analytics to Study the Pattern of Water Bodies Over Time and Possibilities of Their Revival
A Case Study of Sohna MC Water Bodies, Gurugram, India

Khushpal
SGT University

Mamta Dahiya
MRIIRS

CONTENTS

DOI: 10.1201/9781003330875-3

3.1   INTRODUCTION

Spatial data analytics, also referred to as geo-spatial data analysis, empowers us to investigate the behavior and patterns exhibited by various variables within a spatial dataset. For instance, if our objective is to determine the water pattern, land use/land cover [1,2], deforestation, weather pattern, and other changing concentrations over time, geo-spatial analytics can provide easy interpretation, as illustrated in Figure 3.1. We have identified our study area of Sohna Municipal Council water bodies at Gurugram over the time and identified the degradation of the pond over the years.

Water is a very precious natural resource and is essential for survival of human beings. All human settlements are created and sustained by the availability of preferably clean and potable water. However, the often unplanned growth of urban habitation in India, poor management of water resources and weak civic awareness regarding water conservation have put enormous strain on water resources and worked against their sustainability [3]. This has combined with an already low availability of fresh water per person in India to result in a situation where India is on the threshold of a serious water crisis. In urban areas, the difficulties faced by authorities in regulating informal settlements and catering to their requirements for water and sanitation have compounded the problem. Basic needs, especially of the urban poor, and the issue of sustainable use of water resources remain a major challenge in our country.

In India, we have moderate to acute shortage of water from November to mid-June every year, particularly for domestic use. From time to time, government has advocated various water conservation measures that, however, may or may not be

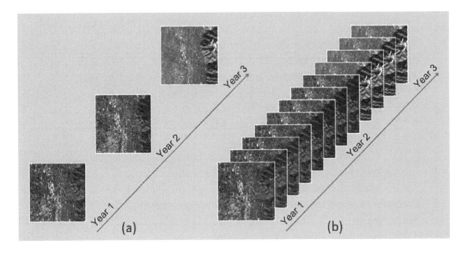

FIGURE 3.1   Spatial data analysis over the time.

followed by urban local bodies, utilities and citizens. The National Water Policy has also elaborated several water conservation measures, including appropriate pricing of water. Ministry of Drinking Water and Sanitation issued guidelines in 2006 for the safe use of waste water and gray water so as to enhance sustainability in a context of water shortage. Currently (June, 2019) Prime Minister launched Jal Shakti Abhiyan throughout India by considering every aspect of water.

On the other hand, growing urbanization in Delhi NCR, Gurugram, Bangalore, Kolkata, and other metropolitan cities have not put proper attention to its natural resources [4], including water bodies, forests or other natural habitats, etc. In Gurugram district, every water body or pond has a natural drainage channel that drains out the extra water. Due the poor planning of government, new buildings and houses were built over many of these ponds, blocking the natural channel of water flow. We have lost the natural ways of drainage. Nowadays, we can only see the forest of concrete around us, not for water or any other natural resources. As a result, all of the city gets flooded even with a few centimeters of rain. Sohna can be stated as the best example of the same trend.

3.2 SPATIAL FEATURES AND LOCATION OF SOHNA MUNICIPAL COUNCIL

Sohna is a town existing on Gurgaon–Alwar Road on the southern side of the Gurgaon City and is a Tehsil as well as Developmental Block of Gurugram District, Haryana, as shown in Figure 3.2. Earlier it used to be a Municipal Committee and

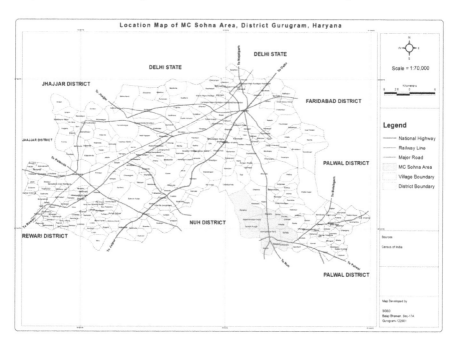

FIGURE 3.2 Gurugram district map highlighting Sohna MC area.

in year 2014 it has been promoted as Municipal Council. In 2012, a master plan had been formulated to divide the MC area into 38 sectors for residential, industrial, commercial, etc., and the urban development has reached from Gurgaon to Sohna, and most of its agricultural land use is being changed in to build up area. The rapid development of infrastructure is taking place in this area; high-rise buildings can be seen coming up in both the sides when we are approaching to Sohna town from Gurugram. In this rapid development drive, natural resources seem to be left behind. One of them is water which is a very precious resource [5]. The conservation of water is very much required, as the ground water is depleting very fast in this area.

3.2.1 Geo-Spatial Feature: Pond/Johad

A pond may be defined as a smaller size of water body formed due to natural or man-made depression. In Indian context, a pond is an essential feature of a village, which is either a low-lying area where the rain water of the area gets accumulated or may be dogged out by the residents to collect rain water [6]. It has been informed that, in some cases, a pond is the main reason for the origin of villages at certain sites. This rain water collected in natural depressions or water brought from canals play a crucial role in the village life. In northern Indian villages, the ponds play multiple functions for villagers.

The villagers take their cattle to the ponds not only to quench their thirst but also allow them to enjoy a free swimming. Kids enjoy bath in the pond, learn swimming in the pond along their buffalos and play different water games. Generally, there is a large, open area around the pond used as a playground or a place to pass free time. It provides water to wash clothes, to make dung cakes, and for day-to-day activities. Ponds are the natural storage of rain water and protect the village from floods. In some villages, when the pond overflows during rainy season, the surplus water is used for irrigation. In certain villages of some areas, the pond water is used for drinking purpose only. Ponds are valuable from biodiversity point of view, and termed as a local ecosystem and local climatic modifier. Such important small water bodies are either lost or completely neglected once a village is added to the urban limits. A village land is generally composed of two components: one is Lal dora land, marked for residential dwellings, and the second one is surrounding agricultural land. There is a transitional zone between these two—common land, and a pond is generally found located in this part.

Once the agricultural land is acquired by the local urban development authority, this common land is susceptible for land speculation. If the Panchayat is not alert enough, it will be gradually grabbed by the land sharks operative in the area. As a result, these small water bodies essential for a village are put to different uses. After some years ponds will disappear from the landscape of the area.

3.2.2 Sohna Pond Natural Catchment Identified by Satellite Image

The natural catchment area of the Sohna pond is existing in its western side from the Aravali Hills of Sohna and Saanp Ki Nangli villages. The water used to reach the Sohna town through one major seasonal stream from north western side of the town from a watershed of 8.94 km² from Saanp Ki Nangli and Sohna area hills. Three decades ago, a check dam of soil had been constructed on this stream before it enters into the town area; and surplus water used to flow toward the town side through its old channel. An overview can be taken from Figure 3.3 and 3.4.

3.2.3   SOHNA POND STATUS (HISTORICAL AND CURRENT)

In year 2005, Sohna land use was agricultural dominant, and the study pond used to get water from the main stream that passes through Mangal Nagar area, and that water used to sustain throughout the year; an overview can be taken from Figure 3.4, but with time developmental activities and city expansion started pace and catchment area got disturbed. In year 2021, the scenario was entirely different; a live pond was dead and dried up, as shown in Figure 3.5.

Watershed catchment of 8.9 Sq Km

Main Stream

FIGURE 3.3   Aster data (DEM) of watershed catchment area of Sohna MC.

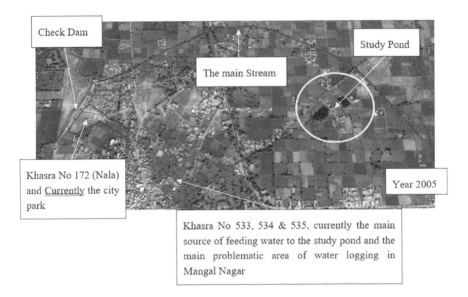

FIGURE 3.4 Watershed catchment area status in 2005 of Sohna MC.

FIGURE 3.5 Watershed catchment area status in 2021 of Sohna MC.

3.3 WATER SPREAD PROBLEM AND REVIVAL OF POND AT STUDY AREA

Currently in Sohna town, the Mangal Nagar area is facing a disaster kind of situation from last one decade. As the Natural Stream (Nala) having Khasra no. 533–535 trespasses through this area, the natural source of water that used to come in this stream has been blocked and the land use has also been changed of the backside stream. The liquid waste/sewage water (black and gray) of the town has been connected in this stream, and a cemented Nala has been constructed on these Khasra numbers. The situation becomes worst during the rainy season, as the surface runoff of the town along with the sewage waste come together into the Nala, the carrying capacity of the Nala does not meet the volume of load and the water spreads into the Mangal Nagar area. An overview can be taken with the help of the following photographs: study has been done through the physical survey, as shown in Figure 3.6 a–d, where problems of water logging in residential area of Sohna MC can be easily noticed everywhere during raining seasons only due to the closing of trespasses or water channels in that area.

Everywhere, it seems to be flooded. So, through the geo-analytics [7], we have identified how the changes have been occurred over the time; earlier these water bodies were full of drinkable water, but now-a-days the picture is entirely different. Either these water bodies are completely dried up or are under miserable conditions.

The condition of the constructed Nala is also very pathetic, and the overall situation has adverse health effects on the residents of Sohna town, as can be seen in Figure 3.7(a), (b), (c), (d). Therefore, it's the demand of time to mitigate the problem.

(a)   (b)

(c)   (d)

FIGURE 3.6 (a–d) Problems occurrence of Sohna MC due to closing of trespasses or water channels.

(a)   (b)

(c)   (d)

FIGURE 3.7   (a), (b), (c), (d) Poor conditions of currently existing water channels in Sohna.

The ways must be found out to counter the problem, and conserve and utilize water in a cultivated manner. Government can still take multiple actions to protect the exiting water bodies or to revive them.

3.3.1   Sohna Study Pond's Revenue Map and Current Status

As per the revenue record (Fieldbook & Massavi), the Sohna study pond is spreading in more than three acres of land under Khasra number 342 shown through Figure 3.5

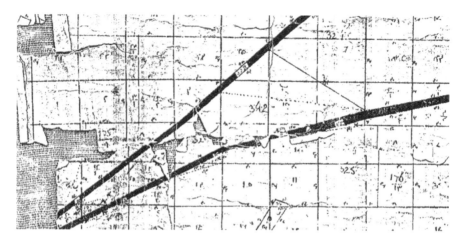

FIGURE 3.8 Sohna study pond's revenue map.

FIGURE 3.9 Sohna study pond's revenue map superimposed on satellite image.

with red color outline around the text. But, at present, the pond has been confined only up to 1.5 acres and has been abandoned. An overview can be taken with the help of Figure 3.8, and later revenue map is superimposed over the satellite image, as shown in Figure 3.9.

3.3.2 CURRENT ISSUE

Currently, the study pond is being abandoned and has no water since few years. The pond has been confined to its half of revenue area and was required to be revived as soon as possible.

3.3.3 Gray and Black Waters

Gray water can be explained as all sources of human waste water, including house waste, excluding bathroom and toilet wastewater or black water [8]. The issue of water management is very popular, particularly in the NCR region where poor waste-water management is one of the key reasons of water pollution and different types of critical diseases. Nowadays, not only have such incidents been identified, but also there is a growing global recognition that reuse of waste water after suitable treatment is necessary and has great potential in enhancing availability of water not only for recharging the ground water but also for different purposes such as irrigation, toilet flushing, floor and vehicle cleaning, etc.

The present scenario seeks to develop and demonstrate a system of treating and re-using gray and black waters for rejuvenating the Sohna water body, and for household toilet flushing and other cleaning applications. Although, as per Central Public Health & Environmental Engineering Organization norms and policies, 70/135 LPCD (Liter per capita per day) is to be supplied by government for rural/urban poor in areas where no sewerage system exists and urban developed areas with sewerage connections, respectively, people residing in Sohna town continue to live under acute water scarcity and under highly unsanitary and unhygienic conditions. The following objectives are proposed to be achieved.

3.4 MAIN OBJECTIVES AND METHODOLOGY OF THE STUDY

- To study the feasibility of water body through its old natural catchment area that lies in Aravalli Hills using spatial analytics.
- Formulation of plan to channelize the rain water mixed with sewerage water to a distant location.
- Suggestion for treatment of water and its reuse in future.

3.4.1 Methodology

To achieve the above-said objectives, the following methodology would be adopted:

- Topographic study of catchment area of the water, and delineation of drainage, slope and relief aspect would be done along with the contours at an interval of at least 2 m.
- Suitable sites' identifications through geo-spatial analysis.
- Topography of depression for the collection of treated water is to be studied and testing the quality and quantity of ground water/water in the depression will be done.
- Eliciting the opinions and suggestions of the residents through focus group discussions, awareness generation cum motivation workshop, etc.
- Construction of two treatment plants: one with Phytorid system and the other with enzymatic system for waste water near the depression. The treated water will be discharged in to the water body.

- Making green fencing and landscaping along the depression for the beautification of the water body and preventing it from silting.
- Training on operation and maintenance.
- Follow-up, monitoring, improvements, etc., where necessary.

3.5 PROPOSAL OF WATER TREATMENT SOLUTIONS THROUGH THE AVAILABLE TECHNOLOGIES

CSIR-NEERI's concepts include a constructed swamp particularly constructed for the dealing of urban and rural wastewater. Solution is depending on different types of grass or plants, like *Iris pseudocorus*, *Pennisetum purpurem*, Cattails (*Typha* sp.), *Phragmites* sp., and *Cannas* sp., generally exist in natural swamps with their percolation and treatment capability. Many other plants varieties such as Bamboo, Golden Dhuranda, Nerium, Colosia, etc. can also be utilized for water treatment and landscaping purposes.

The common concern in wastewater treatment is to segregate pollutants from the polluted water by getting them either to relax or to float, and then separate these unwanted factual. Some components are easily separated. Few of them need to be transferred to a stable form before they can be segregated. Water treatment services are intended in the multiple stages. On every stage either it eliminates particles from the gray/black water or changes melton and deferred material to a form that can be separated from the mixture. Phytorid is essentially a civil structure.

- **Screen chamber, oil, and grease removal system and sump:** Waste liquid is a mixture of rough, refined elements to eliminate that by using bar screens of 3–5 mm hole size for both types of elements. For lubricant and heavy segregation is mixed next to it so that the mixture tank can operate efficiently. The separated effluent is now drove using a cesspit into the deposit container.
- **Deposit container:** The deposit container system is a specified design that allows differed solid waste to relax in the deposited tank and parallelly segregate BOD by exceeding half of it. At this stage, the pH changes and amplifies system to eliminate relax solids.
- **Phytorid bed:** This Phytorid bed works on the rule of consecutive aerophilic and anoxic conduct. This bed is spread with half-water, full-water, decorative and peak varieties of plant where the wastewater flows in a sinusoidal manner to achieve the better efficiency of treatment. It is a sole perplex and fence preparation that surges the interaction time with the microorganisms and the shrub origins, and delivers alternative aerophilic and anoxic stages in the same device foremost to SBR varieties functions. In this unit the crib is filled with different-sized filling media and wetland plants such as *Colocasiae sculenta*, *Canna indica*, *Cyperus alternifolius*, etc.
- **Tertiary handling scheme:** Activated carbon filter and pressure sand filter followed by ultraviolet/chlorine treatment. The methodology being a usual scheme, the process is typically inert and needs slight operative interference

as shown in Figure 3.10. Upholding unchanging movement crossways the wetland structure through in/out alteration is very significant to attain the predictable conduct recital. Specimen of in/out waste will be approved for a retro of 3–4 months every fortnight after steadying of the conduct structures, as shown in Figures 3.11 and 3.12.

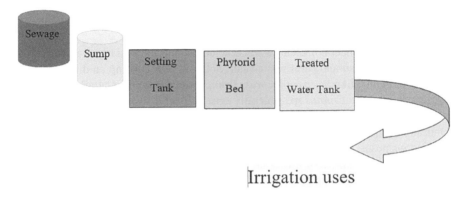

FIGURE 3.10   Tertiary treatment system.

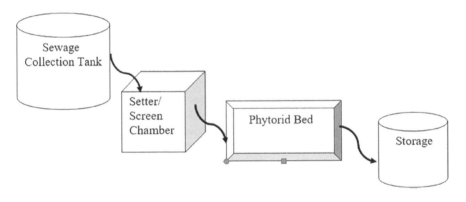

FIGURE 3.11   Stabilization of the treatment systems.

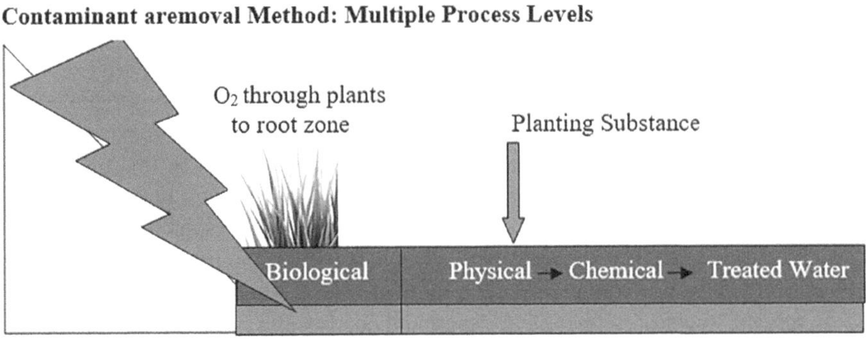

Contaminant aremoval Method: Multiple Process Levels

FIGURE 3.12   The Phytorid system design.

Benefits
- Negligible consumption of electric power
- Able to achieve ideals of 10 mg/L BOD and 10 mg/L TSS in treated water
- This method is easy in plan and process; that's why it required no technical work force for process and conservation
- This scheme has an appealing atmosphere due to beautiful plantations and subsurface water flow
- Insignificant mud creation
- No smell
- Lower costs of producing good-quality water

Healthy and happy surrounding
- Better development and well-maintained values of mess proximal to STP
- Additional various biology
- Concentrated pollutants in available water
- Augmented existence of flora and fauna
- Carbon sequestration
- Easy to clean (mechanism to dislodge clogging is in-built)
- It can handle dynamic shock loads

This concept is also qualified during clean Ganga River National Agenda introduced by Ministry of Drinking Water & Sanitation (MDWS).

3.5.1 ENZYMATIC/MICROBIAL TREATMENT

Introduction of enzymes and bacterial strains in the system ensures that natural bio-chemical and biogeochemical cycles are emulated and re-established in the ecosystem. Once these are established, the water will become clear, enhancing dissolved oxygen levels; a minimum of 3–5 mg/l of dissolved oxygen is necessary for small zooplanktons to survive. Higher levels throughout day and night are required for survival of higher organisms. The bacteria introduced in the system would digest nitrates and sulfates (that will be accumulated along with algal growth), and release these to the atmosphere. It will limit the algal growth and the total nutrients in the lake, the system can be changed to either treating of inflow or of the pond waters as per the direction natural biogeochemistry establishes. It is recommended that the treatment of inflowing waters in water body be taken up simultaneously so as to reduce eutrophication in order to reduce nutrient loading to the pond. This may be done immediately for a period of 6 months in the whole water body, and, thereafter, it may be done for one month in every three months in the deep portion of the pond only. It may not be required once the natural ecosystem is established.

3.5.2 CREATION OF LITTORAL ZONE AND BIRD HABITAT

Emergent vegetation on the lower banks forms an important part of the lake ecosystem, consuming nutrients to convert these into biomass and, more importantly, provide breeding habitat and protection to invertebrates, fishes and birds. This is known as littoral zone. A bench of 4 feet at a depth of 4–5' be created to plant

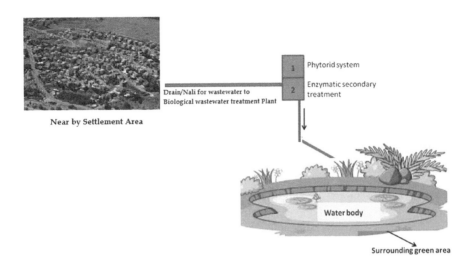

Near by Settlement Area

Drain/Nali for wastewater to
Biological wastewater treatment Plant

1 Phytorid system

2 Enzymatic secondary treatment

Water body

Surrounding green area

FIGURE 3.13   Proposed solution for revival of water bodies.

emergent vegetation—Phragmites sp. and rooted emergent vegetation below this bench—*Nelumbo* sp. and *Nymphaea* sp.

This would ensure easy access to and from island for the various birds. Creation of littoral zone would aid in attracting herons to the water body. This would provide the food—larvae, amphibian, fishes, etc., to them. The littoral zone would also provide breeding habitat for water birds, including Indian moorhen, Waterhen, Spotbills, etc. Herons could nest on Babool trees and lesser whistling ducks on large trees all around the water body. Birds would perform the role of removing fish and thus nutrients from the lake system.

With the above measures implemented, the water quality could be mainlined for aquatic life to thrive. The dissolved oxygen level of minimum 3–5 mg/L is necessary for aquatic organisms to survive. Presence and breeding of birds and fishes in the water body will be the eventual indicator of a restored pond. Proposed plan for revival of abandoned water bodies is shown in Figure 3.13, where waste water from residential area will be utilized to revive the pond after the water treatment. Proposed technology is successfully implemented in various projects to revive the dried-up ponds.

3.6   CONCLUSION

Through geo-spatial technologies-based analytics, the topographic scenario of the catchment area of any water body as well as its historical patterns can be analyzed in an organized way. That helps in understanding the drainage patterns and surface flow of water channels over the time. The contour data helps in understanding the current slopes and depression of the study area that further helps in planning the drainage/sewage systems of any area. In the current study as well, we have taken the help of geo-spatial technologies, and with its use we could reveal the present and past scenario of the study pond, and accordingly suggested the possibility of its revival.

REFERENCES

1. Mamta Malik et al., "Demographic data assessment using novel 3DCCOM spatial hierarchical clustering: A case study of Sonipat Block, Haryana", *International Journal on Computer Science and Engineering (IJCSE)*, Volume 13, Issue 9, Pages 3039–3147, 2011.

2. Martin Breunig et al., "Geospatial data management research: Progress and future directions", *Journal of Geo-Informatics*, Volume 9, Issue 2, Pages 95–110, 2020.

3. Selvam, S., Jesuraja, K., Venkatramanan, S., Chung, S. Y., Roy, P. D., Muthukumar, P., & Kumar, M. (2020). Imprints of pandemic lockdown on subsurface water quality in the coastal industrial city of Tuticorin, South India: A revival perspective. *Science of the Total Environment*, 738, 139848.

4. Derek B. Booth et al., "Reviving urban streams: Land use, hydrology, biology, and human behavior", *Journal of the American Water Resources Association (JAWRA)*, Volume 40, Issue 5, Pages 1351–1364, 2007.

5. A. Roder et al., "Trend analysis of Landsat-TM and -ETM+ imagery to monitor grazing impact in a rangeland ecosystem in Northern Greece", *Remote Sensing of Environment Remote Sensing of Environment*, Volume 112, Issue 6, Pages 2863–2875, 2008.

6. Rawat S.S. et al., "Inventorization of natural water springs of Ravi river catchment of Himachal Pradesh under purpose driven study of national hydrology project", *IWRA Journal*, Volume 11, Issue 1, Pages 33–38, 2022.

7. Zhou, C., Gong, M., Xu, Z., & Qu, S. (2022). Urban scaling patterns for sustainable development goals related to water, energy, infrastructure, and society in China. *Resources, Conservation and Recycling*, 185, 106443.

8. Jan K. Kazak et al., "Changes in water demand patterns in a European city due to restrictions caused by the COVID-19 pandemic", *Desalination and Water Treatment*, Volume 222, Pages 1–15, 2021.

4 Machine Learning Algorithms for Big Data Analytics

Vivek Shahare, Nitin Arora,
Ahatsham Hayat, and Nidhi Mouje
Indian Institute of Technology, India
(University of Madeira) & (ITI/Larsys/
ARDITI, Funchal, Portugal)

CONTENTS

4.1 BIG DATA: AN OVERVIEW

It is an area that collects, processes, and presents information from large sets of data. Although many fields are commonly used in data sets, complexity and size can make it hard to detect patterns and provide statistical power. Big data was initially coupled with concepts like *volume* (*size*), *variety* (*range*), and *velocity* (*speed*). Other challenges in extracting data from large sets include searching, storing, and sharing [1].

The expression "big data" alludes to investigating many informational indexes. Even though it's not the most supportive trait of the new information environment, it can, in any case, discover new examples and relationships to recognize business drifts, and work on the productivity of government and business associations. Most researchers consistently experience difficulties in taking care of enormous datasets.

DOI: 10.1201/9781003330875-4

The rapid growth of the available data has raised storage capacity and the world-wide average daily data size. Because of the growing quantity of digital devices and the amount of data collected, the data volume has grown significantly. Its immense size and complexity make it very challenging to unravel. Converting big data into business intelligence is a daunting task that can be quickly done [2]. According to IDC, the total amount of data collected by 2025 will be 163 zettabytes.

Most of the time, software packages and databases are widely used to visualize data perform responsibilities linked to analyzing and processing extensive data. However, parallelization and analysis are frequently challenging due to the task's intricacy and data. The most successful businesses of the future will be those that can make sense of all their data. This will enable them to expand into new areas and expand their client base. Data scientists may use machine learning and artificial intelligence to assist them in preparing for the massive amounts of data they'll be dealing with [3,4].

Six characteristics describe big data. These features are essential to make the best out of the business data. The features are as follows:

- **Analytical, highly scalable procedures:** Because of their scalability and integration, big data platforms like Hadoop and Spark have grown popular. The amount of data these platforms can analyze at a higher level of performance is practically limitless. This distinguishes it from typical data analysis approaches, such as SQL queries. Traditional methods will not scale until they are integrated into a more extensive analytics framework.
- **Flexibility:** Big data is data that is adaptable. Compared to the previous database kinds of data, today's datasets come in various formats. Based on highly flexible data, business plans are successfully analyzed. Big data necessitates high-speed data transformation and the capacity to interact with unstructured data.
- **Real-time findings:** In most cases, businesses may wait for data analytics results. In the age of big data, high value equates to real-time insights. When employing big data to do activities such as fraud detection, the findings obtained after the facts are of additional value.
- **Machine learning applications:** In this age of big data, machine learning is becoming increasingly essential. Big data is distinguished from traditional data by machine learning. Traditional data was unable to fuel machine learning applications and produce relevant results.
- **Scale-out storage systems:** In the past, data was kept on tape and disk drives. Software-defined scalable storage systems, which isolate data from the underlying storage hardware, are often used in big data. Because not all big data is housed on current storage systems, the ability to quickly transfer data between traditional storage and cutting-edge storage approaches is critical for big data applications.
- **Data quality:** Data quality is always a key consideration. The necessity of guaranteeing data quality within large data sets and analytics processes has grown in tandem with the complexity of big data. A vital aspect of a successful big data process is data quality. These features are essential to make the best out of the business data [5–7].

4.1.1 Types of Big Data

Information has expanded in size from Kilobytes (KB) to Petabytes (PB). Big data is a term that portrays a considerable measure of information that requires the utilization of complex devices and programming to investigate and store [8,9] (Figure 4.1).

Big data is divided as:

4.1.1.1 Structured Data

- Information that can be put away in a proper arrangement is frequently alluded to as organized information. Over the years, various techniques have been developed to work seamlessly with such data. However, various issues are being faced due to the increasing size of such data.
- It provides a good overview of an organization's operations and can be easily accessed using various methods.
- Structured data is kept in a relational database in tables with numerous rows and columns. Another great case of structured data is a spreadsheet. Table 4.1 is presented as a pattern of structured data.

4.1.1.2 Unstructured Data

- Any data that has not been structured or specified in its structure is considered unstructured data. It has several problems with extracting value due to its scale.
- Most of the time, evaluating and extracting value from such data necessitates employing sophisticated software and tools.
- Text, images, music, video, web pages, geographical coordinates, and emails, among other things, are examples of unstructured data.

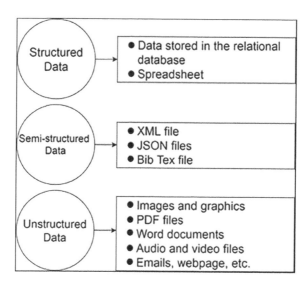

FIGURE 4.1 Types of big data.

TABLE 4.1

A Structured Data Table in a Database Is An Example

Emp_ID	Emp_Name	Sex	Department	Income per Month
4075	Rahul	Male	Education	35,000
1238	Faheem	Male	Medical	25,000
4869	Geeta	female	Transportation	20,000
7826	Priya	female	Development	200,000
1438	Rushi	Female	Education	25,000

4.1.1.3 Semi-Structured Data

- Predefined markup languages, such as text files, .csv files, and XML, are commonly used to create semi-structured online data.
- It's tough to retrieve, store, and evaluate data that isn't well organized. As a result, a software framework that can readily manage semi-structured data must be implemented.

4.1.2 BIG DATA CHARACTERISTICS

Big data is characterized using the following qualities (Figure 4.2):

a. **Volume:** "Big Data" refers to massive amounts of data. When determining the data's value, the data's amount is significant. Data volume defines whether it's big data or not. As a result, "Volume" is important when dealing with big data solutions.

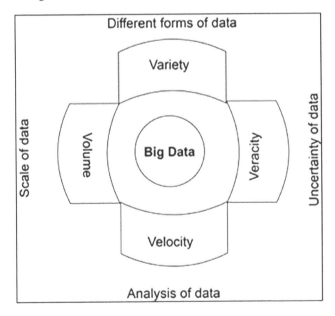

FIGURE 4.2 Characteristics of big data.

b. **Variety:** This is true for organized and unstructured data, and data gathered from various sources. The majority of apps rely only on spreadsheets and databases for data. Analytic software includes emails, photos, videos, monitoring devices, PDFs, and audio. Unstructured data is difficult to store, retrieve, and analyze.

c. **Velocity (speed):** Velocity is the speed at which information is made and prepared. It advises us about the information's prospects.

d. **Variability:** This alludes to the occasional irregularity that information may have, discouraging the course of effectively preparing and overseeing information.

4.2   BIG DATA ANALYTICS' IMPORTANCE

Big data analytics uses sophisticated techniques to analyze structured, semi-structured, and unstructured data from terabytes (TB) to Zettabytes (ZB). Informational indexes are excessively huge or mind-boggling for average social data sets to assemble, oversee, and break down immediately. Huge information contains numerous volumes, numerous speeds, and much assortment. Information sources are becoming progressively complex because of computerized reasoning (AI), cell phones, web-based media, and the Internet of Things (IoT). Sensors, video/sound, organizational log records, value-based initiatives, and online and web-based media create information continually and broadly [3,10].

Big data analytics might help settle on upgraded and faster decisions, demonstrate and estimate forthcoming events, and improve business insight. As you develop your big data strategy, consider open-source tools like Apache Hadoop, Apache Spark, and the whole Hadoop ecosystem as business, flexible data preparation, and limit courses of action [11].

Big data analytics is a time-consuming procedure of analyzing the massive volume of data to expose secreted patterns, correlations, market trends, and client preferences that may help the industry make a better decision. Companies employ data analytics to examine data sets and obtain new insights. Business intelligence (BI) addresses questions about company operations and performance. Robust data analytics software and technology may assist organizations in making decisions based on data that enhance business outcomes. Marketing effectiveness, additional income opportunities, customer customization, and enhanced working effectiveness are a few compensations. These advantages can offer a competitive advantage if used correctly [12].

Analysts, predictive modelers, data scientists, statisticians, and others collect raw data from a variety of sources, process and clean it using data analytics techniques so that computing systems can understand it, and then analyze this massive volume of structured transactional data using ML and AI algorithms to gain valuable insights. The big data analytics process is usually separated into four phases.

• **Data collection:** Raw or unprocessed data comes from various sources and might be in organized, semi-structured, or unstructured formats. Some sources are Internet data, online servers, cloud and mobile apps, social networking sites like Facebook, health devices, machine process data, etc.

- **Data processing:** Data from data warehouses or lakes is cleaned, that is, configured, structured, organized, partitioned, and so on, in computing language, before being made available for analytical queries.
- **Data cleaning:** Inconsistencies, mistakes, duplications, and formatting problems are corrected utilizing business software and scripting tools.
- **Data analysis:** In the big data examination, the information is analyzed utilizing instruments, for example, social information mining apparatuses, profound learning devices, prescient demonstrating devices, measurable investigation programming for text mining, BI, AI, perception devices, etc. [13].

Businesses frequently anticipate storing the history of company data to obtain relevant results and gain fresh insights to help them develop. As a result, significant data analysis needs technical innovation and data science expertise.

Models for significant data analysis were investigated and utilized to build a general conceptual architecture to make things more transparent. The graphic depicts how various sectors use data in different ways.

The following are some examples of how big data analytics may assist organizations:

- **Business decisions:** Online retail companies like Amazon look forward to making decisions based on past "Prime day" sales and consider the best-selling items to be repeated for the next sale.
- **Insight into data and business:** A company located in multiple locations using their sales data can get an insight into which location has the maximum sales for the last financial year.
- **Interpretation of outcomes:** The data can be estimated in the nearest time range based on pattern-based analysis.
- **Data visualization:** Graphical representation of data can show the behavior of a business.
- **Predictive analytics:** Using mathematical and scientific techniques applied to historical data, future data can be predicted with appropriate variables to a certain confidence level.

4.2.1 Advantages of Big Data Analytics

- They quickly evaluated colossal amounts of data from several sources in various formats and types.
- They make better-informed decisions quicker, which may strengthen the supply chain, operations, and other strategic decision-making areas.
- Process efficiencies and optimizations may reduce costs.
- Consumer needs, behavior, and sentiment may produce more precise marketing insights and product design data.
- Better risk management strategies using big data samples. Customer retention, product decisions, and marketing or business strategy decisions are aided by social data from numerous sites and search engines such as Twitter, Facebook, etc.

- Forecasting insights, forecasts, and trends provide easy access to business intelligence.
- NLP features may be used to measure customer happiness, handle concerns, and offer basic product information, among other things.
- When massive amounts of data are well-analyzed and used to adjust goods, services, risk mitigation, security concerns, and so on, improved operational efficiency follows.
- Early mistake detection lowers the chance of supplier services or products being harmed.
- Big data analytics produce massive data warehouses for integrating diverse sources, technologies, and processes.

4.3 CHALLENGES IN ANALYZING BIG DATA

Big data is defined by its high dimensionality and colossal sample size. Three problems arise from these two characteristics: Big data samples are compiled from different sources, times, and methods. Large sampling in big data is generally compiled from various sources and uses various methods. We need more flexible and durable techniques to cope with heterogeneity, trial variations, and numerical bias [6,13]. The following are the significant challenges in analyzing big data:

- **Quality of data:** With the pace at which business organizations are growing and the volume of data increasing daily, storing such huge volumes, managing data to be consistent, and avoiding duplicating data transformations and processes are significant challenges.
- **Security and privacy:** Securing the data from getting accessed and lost is challenging. This requires extensive data managers and teams to create user-specific access and encryption of data while transferring from one system to another.
- **Lack of talent:** The lack of professionals who manages big data, maintains big data, develop solutions out of big data, and data scientists who identify techniques and algorithms that solve business problems are comparatively less.
- **Various sources of data:** Managing data flowing into the ecosystem from various sources and formats at high velocity is challenging.
- **Identify value-added insights:** With the challenges mentioned above, if we analyze wrong or inconsistent data, the result will be "Solving the wrong problem," which loses the business value.
- **Inaccessible data:** Putting information into a unified framework has little impact if individuals who need it can't get to it. Leaders and risk supervisors require access to every association's information to know what's happening. Data investigation should be straightforward. A very much planned data set will dispose of any troubles with openness. Approved laborers will safely access or update information from any area, showing authoritative changes and working with fast dynamics.

- **Scaling data analysis:** Finally, an examination can become testing to scale, as an association's information assortment grows. Gathering information and delivering reports is becoming more intricate. You'll need a scalable framework to handle this problem. Information examination is worth the effort required to overcome these barriers. Consider an information exam response for your business now. The Claims, Incident, and Risk Management System from ClearRisk is cloud based, with robotized information input and boundless report prospects. The investigations you start to deliver will wow your supervisors!
- **Statistical significance:** It's critical to attain statistical significance and not be deceived by chance.
- **Distributed mining:** It's not easy to disable many data mining algorithms. Much study is required to have distributed versions of some procedures, including practical and theoretical analysis.
- **Data that changes over time:** Because data changes over time, big data mining algorithms must be able to adapt and, in certain circumstances, identify change first.
- **Compression:** When managing much information, the extra room required is vast. Two principles draw near: robustness, in which nothing evaporates, and examining, in which we select the data that is a general agent. We might think about pressure as a change from time to space, since it requires some investment and occupies less room. We lose data when we test, yet space advantages may be significant.
- **Visualization:** Presenting the information is one of the aspects of investigating big data that presents one of the greatest challenges. Since the information is so enormous, discovering easy-to-use portrayals is very difficult.

4.4 MACHINE LEARNING

ML is a subset of artificial intelligence (AI). It enables gadgets to gain from their encounters and work on themselves without doing any coding. AI centers around creating PC programs that can get information and use it to find out independently.

The learning framework starts with estimations or data, such as models, direct knowledge, or direction, to seek plans in data and create better judgments using models. The aim is to let PCs adapt without human interference and alter workouts as anticipated.

There are four basic categories of machine learning algorithms, which are referred to as supervised learning, unsupervised learning, semi-supervised learning, and reinforcement learning [14], as illustrated in Figure 4.3.

- **Supervised:** In AI, supervised learning is the work of learning a capacity that maps a contribution to a yield dependent on model information acquiesce sets [15]. It utilizes a named prepare in sequence and a cluster of prepared models to derive competence. Supervised learning is utilized when specific objectives are set up to be proficient from an exact agreement of in-sequence sources [16], i.e., an assignment-driven technique. The most

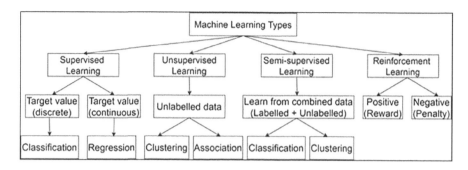

FIGURE 4.3 Types of machine learning.

successive administered errands are sequence indifference (arrangement) and sequence fitting (relapse). For instance, a directed learning model is message agreement or anticipating the class name or feeling of a portion of messages, such as a tweet or an item survey.

- **Unsupervised:** Unsupervised learning investigates unlabeled datasets without requiring a personal obstacle, i.e., an information-driven interaction [16]. This is generally utilized to separate generative mechanism, individual major pattern and design, group in the outcome, and trial purpose. The most widely recognized unaided learning assignments are group, thickness appraisal, highlight learning, dimensionality shrink, discovering association rules, inconsistency innovation, and so forth.

Semi-supervised learning combines supervised and unsupervised discussion, since it works with named and unlabeled sequences [16]. Accordingly, it lies someplace in the center between knowledge "with no oversight" and learning "with management." In the real world, name information might be inadequate in different situations, yet unlabeled information proliferates, making semi-supervised learning gainful [15]. A definitive point of a semi-supervised wisdom model is to offer a preferable predicted result over that acquired from the model's specific information unaided. Machine analysis, misrepresentation recognition, marking information, and message grouping are instances of semi-directed learning applications.

4.4.1 REINFORCEMENT LEARNING

Reinforcement learning is an AI technique that naturally permits program specialists and technology to consider the most excellent behavior in a given situation or climate to build effectiveness [16]. In light of remuneration or discipline, a definitive goal of this type of learning is to utilize experiences acquired from natural activists to work on the reward or decrease the peril [15]. It's an indispensable resource for planning AI models that may help further foster robotization and practical usefulness in complex structures like robots, free driving, gathering, and stock organization collaborations; in any case, it isn't attractive to use it to handle fundamental or straightforward issues.

Few machine learning algorithms are as follows [15,17–19]:

- **Binary classification:** In binary classification, a task involves identifying the data classes that belong to the two groups. For instance, if a task has two classifications, one is the normal state, while the other refers to the abnormal state. These two classes may be labeled as "1 and 0," or "yes and no," or "true and false." "Cancer not originate" is the normal state of a work concerning a check-up, as "cancer identified" is the pathological situation.
- **Multilabel classification:** Multilabel classification mainly represents multiple classes or labels. It is possible to classify an example into more than one class, depending on its level of text classification. The problem's classes are organized in a hierarchical order. Consider a multilevel text classification example: the same Google news may be classified and displayed as "latest news," "technology," or "city name," among other terms. In contrast to classical classification problems in which class labels are incompatible, Multilabel classification uses advanced machine learning algorithms to predict a large number of mutually nonexclusive labels or classes.
- **Naive Bayes (NB)**: The classification technique is based on Bayes' theorem, which assumes that every pair of features is distinct. It performs effectively in various real-world scenarios, including document or manuscript classification, spam filter, and so on, and can handle binary and multiclass categories. The NB classifier can correctly categorize the data's noisy samples and create a powerful prediction model. The primary benefit is that it takes a small amount of training data to approximate the needed parameters rapidly compared to more complex algorithms. However, its performance may be hindered due to its robust feature independence assumptions. NB classifier has various variants, and some common ones are Multinomial, Gaussian, Categorical, Bernoulli, and Complement.
- **Principal component analysis (PCA):** Huge datasets prevalent nowadays are challenging to understand. PCA is a method for sinking the dimensionality of such datasets while retaining as much information as possible. It does this by successively creating new uncorrelated variables that optimize variance. PCA minimizes the time needed to find additional variables or principle components when addressing an eigenvalue/eigenvector issue. The dataset settles the novel variables at hand rather than the a priori. Principal components and orthogonal are terms used to describe the eigenvectors of a covariance matrix. It's also flexible in a different manner, as several variations of the technique have been created for other data kinds and structures. The dataset, above all, must be scaled and based on the PCA techniques to be utilized. The finding also looks to be sensitive, based on the relative scale. It may be regarded as a method of data summarization.
- **Linear discriminant analysis (LDA):** A linear assessment edge classifier is LDA. It's created by using Bayes' theorem to data and fitting class acting entity. This approach projects a dataset into a less-dimensional space, decreasing the model's complexity or processing costs. Assume that all classes have the same covariance matrix; LDA yields each Gaussian density. Like regression analysis and ANOVA (analysis of variance), LDA describes one reliant variable as a sequential grouping of other variables.

- **Logistic regression (LR):** In machine learning, LR is a prominent probabilistic-based statistical approach for solving categorization and regression issues. However, it is more commonly employed for categorization. In LR, a logistic function, usually identified as the hypothetically defined sigmoid function (Eq. 4.1), is used to estimate probabilities. It can over-fit high-dimensional datasets and works best when data can be split sequentially. Normalization techniques are used to circumvent over-fitting in such instances. LR's fundamental drawback is the hypothesis of linearity between the dependent and independent variables.

$$g(z) = \frac{1}{1 + \exp^{-z}} \tag{4.1}$$

- **Linear regression:** Linear regression is a well-known approach for modeling the connection between one or more independent variables designated as "x," and represented in a linear form and a dependent variable "y." The term linear refers to a relationship between the dependent and independent variables in which the dependent variable is proportionate to the independent variables. There are a few more things to consider. Because whether "x" is increased or reduced, "y" changes linearly; it must be constant. The mathematical representation is expressed using Eq. (4.2):

$$y = Ax + B \tag{4.2}$$

- where A and B are constant variables, the fundamental goal of supervised learning using linear regression is to use data sets to discover the precise value of Constants "A" and "B." These values, i.e., the Constants' values, will then help forecast future values of "y" for any value of "x." Simple linear regression is used when there is only one independent variable. In contrast, multiple linear regression is used when there are several independent variables.
- **K-nearest neighbors (K-NN):** The supervised learning approach is used in K-Nearest Neighbors—a basic machine learning algorithm. It is a model of learning that is based on instances. As the algorithm saves the available data, the K-NN model verifies the similarity between the new and existing data, and places the new data point in the category most similar to the existing categories. This implies that the K-NN algorithm can swiftly classify it into a well-suited group of data items based on Euclidean distance anytime a new data point is created. The nonparametric K-NN method makes no data assumptions. K-NN is used for regression and classification. Classification is its main use. K-NN is a "lazy learning" approach, since it keeps the training set and classifies it later. The quality of the data determines the accuracy of K-NN, and the method is highly resilient when dealing with noisy training data.

- **Support vector machine (SVM):** Another supervised machine learning approach is the Support Vector Machine (SVM). SVM, like K-NN, is used to solve both regression and classification issues. However, it is mainly utilized to solve classification problems. The SVM algorithm's goal is to find the decision boundary. In other words, we can say the best line for categorizing the n-dimensional space where n is several features. Future data may be categorized. Hyperplane defines the optimal decision boundary. The SVM constructs the hyperplane using extreme points or vectors called support vectors. It works well in high-dimensional environments and behaves differently depending on kernel functions. SVM classifiers use linear, polynomial, sigmoid, RBF, and other kernel functions [19]. When a data set contains additional noise, such as overlapping target classes, SVM does not necessarily perform well. Figure 4.4 depicts the categorization process of locating the hyperplane that separates data into two classes.
- **Decision tree (DT):** Another well-known nonparametric supervised learning approach is the decision tree (DT). For both the regression and classification problems, DT learning techniques are utilized. The DT structure's internal nodes reflect a dataset's characteristics, whereas the leaf node represents the output. The branches of the DT represent the decision rule. DT sorts instances from root to leaf nodes. These instances are now classified by the node's attribute, beginning with the tree's root node and going down the appropriate branch. The most important thing to remember is to choose the appropriate method for the dataset and task at hand. DTs are simple, because they mimic human decision making. Decision trees are easy to understand because of their tree-like form.
- **Random forest (RF):** A RF classifier is a typical example of ensemble learning, combining many classifiers to solve a complicated problem and improve overall model performance. RF is a classification technique that averages several decision trees applied to distinct subsets of a dataset to increase the dataset's prediction capacity. As a result, the RF learning model with numerous decision trees is extra exact than a solo decision tree.

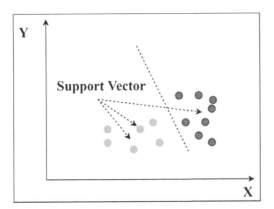

FIGURE 4.4 SVM classification.

As a result, the more trees you have, the better your accuracy will be, and you'll be able to avoid over-fitting. It applies to classification and regression problems, and works well with continuous and categorical standards. RF can handle large datasets with high dimensionality.

4.5   BIG DATA MEETS MACHINE LEARNING

Big data is a term that describes extraordinarily vast amounts of organized and unstructured data that cannot be managed using standard approaches. By discovering examples and models, Big information examination helps recognize the data. With the aid of dynamic computations, AI can speed up this connection. It can portray moving toward data, perceiving floats, and changing the information into fundamental business pieces of information. As the number of training datasets rises, machine learning algorithms become increasingly influential. So when we join Big data with AI, we gain twice; the calculations assist us with staying aware of the consistent surge of information, and the calculations assist us with staying aware of the nonstop deluge of information. Conversely, the volume and assortment of similar information feed the calculations and help them develop [20].

Let's have a look at how this procedure may work:

We may anticipate observing specified and analyzed outcomes, such as hidden patterns and analytics, when we input extensive data to a machine learning algorithm, which can help with predictive modeling. These algorithms can automate human-centered tasks for certain businesses. A company will evaluate the algorithm's results for insights that will assist them in operating their business [21].

This is where people return to the picture. While AI and data assessment run on PCs that beat individuals intensely, they need explicit unique limits. Computers by and by can't copy human credits, similar to fundamental thinking, objective, and comprehensive techniques. Without an expert to give the correct data, the value of computation-made outcome decreases. Without an expert to interpret its yield, thoughts made by a computation may mull over decisions [4].

4.5.1   AI APPLICATIONS FOR BIG DATA

We should gander at some genuine-world instances of how big data and AI may complement each other [16].

- **Cloud networks:** An assessment firm has much clinical information it needs to consider. To do such on-premises, it needs servers, online limit, frameworks organization, and security assets, all of which add up to an unbelievable expense. The firm decided to place assets into Amazon EMR, a cloud organization that offers data examination models inside a supervised framework. Computer-based intelligence models of this sort fuse GPU-accelerated picture affirmation and text gathering. These computations don't adjust once passed on to be spread and maintained by a substance transport association. Take a gander at LiveRamp's quick and dirty graph portraying a critical data environment development to the cloud [12].

- **Web scraping:** We should envision a maker of kitchen machines finding out about showcasing propensities and consumer loyalty patterns from a retailer's quarterly reports. In their longing to discover what the reports may have forgotten, the maker chooses to web-scratch the colossal measure of existing information related to online client input and item audits. By conglomerating this information into a profound learning model, the maker figures out how to improve and better depict its items, bringing about expanded deals. While web scraping generates a massive amount of data, it's worth noting that choosing the sources for this data is an essential part of the process.
- **Mixed-initiative systems:** Community sifting is utilized in the Netflix suggestion motor, which proposes titles on your landing page: Big data is utilized to follow your (and every other person's) past, and AI calculations are utilized to figure out what it ought to propose straightaway. This model shows how extensive information and AI crash in blended drive frameworks or human–PC associations where results are controlled by human and machine drive. Creative vehicle producers also utilize considerable information and AI in the prescient investigation frameworks that power their vehicles. Tesla vehicles, for instance, speak with their drivers and react to outer improvements by utilizing information to settle on calculation-based choices.
- **What to remember:** A couple of necessities for getting dependable outcomes utilizing AI. Clean information, adaptable instruments, and an unmistakable comprehension of what you need to accomplish are needed, notwithstanding an all-around planned learning calculation. While some might see these standards as detours to understanding the advantages of enormous information and AI, each organization that utilizes this innovation appropriately ought to put resources into them.
- **Data hygiene:** Learning from sanitized or inaccurate data may be costly, just as practicing for a sport can harm injury-prone individuals. As mentioned in the essay *Towards Data Science*, incorrectly trained algorithms create results that cost firm money rather than saving it. You should have the option to confirm the quality and fulfillment of your informational collections, just as their sources, because mislabeled, missing, or immaterial information may influence the exactness of your calculation [20].
- **Practicing with real data:** Let's say you want to develop a machine learning algorithm but don't have the necessary data to train it. You heard that derived calculated data may be used in place of actual data that you created. However, an ideal algorithm should address a problem requiring specific data to learn. Because derived data seldom resembles the algorithm's accurate data to solve the issue, employing it practically assures that the trained algorithm will not perform as expected. The safest way is to experiment with actual data.
- **Knowing what you want to achieve:** Don't let the buzz about machine learning and big data cloud your problem-solving abilities. If you don't know how to use your data to solve a complex problem, you risk providing your algorithm with erroneous or wrongly used data. Before digging into an

algorithm, we advocate taking the time to build your data to leverage the potential of big data. That way, you can learn about your data and apply (and train) an algorithm suited for your problem when the time comes.

- **Scaling tools:** Big data expands our knowledge base, while AI improves problem-solving abilities. When combined, the two have the potential to grow whole enterprises. We also need to scale our other instruments.
- **Doing statistical surveying and division:** The cornerstone of each business is the target audience. To be victorious, each business must first recognize the spectators and market its desired goal. Businesses must do market research to dive deep into potential customers' brains and deliver usable insights. Machine learning can help by accurately interpreting customer patterns and behaviors using supervised and unsupervised algorithms. The media and entertainment industries use machine learning to identify viewers' preferences and tailor their material.
- **Exploring customer behavior:** After you've drawn an image of your primary interest group, AI doesn't end. It likewise helps associations dissect crowd conduct and build a robust system for their customers [22]. Client displaying an AI framework is an immediate aftereffect of human–PC connection. It mines information to understand the client's brain and assist organizations in settling on better choices. Facebook, Twitter, Google, and different organizations to become more acquainted with their clients and propose practical proposals [20] utilizing client-demonstrating frameworks.
- **Personalizing recommendations:** Customers demand personalization. Companies must close relationships with consumers through smartphone or video content to explain what's essential. Machine learning with a large amount of data is best used in a recommendation engine. It mixes setting with forecasts of client conduct to impact client experience dependent on their Internet-based movement. In this methodology, organizations want to make the right ideas that clients would discover engaging. Netflix prescribes the appropriate material to its clients utilizing AI-based recommended calculations.

4.5.2 PROPER STEPS FOR SUCCESSFUL PROGRESS TO MACHINE LEARNING

The transition to machine learning may be a significant step for companies, and it is not something that can be accomplished by top-level integration. All modules, including analytics, workflows, architecture, data collection and storage, and so on, will need to be redesigned. The scope of the system should be determined and adequately conveyed to the appropriate parties. As clichéd as it may sound, a systematic strategy is preferable for any such change. Primarily, businesses must have a solid AI and machine learning strategy aligned with their business goals. Second, they must keep in mind that high-quality data is necessary to use the potential of machine learning technologies fully. Organizations need an information-based culture. The perfect individuals and the right information can have a tremendous effect.

At last, time is of the pith, and organizations need to move quickly [3]. As data volumes expand, companies must put more effort into acquiring and managing it. After all, gathering data is just half the battle. Manage and derive meaning from data to increase marketing strategy and revenue. Machine learning for big data analytics is a technological improvement I would recommend for your company if you want to get the most out of your big data.

REFERENCES

[1] T. Breur, Statistical power analysis and the contemporary "crisis" in social sciences, *Journal of Marketing Analytics*, 4(2–3) (2016), 61–65.

[2] O. J. Reichman, B. J. Matthew, and M. P. Schildhauer, Challenges and opportunities of open data in ecology, *Science*, 331(6018) (2011), 703–705.

[3] A. Nitin Arora and K. Preet Singh, An approach towards real time smart vehicular system using internet of things. *International Journal of Research in Engineering, IT and Social Sciences*, 08(10) (October 2018), 52–56.

[4] A. Katal, V. Sethi, and T. Choudhury. Potential of blockchain in telemedicine. In T. Choudhury, A. Katal, J. S. Um, A. Rana, and M. Al-Akaidi (Eds.), *Telemedicine: The Computer Transformation of Healthcare*. Springer, Cham; (2022).

[5] A. Kakde, Multi spectral classification and recognition of breast cancer and pneumonia. *Polish Journal of Medical Physics and Engineering*, 26(1) (2020), 1–9.

[6] K. Singh, Role and impact of wearables in healthcare, *Proceedings of the Third International Conference on Computational Intelligence and Informatics*, Springer, Singapore, (2020), 735–742.

[7] W. Li, Y. Chai, F.Khan, S. R. Jan, S. Verma, V. G. Menon, and X. Li, Comprehensive survey on machine learning-based big data analytics for IoT-enabled smart healthcare system. *Mobile Networks and Applications*, 1(19) (2021), 234–252.

[8] A. H. Gandomi, F. Chen, and L. Abualigah, Machine learning technologies for big data analytics. *Electronics*, 11 (2022), 421.

[9] A. Ahatsham, V. Singh, B. Shahare, and N. Arora, An efficient system for early diagnosis of breast cancer using support vector machine. *International Journal of Engineering and Advanced Technology (IJEAT)*, 9(1) (2019), 7029–7035.

[10] I. H. Sarker, Machine learning: Algorithms, real-world applications and research directions. *SN Computer Science*, 2(3) (2021), 1–21.

[11] Y. S. Jeong, H. Hassan, and A. K. Sangaiah, Machine learning on big data for future computing. *Journal of Supercomputation*, 75(6) (2019), 2925–2929.

[12] A. Hayat, F. Morgado-Dias, B. P. Bhuyan, and R. Tomar, Human activity recognition for elderly people using machine and deep learning approaches. *Information*. 13(6) (2022;), 275.

[13] M. M. Najafabadi, F. Villanustre, T. M. Khoshgoftaar, N. Seliya, and R. Wald, Muharemagic, deep learning applications and challenges in big data analytics, *Journal in Big Data*, 2(1) (2015), 1–21.

[14] N. Sharma, S. K. Gautam, A. A. Henry, and A. Kumar, Application of big data and machine learning. In U. N. Dulhare, K. Ahmad, and K. A. B. Ahmad (Eds.), *Machine Learning and Big Data*. Scrivener Publishing LLC; (2020).

[15] D. Javed, *Big Data Mining and Machine Learning*. John Wiley & Sons, Inc., Hoboken, NJ; (2019).

[16] J. Singh, Big data analytic and mining with machine learning algorithm. *International Journal of Information and Computation Technology*, 4(1) (2014), 33–40.

[17] J. Qiu, Q. Wu, G. Ding, Y. Xu and S. Feng, A survey of machine learning for big data processing. *EURASIP Journal of Advanced Signal Process*, 2016(1) (2016), 67–83.

[18] S. Jain, V. Shahare, N. Arora, Real time human activity recognition using smart phone. *Advanced Science, Engineering and Medicine*, 12(9) (2020), 1200–1203.

[19] A. Nitin, S. Anupam, M. Z. Nayef Al-Dabagh, and S. K. Maitra, A novel architecture for diabetes patients' prediction using *K*-means clustering and SVM. *Mathematical Problems in Engineering*, 2022 (2022), 9.

[20] J. Dean, *Big Data, Data Mining, and Machine Learning: Value Creation for Business Leaders and Practitioners*. John Wiley & Sons, Hoboken, NJ; (2014).

[21] W. Abu-Ulbeh, M. Altalhi, L. Abualigah, A. Almazroi, P. Sumari, and A. Gandomi, Cyberstalking victimization model using criminological theory: A systematic literature review, taxonomies, applications, tools, and validations. *Electronics* 10 (2021), 1670.

[22] J. C. Priya, T. Choudhury, and A. Khanna, Blockchain-based transfer learning for health screening with digital anthropometry from body images. *Network Model Analysis in Health Informal Bioinformatics*, 11 (2022), 23.

5 A Modern Approach to Sentiment Analysis in Big Data
Methods, Tools, Applications, and Open Challenges

S Santhiya, M Shalini, and C Sharmila
Kongu Engineering College, Perundurai,
Erode, Tamilnadu, India

CONTENTS

DOI: 10.1201/9781003330875-5

5.1　INTRODUCTION: SENTIMENT ANALYSIS

Sentiment analysis, also known as opinion mining, is a branch of knowledge that examines mankind's points of view, emotions, sentiments, assessments, and attitudes hidden within a body of text or similar large data. It illustrates a massively problematic scope (adapted from Katrekar 2005). The various titles and tasks of sentiment analysis include opinion mining, opinion extracting, sentiment mining, subjectivity analysis, emotion analysis, and review mining. Sentiment analysis may be an approachable way for organizations to determine and categorize opinions about a product, service, or idea.

5.2 PRE-EMINENCE OF SENTIMENT ANALYSIS IN BIG DATA

The expressions' positive and negative take a predominant part every day. Indeed, positive feedback is a confidence booster that shows people are esteeming them. Negative feedback can help to get back on the right path. Sentiment analysis is the process of identifying positive or negative sentiments in a text (based on Shayaa et al. 2018). Feedback on the product is essential for gaining a clear picture of what the user thinks. Consider devoting the weekend to the family; the first and foremost item on the list would be a movie because people always want things to be worth it when they spend their money and time. People then search for the movie review, compare it, and decide which one to buff. Limited sources of user feedback data are available when talking about a product's review. People look deeper into shopping portals like Amazon, Alibaba, Flipkart, Myntra, and others, as well as social media platforms like Twitter, Twitch, and Facebook for data sources. Sentiment analysis helps to decipher the mood and emotions of the public, and gather insightful information regarding the context.

5.3 LEVELS

Sentiment analysis has been contrived at several levels.

5.3.1 DOCUMENT LEVEL

Based on Shirsat et al. (2017), document-level sentiment analysis is accomplished throughout the document, and one deviation is provided throughout the text. Such a type of emotional analysis is not widely employed (adapted from Balaji et al. 2017). The reader could be considered a novice in terms of categorizing a book as positive, bad, or neutral. Text can be separated using both supervised and unsupervised learning levels. Sentiment analysis of different domains and languages are the two most important issues in analyzing the emotions of a documentary approach. Domain-specific emotional analysis shows astonishing accuracy while it remains highly sensitive to the domain. The feature vectors are required for such a level. The feature vector represents the input features for prediction in machine learning models.

5.3.2 SENTENCE LEVEL

Each sentence is determined and analyzed by correlating polarity. It is especially useful if the document has a wide range of emotions associated with it. The level is associated with the classification. The variety of each sentence will be determined independently using the same levels as the document level but with larger training data and processing resources. The differences in each sentence can be combined to get the feel of the document to be used individually.

5.3.3 PHRASE LEVEL

Sentiment analysis is used when the words or ideas are drafted in the form of sentences by dividing them into categories. Each phrase may contain more than one element (Joshi et al. 2017). It may be considered a useful review for many products, as it is recognized that one element is expressed in a sentence. It has been a hot topic for researchers in recent times. The textual analysis focuses on classifying the whole document as self-centered, good, or bad. Sentence structure analysis has great benefits. The document contains both positive and negative statements. The word is the most basic part of the language. Its diversity is closely related to the subjugation of the sentence or document from which it originates (Pawar et al. 2015). A sentence that contains an adjective has a greater chance of being a straight sentence. Furthermore, the term is chosen to represent the mathematical characteristics of individuals, such as gender and age, as well as desires, social status, personality, and other psychological and social factors. As a result, the term serves as the basis for the emotional analysis of the text.

5.3.4 ASPECT LEVEL

Each sentence may contain many elements. As a result, the emotions of the aspect level are being examined. The emphasis is on all the sentence's elements and assigns variation in all aspects after calculating the aggregate sentiment across the sentence.

5.4 METHODS

In this section, we will look at the methods used in sentiment analysis.

5.4.1 KEYWORD-BASED METHOD

The keyword-based method categorizes text based on the presence of positive or negative words like happiness, joy, happiness, sadness, sadness, shock, and indifference. The main disadvantage of keyword-based segregation is the inability to distinguish opposing words and polarity, because the approach is dependent on more factors. Another disadvantage is that it is based on the obvious presence of positive or negative polarity. However, a post may occasionally convey a feeling or an idea in a lower sense than the obvious variation in words.

5.4.2 LEXICON-BASED METHOD

Dictionary-based methods generate a list of automatically labeled words with positive and negative polarity, and it constructs a polarity effect for each word. The built-in dictionary computes the entire range of sentiments in a post or text. The lexicon-based method has the significant advantage of not requiring training data. The lexicon-based approach has been used widely in general texts such as reviews, forums, and blogs. Dictionary-based methods are less likely to be used for the massive amounts of data published on social media websites. The irregular format and nature of social media websites is the primary reason. Although dictionary-based methods outperform keyword separation, they are not without drawbacks. Because it works at the word level, discarded and descriptive posts cause lexicon polarity score estimates to be incorrect. Second, lexicography and polarity schools are often biased toward texts cited by the linguistic organization's source. As a result, regardless of application background, developing a standard model is difficult.

5.4.3 MACHINE LEARNING-BASED METHOD

Machine learning research has become an important activity in many workplaces. In recent years, machine learning has been wonderfully designed with high-volume data management algorithms to solve real-world problems. The machine learning algorithms used are supervised learning and unsupervised learning algorithms. End-users would benefit from supervised learning algorithms to train and learn from a training model that is re-evaluated and analyzed using test data. The important one of supervised machine learning algorithms is the requirement to develop a training model. The training model must be sufficient to make the algorithm functioning and reliable enough to separate the sample from the test data. Unsupervised learning algorithms are another type of machine learning algorithm. The basic idea behind this algorithm is to find hidden entities in unwritten data. The calculation of similarity differences between data is the foundation of supervised learning methods. For example, it computes k-methods, which compute similarities between data based on proximity measurements such as the Euclidean distance.

5.5 TOOLS

The various available tools in sentiment analysis are:

- Brandwatch
- Critical Mention
- Lexalytics
- Repustate
- Talkwalker
- Social Mention

5.5.1 BRANDWATCH

The most important tool of Brandwatch is the "photo detail" tool, which can identify images related to the product. For example, suppose the logo for one product is uploaded, and Brandwatch searches the internet for images that represent that logo. Then, combine the images into a list, and highlight the source of the product logo.

Furthermore, the Brandwatch software provides interesting information on each image received. Metrics, such as spoken volume, integrated fans, and recent activity, are included. With Brandwatch, one can see where the product images are coming from, and how they are resonating with the target audience.

5.5.2 CRITICAL MENTION

Keywords are distinct from the other options in the list. It analyses news and other publications that are relevant to the business. It's the only way to see the emotions behind the community's most visible news. Since the news is covered constantly, it is helpful to have tools that can track online activity and may alert if there is any buzz regarding the company.

Any organization can be alerted when news reports appear on television using Critical Mention. By browsing through video files, employees can easily exchange company videos with one another to educate them about the company. If a company has a good reputation for live streaming, videos can be accessed and shared on social media channels. It aids in creating effective online content that helps in effective marketing.

5.5.3   Lexalytics

Lexalytics is a text analysis tool that explains why a consumer reacts to the firm in a particular way. It analyses text using natural language processing and then applies emotional analysis to identify the intent of a customer message. Lexalytics completes the process by integrating the information it receives from the user into an easily readable and shareable representation. There are many emotional analysis tools to determine how customers are feeling. Lexalytics stands out from other emotional analysis tools, because it explains why customers are feeling the way they are.

5.5.4   Repustate

Repustate has an advanced text analysis API that accurately determines the emotions underlying a customer's responses. The software can recognize text in short and slang forms such as ROFL, LOL, and SMH. It also examines emojis to determine what they mean in the context of the message. For example, if usage of an emoji is in a conversation, Repustate predicts whether it is a positive or negative sign in it. A language filter is an industry-specific tool that can be customized using the Repustate API. Secrets can be edited using the Repustate program if there is a slang word or are different meanings of words. Complete control is there to see how the software analyses the customers' responses.

5.5.5   Talkwalker

A large customer service platform is associated with "Talkwalker Quick Search." The technique works best with social media platforms, since it can identify how users feel about company brand profiles on social media. Quick Search analyses comments, engagements, and other data to provide a more comprehensive picture of how customers react to social media activity. It assists the team in planning and executing effective campaigns that attract the target audience.

5.5.6   Social Mention

A free social media analysis tool called Social Mention offers users bang for their buck. Users need to visit the website and search for the keyword in any search engine, instead of downloading software and setting up an account. When starting the search,

Social Mention gathers information about the keyword from all social media platforms and assembles it into a detailed summary.

It can provide useful information like the proportion of people expressing positively about the keyword compared to those speaking badly. Additionally, it might reveal the percentage of users who are likely to keep using the keyword and the level of popularity of the brand on social media. Social Mention is an excellent choice for persons who want to receive a quick overview of their social media reputation.

5.6 APPLICATIONS

In this section, we discuss the numerous applications of sentiment analysis using big data.

5.6.1 SENTIMENT ANALYSIS IN BUSINESS AS BUSINESS INTELLIGENCE

Business information can help achieve a competitive edge by starting to use the information on the product and processes within the company (Shayaa 2018). Sentiment analysis could encourage finding this information and understanding what the prospects want in the respective commodity. To use it properly, let's understand what emotions are used in the analysis, and how to analyze emotions to benefit the cause. Predicting future market conditions is one of the major factors to be done nowadays in a competitive business environment. Business intelligence is something that is of complete comprehension of aspects both inside and outside the organization by the company. This has a consequential impact on the business's capacity to boost productivity, sales figures, and general profitability. The real basis for business intelligence is data. Approaches to analyzing data help in driving strategies using real, past, and present facts and statistics. Companies could develop solutions and implement changes in the specific areas of the business that will have a stronger influence on reaching business objectives by leveraging data processing. Data, however, only provides a portion of the narrative. The actual mastery of big data is in the use of technology to unearth critical information that was hidden in haphazard internal and external data. To gather the data, the organization must determine the quickest and most precise method of gathering crucial data, wherever it may be housed, and then analyze the leads and trends that would help it better anticipate future market circumstances. This method makes the procedure simple and automatic in place of the conventional manual techniques. The simplest method to do this is through AI Business Intelligence, where innovative thinking assists organizations in meaningfully organizing and searching their data. Make the finest company judgments by listening to the customer's voice.

5.6.1.1 How Are Business Pieces of Information Found Using Semantic Business Search?

With a single click, browse individuals, businesses, genres, goods, and locations. The biggest problem on this very day was addressed by the creation of Semantic Enterprise Search (SES). To assist businesses and governments to discover important business information, which is buried deep, can be quickly and accurately handled by SES. Machine learning algorithms are used by Semantic Search APIs for Business to locate all subjects and organizations in corporate text datasets. This enables its information providers to perform a mathematical or contextual search on the documents. Businesses will be able to quickly search for individuals, organizations, genres, goods, places, and anything else they can think of utilizing the business intelligence search engine.

5.6.1.2 What Specific Details about the Business Might Help in Understanding Emotional Analysis?

Drive the company into an inter-economy. Since in the present-day world businesses must be customer-focused, a business needs to know the business feelings of its customers so that it provides them with as much personal and advanced product information as possible. To begin to better understand customers, the company needs to have an emotional analysis as part of the context strategy, and appropriate technology to begin discovering and analyzing the information found in the text. Knowing what the consumers believe will help enterprises make the correct judgments and the necessary changes to make it a true business growth, regardless of whether they are indifferent, reluctant, or confident about the many components of the firm.

5.6.2 Sentiment Analysis in Healthcare as the Patient Voice

A healthcare survey by the Health University of Utah predicted that the first and foremost barrier to providing an outstanding patient experience is not granting enough time to patients. According to the survey, patients seek to be heard rather than spend time with their providers. As clinicians provide a surplus of time to patients related to medical care, they find it difficult to allot time for patients' mental needs. How can we break down barriers and provide a setting where professionals can get to acknowledge and accept their patients better? We could try a completely electronic health record in the hospitals instead of clinicians spending their time and energy; possibly they would simply feel less rushed.

5.6.2.1 Patient Voice

The healthcare sector evaluates patient feedback or "patient voice" to enhance the patient experience, safety, and quality of care. Patients' opinions and sentiments are recorded via sources such as phone calls, post-appointment service questionnaires at clinics, and feedback web forms. To create a more satisfying patient experience, healthcare practitioners are investigating the best ways to comprehend the patient voice and assess the quality of their services. The practice of the healthcare industry that analyzes patients' feedback and experience, and how those connect to the medical treatment patients receive and take efforts to improve at all costs is known as patient voice. Numerous organizations, including clinics, hospitals, and doctor's offices, use this data and analyze it to enhance patient safety, care quality, and satisfaction. Sources like in-clinic questionnaires, post-appointment surveys, phone calls, and feedback web forms are used to represent the thoughts, feelings, and feedback of patients. Healthcare practitioners are searching for the best ways to detect the patient voice to give a more positive patient experience.

Healthcare professionals are aware of the value of examining a patient's response and how it might enhance their understanding of treatment initiatives. However, many organizations rely on cumbersome and slow techniques to gather the information they require to better comprehend what their patients are attempting to convey.

Communities like hospitals and even health insurance providers can learn useful information about where they are doing good work within their organizations and where they might need to fill a specific position by analyzing data from new patient voice platforms. Additionally, they can apply mathematical methods to discover "why" they do well or poorly. It's not necessary to find this visual patient irritating.

5.6.2.2 Is the Patient Voice in Health Care Important?

The organizations try to engage their patients in conversation at various points throughout the patient's healthcare journey. Utilizing outreach, the patients' stories about their care are obtained. Text messages, emails, marketing efforts, patient portals, and even mobile apps may be a part of this outreach. It has been demonstrated that engaging in conversation and paying attention to patient opinions increases patient satisfaction with care. Now there are several social media gatherings created by vendors which serve as an opinion mining platform. Social networks such as Twitter, Google, and FB gauge the patients' progress more positively and provide a holistic experience for them. Setting up a patient voice and monitoring patients' development will undoubtedly help healthcare organizations meet patients' requirements. These communications could take the form of advertisements, messages, emails, patient websites, and mobile apps. It has been demonstrated that having a conversation and paying attention to the patient's viewpoint increase engagement, enhance the care experience, and boost patient happiness.

5.6.2.3 What Applications of Sentiment Analysis Are There for Patient Voice?

To identify a patient's emotions and opinions, sentiment analysis is implemented using natural language processing (NLP) techniques. The sentiment analysis continues, as patient voice surveys gather responses to survey questions by manipulating what patients said in their research to identify where change is needed by gathering feedback through patient voice notes, surveys, reviews, and social media. This can be performed by determining whether their information is favorable, neutral, or negative. Patient's emotional responses are gathered by fusing their voices with their feelings. In countless sectors, the effectiveness of a large response solution is widely acknowledged.

5.6.3 Sentiment Analysis in Social Media as Social Media Listening

In this digital age, one of the most popular platforms for the average person to express his thoughts, feelings, and emotions about his preferred products is social media. There is no other channel that would provide as much insight into what the client's desire in a product as a social network, regardless of how many surveys they fill out.

People disclose every part of their lives online. Through the most accessible social networks, customers share their opinions through tutorials, product reviews, and recommendations. Every day on social media sites like Facebook, Twitter, YouTube, and Instagram, millions of product discussions take place.

By highlighting phrases like competitors and topics, listening to social media enables businesses to keep an eye on social media. After that, the information is gathered for analysis to gauge client response. There's an efficient chance to get to the heart of the customers' reactions, regardless of whether they are in response to new or existing products, customer service, shipping, or anything else.

Companies must have the technology and techniques required to capture data based on consumer feedback for some of these critical comments, conversations, and upgrades to be beneficial to them. Being able to find and extract pertinent information, and then analyze it to obtain a sense of a social networking site will provide companies more clout, whenever it comes to bettering the user experience and outpacing the competition.

By reacting to harsh or direct statements at the appropriate moment, companies may better assist their consumers thanks to the emotional analysis made possible by public listening technologies. This crucial tool will assist businesses in adapting their offerings to please existing clients and draw in new ones.

5.6.3.1   Is There a Distinction between Digital Network Listening and Web Analytics?

While public listening focuses on recognizing and responding to each product on social media, public monitoring focuses on the response to public discussion and participation. On the other hand, public listening gathers information through extensive consumer interviews and public discourse to help customers make smarter decisions. The difference between social media listening and public monitoring is the human element in written and interpersonal communication. Key elements of social media monitoring include keeping in touch with customers and the notion of listening to what others are saying about the company. Metrics are used to guide public listening, which is successful, even though both are crucial components of a customer's voice strategy.

5.7   OPEN CHALLENGES IN SENTIMENT ANALYSIS

5.7.1   AUDIO INPUT

5.7.1.1   Challenge

Translating the voice message into wordings could be complex, and it may be even more complex to acknowledge the written word. When attempting to examine a sizable amount of data that may contain both direct and indirect solutions, things start to go awry. Finding certain emotions and properly correlating them with the right tone could be challenging for brands.

5.7.1.2   Remedy

Any effective sentiment analysis tool must have the capacity to distinguish between appropriate and plain remarks, and choose the appropriate tone for each. For instance, the self-centered notion that "A commodity is pricey yet good" results in the product being undesired because of its price. Companies can express such distinctions in tone and intensity using the smart sentiment API.

5.7.2 POLARITY

5.7.2.1 Challenge

Words like "good" and "evil" are on the high rise in points and have a polarity of (+1) and negative (−1). This is unchallenging to understand. But there is a connection between words like "not so good," which could mean "average" and then between polarity (−75). These kinds of words are occasionally omitted, which decreases the grade.

5.7.2.2 Remedy

Those midst-word phrases which give an absolute view of the comments could be predicted by sentiment analytics tools assuredly. In this context, article-based sentiment analysis may provide a comprehensive analysis; nonetheless, thought-based sentiment analysis allows for a more thorough examination of many aspects of comments.

5.7.3 CONTEMPT

5.7.3.1 Challenge

In everyday discussions and social media memes, people make fun of and mock other people. It can be challenging for emotional analysis techniques to ascertain the underlying context of a response when negative feelings are expressed through the use of flattering remarks about the respondent. This problem always causes a lot of miscommunications, turning "good" ratings into bad ones and vice versa.

5.7.3.2 Remedy

A top-notch emotional analysis API would be able to identify the language context and all other factors that go into establishing a genuine emotion when someone publishes something. In this instance, the language database used to train the emotional analysis model must be both accurate and substantial.

5.7.4 EMOJI

5.7.4.1 Challenge

Emoji overuse on text-based social networking platforms like WhatsApp, Twitter, and LinkedIn is a problem. Language interpretation is accurately trained in NLP processes. Emojis are not the language itself, yet they can be used to extract words from parallel images. Emoji are frequently treated as special characters that can be retrieved from data during text excavation in emotional analysis software. However, doing so means that businesses won't get all the information from the data. For instance, "😱" designates a scream, although some of us use it to convey surprise.

5.7.4.2 Remedy

The organization needs to employ an emotional analysis technology that can deduce the meaning of emojis and not link them with special characters like commas, spaces, or stops to meet these analytical obstacles.

5.7.5 IDIOMS

5.7.5.1 Challenge

The metaphor is not understood by machine learning algorithms. For instance, the algorithm will be confused by the expression "dog with two tails," because we understand things practically. As a result, if a term is used in a remark or review, an algorithm may interpret it incorrectly or overlook it. The emotional analysis platform requires idiom comprehension training to resolve this conundrum.

5.7.5.2 Remedy

The neural networks in the emotional mining API have been specifically trained to comprehend and interpret expressions, and this is the only way this task can be met with the precision of sentimental analysis. Nouns that convey emotions like rage, excitement, tenacity, success, etc., are used to map out sayings before the models are adequately trained. It should go without saying that only then will an emotional analysis technology be able to accurately extract information from a text like this.

5.7.6 DENIAL

5.7.6.1 The Problem

Denial, given by words like no, cannot, never-ever, etc. could make the ML model unclear. For instance, a computer algorithm must comprehend that the words, "I have barely seen anyone in the gym class today" means that there is no way that they could have seen anyone in the gym class.

5.7.6.2 Solution

The emotional analysis field should be equipped to understand that two negatives are superior to others and to revamp a sentence into a positive. This can only be done if there is an adequate corporative training algorithm, and also which has the highest number of opposing words and makes it possible to create the total number of permits and combinations.

5.7.7 COMPARISON SENTENCES

5.7.7.1 Challenge

Comparison sentences might be challenging, because they don't always convey an idea. It is crucial to give it a lot of thought. For instance, when someone says, "Jupiter is bigger than the earth," they are not expressing any kind of good or negative sentiment; rather, they are expressing a relative ranking of the two planets' sizes.

5.7.7.2 Solution

When a machine learning model compares the degree of a business at one location to a bigger or lesser category than another, the accuracy of the sentimental analysis can be attained. Then connect that to a bad or good sensation. It is not enough to merely have a language to express positive or constructive feelings.

5.7.8 CODE-SWITCHING

5.7.8.1 Challenge

Code-switching is the process of transitioning from one language to another. When multilingualism is spoken, the problem is uncountable, and the model might become confused. If a machine learning model is trained merely using insufficient training languages, then multilingualism could be a tremendous tragedy. For example, "Anna" is a word that specifies a name of a girl in English, but in Tamil, it means brother, and in Arabic, it signifies a boy's name.

5.7.8.2 Remedy

The machine learning model is to be trained to deal with multilingualism so that it comes to be effective and does not confront this variety of challenges.

5.8 CONCLUSION

The preceding chapter in this series delivered a brief overview of sentiment analysis. The purpose of this chapter is to apply this information to the development of sentiment analysis in every possible room. The discussion in this chapter begins with a summary of sentiment analysis and continues with its methods, tools, and open challenges of this process today.

REFERENCES

Balaji, P., O. Nagaraju, and D. Haritha. "Levels of sentiment analysis and its challenges: A literature review." In *2017 International Conference on Big Data Analytics and Computational Intelligence (ICBDAC)*, pp. 436–439. IEEE, 2017.

Joshi, M., P. Prajapati, A. Shaikh, and V. Vala. "A survey on sentiment analysis." *International Journal of Computer Applications* 163, no. 6 (2017): 34–38.

Katrekar, A. "An introduction to sentiment analysis." *GlobalLogic Inc* (2005).

Pawar, K., P. S. Pukhraj, and R. R. Deshmukh. "Twitter sentiment analysis: A review." *International Journal of Scientific & Engineering Research* 6, no. 4 (2015): 957–964.

Shayaa   S. "Sentiment analysis of big data: methods, applications, and open challenges," *IEEE Access*, 6, 2018: 37807–37827.

Shayaa, S., N. I. Jaafar, S. Bahri, A. Sulaiman, P. S. Wai, Y. W. Chung, A. Z. Piprani, and M. A. Al-Garadi. "Sentiment analysis of big data: methods, applications, and open challenges." *IEEE Access* 6, (2018): 37807–37827.

Shirsat, V. S., R. S. Jagdale, and S. N. Deshmukh. "Document level sentiment analysis from news articles." In *2017 International Conference on Computing, Communication, Control and Automation(ICCUBEA)*, pp. 1–4. IEEE, 2017.

6 Big Data Analytics, Internet of Things (IoTs) and Bio-Robotics

A Budding Trio for Prospective Prevention of Plant-Related Emerging Disease Distribution, Monitoring, and Management/Control

Bright E. Igere
Western Delta University

Mercy A. Igere
Delta State University

Uzezi E. Isiosio
Western Delta University

Temitope C. Ekundayo
Durban University of Technology
University of Medical Sciences

Oluwatosin A. Ijabadeniyi
Durban University of Technology

DOI: 10.1201/9781003330875-6

CONTENTS

6.1   INTRODUCTION, SUMMARY AND FOCUS

In the recent times, there had been an increasing spread of diseases among diverse plant species affecting different plant parts (leaves, roots, fruits, etc.) and resulting low farm produce as well as reduction of food availability and effect on consumers. Interest toward the study of such emerging concerns continues to rise, especially among science-based researchers, practitioners and farmers of different products. Diverse strategies have been employed by various farmers and researchers with a view to reduce the growing impact of plant-related infections, employing some specific area of information resource tagged as big data. As a contribution to enhance the growing interest in management of risk in plant-related diseases, we present this study which aims at appraising the relevance of big data, data analytics, Internet of Things (IoTs) and bio-robotics as well as its future prospects in the management, monitoring and control of plant-associated diseases. This would both encourage/promote risk identification and improve efficiency of plant production. This study describes the meaning of big data, bio-robotics and data analytics, the potential models of proposed application of the trio as IoT subjects, factors affecting plant detection using image acquisition and segmentation, economic relevance of plant diseases and types, gap in plant disease detection, theodolite of machine learning, integrated IoTs for agro-expansion, diversity of machine learning language, factors affecting machine learning choice, application of IoT in plant disease detection, characterization and management, and future prospects. Farm automation and smart farming approach for the management of plant diseases, monitoring/surveillance and control possess the potential for advancement in food production, since it would reduce disease distribution. The application of IoTs and robotics remains the future for control of plant-associated diseases.

6.2 BACKGROUND AND DETERMINANTS OF STUDY

There had been a growing trend in the relevance of bio-robotics and IoT in the recent times, which may be effectively applied using stored data and information resources. Coincidentally, stored data or data repository center has remained the world essential indices without which it may be adjudged as drifting toward failure or non-existence. This is further buffered, as data have been implicated as excellent driver of global social, scientific, financial and technological advancement. Surprisingly, applying the trio (data–bio-robotics–IoT) continues to expand as major determinants for continuity and survival of various systems, including biological processes and abiotic activities (Elgendy and Elragal, 2014); hence, the expansiveness and largeness of data has been named with the term big data. The term had not been in use for some time now; however, it was first applied scientifically in 1990s by an American computer scientist named John R Mashey. He describes big data as datasets that have grown so large that it becomes cumbersome to apply in traditional tolerance, scientific advancement, software usability, storage and database management systems (Kubick, 2012). Its size ranges in a single data set from terabytes (TB) through petabytes (PB) to Zettabytes, which are regularly sourced while considering and/or discussing scientific advancement, management and control in diverse discipline. Additionally, it is imperative to note that when the assessment of such big data is aimed at revealing their relevance in medicine, pharmacy and drug delivery, biological sciences, Agriculture and biotechnology etc., then big data analytics becomes the drafted discussion (Russom, 2011). When such stored big data are analyzed for quick assessment and control of plant-related diseases or agriculture, it would both encourage/promote risk identification and improve efficiency of plant production.

The Internet of Things (IoT), one component of the trio that promotes intelligent utilization of information resources, has also made its mark on the realms of smart farming and big data, influencing various aspects of everyday life. Such application of smart and advance farming approach is employed today as IoT. IoT is a technology that applies the network of physical smart devices such as temperature monitoring systems, RFID (Radio Frequency Identifier), IP (Internet Protocol) cameras, smart sensing devices, etc. with details recovered from big data. The devices are distributed/dispersed to work independent of themselves, while focusing on related concern to meet a specified need. IoT is the third global advancing science-based technology that is next to the computer, mobile communication networks, information resource and internet (Ruan et al., 2019; Angadi and Reddy, 2018; Angadi, 2019; Atzori et al., 2010; Chandra et al., 2017a, 2017b; Sarma and Girão, 2009). Such physical smart devices may be embedded with electronic softwares, sensors, and network connectivity wired or wireless in vehicles, buildings and other items which may enable diverse objects to be collected, processed and exchange data/information via remote access. It may also enable the management of information/data and integrated interactive services. IoT, in addition to other members of the trio, possesses the potential for environmental, economic and social impact toward adaptation and application (De Mauro, 2023). This concept of the trio has been applied in diverse domains like smart home, precision agriculture, smart city, smart system and breeding, electro-metric medicine, smart environmental monitoring and public safety, etc. Figure 6.1 shows the various areas where IoT–big data–robotic may be applicable. The focus on applying the trio in agriculture/plant disease monitoring and management is driven by the numerous challenges of farmers arising from pathogens and possible poor yield of farm produce. These potential pathogens range from bacteria, protozoans, nematodes, fungi and viruses. An IoT–big data–bio-robotic-based application in farming and control/management of plant diseases entails a computer built-in system of devices that aids monitoring of various changes in the plant developmental stages (Vidya et al., 2020). These data systems are embedded and/or contained in a sensor and a monitor from a remote location that automatically activates a signal in the monitor, indicating a particular disease as early as the initiation stage of the disease development. Such early detection enhances appropriateness in the control and management of the disease. Suffice to say that the sensor must contain some disease

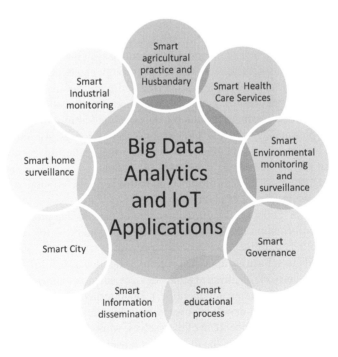

FIGURE 6.1 Application of big data analytics, Internet of Things (IoTs), and bio-robotics and subsets.

detection algorithm linked with machine learning and image processing device. This incorporation of soft and hard devices to the IoT system or data science/technology also enhances leaf disease identification (in addition to other plant-related diseases) in the early stage and encourages remote farm monitoring. This application may also be referred to as robotic monitoring/management of farm (robotic farming). The above show the various IoT subsets as the nine subsets represent alphabets A, B, C, D, E, F, G, H, I, while IoT is the Universal set.

6.2.1 ROBOTICS AND BIO-ROBOTICS

Following the recent technological advancement and the rapid modernization of the world systems, novel categories and classes of service delivery agents are being designed with a view to meet the requirement of an advancing world and also maintain quality of life. One most sourced approach is the application of robots while focusing on the need to make robots as close as possible to humans to serve the needs of man (Car, 2014). Such approach has to a greater extent re-invented and revolutionized the human resource management (HRM) system globally (Ancarani et al., 2019), with specific impact on the intelligence and practice. It has also resulted the term artificial intelligence and automation of processes, which were previously applied by man (Lariviere et al., 2017). Robots are man-made socio-economic machine designed with autonomous movement ability and the capacity to perform variety of expanding set of tasks in a short time, which the normal human may not be able to accomplish within a short time (Graetz et al., 2018). Although the acceptability of such emerging technology yet seems vague (Mubin et al., 2013; Sabanovic, 2010), there is a growing need for its application in diverse field of study. Several society and systems now demand a possible new design for robots that would assist them in meeting specific targets and harks back to the initial purpose of the concept of robots (Gruber and Wood, 2022). It is important to note that in the early 1920, researchers transmitted scientific fiction into an imaginary being to serve as servant of man. This was the genesis of the term robots (Mora et al., 2011; Gruber and Wood, 2022). The current re-emergence of robot now employs sensing of the environment, control, seeing an environment, touching, and consideration of proximity of objects to robot and intelligence (Demetris et al., 2022; Brunke et al., 2022). This new concept (known as robotics) has shown potential applicability in diverse field, including marketing, farming, industry production, security, etc. It has also enhanced other areas such as industrial robots, traditional robots, warfare robots, mobile robots, etc. to address research-based solution-driven strategies and technical necessities (Mora et al., 2011; Gruber and Wood, 2022). These new trends (robotics) also employ the use of data or information that are commanded into the machine to perform specified task with the research goal of getting robots as close as possible to human's socio-economic needs (Garcia et al., 2007; Brunke et al., 2022).The question of controlling the robots has been saddled with so much responsibility and capability; however, some recent investigators opined that such application of information command provides necessary solution for the control of robots in any challenging and changing environment, since its operation is loop controlled. This is the target of the trio in enhancing disease management in an advancing but dynamic environment.

6.3   AGRICULTURE, FARM PRODUCE AND THE BUDDING TRIO

To say the less, agriculture has been seen as a pivotal facilitator or driver of growth and development, following the day-to-day economic growth of a country, which is applied by subsistent farming or traditional/local farming. The traditional/subsistent farming strategies have not left up to its practice, as it has resulted food shortage due to low productivity arising from pathogens-based diseases (Mangla et al., 2020). Such occurrences are attributable to poor application of standards which big data and analysis of available related data promises to provide. Addressing the diseases of plant has welcomed concerted efforts from diverse experts and yet remains a global concern of both research-based knowledge and idea-driven strides. The identification of such disease type/pathogens type is also another area of growing interest among recent agro-experts and scientists. Some approach employed by various investigators have further compromised/contaminated and encouraged the spread of diseases due to the procedural sensitivity and the ubiquitous nature of such pathogens. The need for smart farming approach has been suggestive, as it possesses potential of preventing possible contamination and avoidance of pathogens spread. This approach has the tendency of helping and benefiting farmers in diverse ways, including reduction of manual labor, prevention of contamination, resolution of critical environmental factors issues, increased productivity, etc. It also has the potential of eliminating the problem of pathogen detection and/or characterization in most plant disease cases. It involves the early detection/identification of pathogens, disease etiology, class of parasite, disease impact on plants and encourages management of such diseases with improved yield of farm products at lesser efforts.

6.4   CATEGORIES, TYPES AND CHALLENGES OF BIG DATA

The term big data describes large, stored data that may be analyzed employing a complex series of techniques, including machine learning, Map Reduce and No SQL (Shreyas et al., 2022). It is categorized into structured data, unstructured data and semi-structured data. Structured data are data that possess pre-defined organizational properties that are orderly presented in a tabular scheme for easy sorting and analysis. Unstructured data are a collection of large datasets that lacks pre-defined data model, or data that lacks an organized and any pre-defined structural data model, which may consist of numbers, dates as well. Examples include medical records, social media records, business documents, images, video and audio media contents, survey responses, communications-live chat, messaging and web meetings, publications and listings, web pages, etc. Semi-structured data are a form of structured data that are not ordered in a tabular data model, which may not be employed in a relational datasets. It may contain meta tags of photo and/or video that associate dates, location or geographical position, and time of data retrieval; however, the data are not well structured and/or lack structural model (Russom, 2011; Baker et al., 2020; Shreyas et al., 2022).

The appropriate application of such data types and categories has been shown to possess diverse challenges that are tagged the '4 Vs'. These include Volume, Velocity, Variety and Veracity, as itemized below.

6.4.1 VOLUME

This is the power of computing and capabilities to store only required and needful information resources.

6.4.2 VELOCITY

This describes the speed at which data is created and the expected needs for such real-time prepared information analysis.

6.4.3 VARIETY

This is the multifaceted nature and copiousness of different dataset types ranging from their purpose to their sources.

6.4.4 VERACITY

This describes how reliable, viable, quality and dependable a dataset may be based on certain justifiable conditions and applying specific determinants (Hey et al., 2009; Russom, 2011; Baker et al., 2020; Srikant, 2016).

6.5 MODELS OF PROPOSED APPLICATION OF BIG DATA AND DATA ANALYTICS

The examined novel discussion on big data, data analytics IoTs and bio-robotics has gained and welcomed lots of research interest, as a result of their perceived unprecedented benefits and opportunities. This dispensation of information resource is currently depositing high-velocity data and voluminous varieties of datasets that lay intrinsic details and patterns of hidden knowledge, which should be extracted and utilized (Shreyas et al., 2022). The application of big data have been proposed by employing specific models, since its updated application covers governments, private organizations and individuals. The application of big data involves traffic control, route planning, intelligent transport systems, congestion management (by predicting traffic conditions), etc.

6.6 MODELS OF PROPOSED APPLICATION OF IoT

Various investigators have proposed diverse models for the detection of plant diseases using the machine learning and image processing technique. According to Aarju Dixit and his colleagues, the device regularly acquires the image of the plant and processes the collected image. The regions around the image with suspected expression is then segmented as infected region, which is thereafter extracted and saved. The saved information then applies the algorithm of machine learning (SVM) to uncover or characterize the disease type by regression (Dixit et al., 2018). In a similar proposal of related model by Shufen Zhang and his group, it was reported that using IoT to monitor and control wheat diseases would contain a system of data acquisition or image acquisition, processing of acquired data, transmission of data, remote manipulation of equipment and monitoring of activity by expert (Zhang et al., 2014). It can be seen that both the proposed models use similar mechanism, except that the transmission system uses a Wi-Fi and 3G or 4G, and an expert monitoring is required. The designed remote device may also be applied in the control of linked equipment as well as relay control circuit, which may help users to manage information acquired as gateway, control node, equipment parameters and acquisition node; and this equipment can be controlled directly by using computer and mobile phones.

6.7 FACTORS AFFECTING PLANT DETECTION USING IMAGE ACQUISITION AND SEGMENTATION

Various factors have arisen from the use of image acquisition and segmentation, including the following:

- Distorted images due to angle of capture and structure of plant
- The low-frequency objective and improper configuration of the trap change over time, resulting in overlapping images.
- Presence of dust, debris and other artifacts
- High variability of captured images in the field
- Specimen contrast with notable environmental conditions
- Failure to detect specimens at early stages of development
- Uncontrolled environmental dynamics and objects in the farm land may result confusion
- Visual similarities of disease symptoms
- Poor cameras built-in functions

6.8 ECONOMIC RELEVANCE OF PLANT DISEASES AND TYPES

Various plant diseases have been observed among plant species with pathogens ranging from bacteria, viruses, nematodes, fungus, and other parasites. The diseases range from known plant physical expression specific to plant part to other unknown expressions associated with diverse pathogens. Bacterial diseases affect roses, pears, tomatoes, apples as well as other fruits and stems/roots of plants. The severity of diseases at any given time or season determines the specificity of symptoms and characteristics of the disease. During wet seasons, bacterial diseases are favored among most plants, as the season encourages proliferation of bacterial pathogens and spread to other plants (Mangla et al., 2020; Igere et al., 2022, 2021a, 2021b). The growth of bacteria pathogen into plant tissues is preceded by discolouration of the leaves and stems or fruits, with generalized patches on affected areas. Some of these bacterial pathogens are also source tracked to other additional nutritional application by farmers into farmlands, which on application encourages the proliferation of pathogens. Fungal diseases also present similar expressions, as it affects soybean, cotton, rice, banana, mango, strawberry, pomegranate, guava, olives, papaya, etc. However, in addition to the various discolouration and curling of leaves, it also produces powdery spores with dry, circular, dark-to-brownish spots in infected plants. Fungal diseases also affect plant leaves, branches, roots, stems or twigs, and wet seasons also favor their proliferation as well as spread (Plantix, 2019). Other pathogen types (virus and nematodes) and the diseases caused by them are shown in Table 6.1. Although some of these pathogen types have been used in the control and management of diverse diseases of the plants that affect leaves, crops, stem, fruits, roots, etc. (Borah and Roy, 2020), they have been implicated in diseases as listed in Table 6.1.

TABLE 6.1
Plant Diseases and Various Pathogen Types

Pathogen Category	Pathogen General and Species	Associated Disease Type	Affected Plant Type and Parts
Bacterial			
Varying	Various bacteria	Blotch	Leaves and fruits
Varying	Various bacteria	Blight	Leaves and fruits
Agrobacterium	*Agrobacterium* species	Crown gall	Stem and soil around plant
Clavibacter	*Clavibacter* species	Canker or wilt	Stem and leaves
Erwinia species	*Erwinia amylovora*	Wilt, gall, soft rot	Fruits, leaves, crops, and roots
Phytoplasma	*Phytoplasma* species	Phytoplasmosis	Root, leaves, and growth
Pseudomonas species	*Pseudomonas syringae*	Brown spot	Stem, leaves, and fruits
Xanthomonas	*Xanthomonas* species, e.g. *X. campestris* Pv. *vesicatoria*, *X. campestris* Pv. *vitians*, *X. campestris* Pv. *Malvacearum*	Blight, brown spot or leave spot	Leaves of rice, tomato, grape, cotton, etc.
Fungus			
Ramularia	*Ramularia areola* ATK	Gray/black mildew	Cotton
Elsinoe	*Elsinoe ampelina*	Anthracnose and spot anthracnose	Grapes and leaves
Varying fungus		Blackleg or pycnidia	Leaves and stem
Varying fungus		Blackspot	Leaves and stem
Alternaria	*Alternaria solani*	Blights	Tomato leaves and fruits
Varying fungus		Blotch or yellow ring in leaf	Leaves and stem

(Continued)

TABLE 6.1 (*Continued*)
Plant Diseases and Various Pathogen Types

Pathogen Category	Pathogen General and Species	Associated Disease Type	Affected Plant Type and Parts
Plasmopara	*Plasmopara viticola*	Downy mildews	Grapes and leaves
Taphrina	*Taphrina* species	Leaf blisters and leaf curls	Peaches and leaves
Septoria	*Septoria lycopersici*	Septoria leaf spots	Tomato leaves and fruits
Pseudocercospora	*Pseudocercosporafuligena*	Molds or Cercospora leaf mold	Tomato leaves and fruits
Erysiphe	*Erysiphe necator*	Powdery mildew	Grapes and leaves
Varying fungus		Rots	Stem, trunk and branches
Varying fungus		Rust or small pustules with a mix of orange/red color on leaves	Leaves and stem
Varying fungus		Scab	Leaf/fruit of apple and orchards
Varying fungus		Snowmolds identified by patches of white/pink-purple coloration	Leaves of golf greens or plants
Varying fungus		White rusts	Leaves and crops
Fusarium	*Fusarium oxysporum*	Wilt	Cotton
Alternaria	*Alternaria macrospora*	Altenaria	Cotton
Cercospora	*Cercospora gossypina*	Cerespora	Cotton
Nematodes			
Insects	Varying insects	Sooty mold	Leaves
Mites	*Calepitrimerus vitis*	Rust	Grapes and leaves
Oomycetes	*Phytophtora infestans*	Blight	Tomato and leaves
Viruses			
Tobacco mosaic virus	Varying	Stunted growth, leaf curl/leaf yellowing	Leaves and soil
Tomato yellow leaf curl virus	Varying	Yellow leaf curl	Tomato and leaf
Cucumber mosaic virus	Varying	Chlorotic mosaic patterns on leaves	Leaves, stem and fruits

(*Continued*)

TABLE 6.1 (*Continued*)
Plant Diseases and Various Pathogen Types

Pathogen Category	Pathogen General and Species	Associated Disease Type	Affected Plant Type and Parts
Tomato spotted wilt virus	Varying	Leaves turning yellow at margins	Leaves and fruits
Potato virus y	Varying	Leaves mottling and mosaic	Leaves, soil and tuber
African cassava mosaic virus	Varying	Leaf discoloration, dwarf/stunted growth	Leaves and soil
Cauliflower mosaic virus	Varying	Chlorotic spotting and leaves chlorotic mottling	Leaves, stem and fruits
Plum pox virus	Varying	Chlorotic spots, brown lesions and deformation of leaves	Leaves, stem and fruits
Potato virus x	Varying	Chlorosis and decreased leaf size	Leaves and soil
Brome Mosaic Virus	Varying	Patterns/lines of mosaic character on leaves with characteristic dwarf and stunted plants growth	Leaves and soil

6.9 GAP ON PLANT DISEASE IDENTIFICATION

The detection and characterization of various plant diseases have been a long practice by farmers and agro-experts. The relevance of food production to the economic state of a country and the availability of food product that is mainly sourced from plant/farm has influence on the detection of plant diseases. The study of plant diseases, distribution, occurrence, epidemiology, including transmission/spread and diagnostic detection, has shown noteworthy importance in yield and quality of farm products. The basic integrated approach of disease management, including cultivation of resistant cultivars, cultural methods, biological control, improved soil tillage, use of botanical chemical methods as well as biotechnological methods, has shown potentials for appropriate management of plant diseases (Joshi et al., 2020; Mangla et al., 2020). However, the characterization of various pathogens and disease types continues to create a burden on farmer because of the techniques and ubiquitous nature of such pathogens. Most of their disease characterization studies are based on extracting disease information by observing segmented image sections (Joshi et al.,

2020; Mangla et al., 2020; Bergougnox, 2014; Nutter et al., 2006). Others utilize observation of neural networks to identify bacterial diseases. However, most of these strategies were greeted with numerous anomalies, as some of them fail to confirm the specific diseased plant due to the diversity of causal pathogens. It is also limited or narrowed to particular plant disease, e.g. soy plant, poor images sizes, and poor accuracy. This created a gap in the detection and characterization of plant pathogens, which also impacted the management of plant diseases. In a recent study, some investigators utilize support Vector Machine to develop an algorithm that is plant species specific, which detects pathogens of diverse classes, including bacterial, fungus, virus, etc. (Lindgren, 2020; Nazki et al., 2019). The algorithm is focused on an improved plant disease identification or characterization that may also be applied in disease management strategies. The mechanism has been proposed to follow a prescribed methodology to achieve the need goal. Figure 6.2 is a schematic representation of some proposed model for IoT used in diagnosis and management of plant diseases. Suffice to say that some of these strategies have been applied by various investigators. While studying the strategy on tomato, Verma and his colleagues reported appreciable success in the production of tomato (Verma et al., 2018). In a similar and related study, Patil and his group reported noteworthy achievement on grape production (Patil et al., 2016). Other investigators, such as Tanmayee (2017) on rice, Sarangdhar et al. (2017) on cotton, Zhang et al. (2014) on wheat, etc., reported an improvement in the production of the various crops while applying the IoT strategies in management of farm or employing smart farming.

6.10   THEODOLITE OF MACHINE LEARNING

The term machine learning was first coined in 1950 by Arthur Samuel, which has become a buzz word in diversity of application. It can be applied in agricultural practices as was reported in Badage's studies (Badage, 2018). They applied machine learning techniques in crop disease detection and proposed a two-phase model. The first phase involves training of dataset, while the second phase emphasizes monitoring/

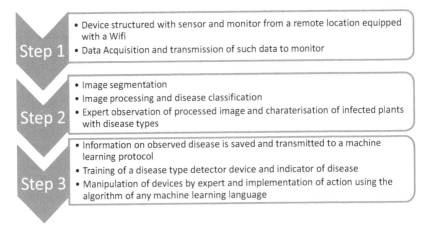

FIGURE 6.2   A schematic flow of IoT in plant disease detection and management.

identifying crop disease using Canny's edge detection algorithm. According to Sarangdhar et al. (2017), who employed linear regression as a model for detection of cotton leaf disease, a similar machine learning model was also proposed for predicting plant diseases which applies a decision tree, Naïve Bayes and Artificial Neural Network (ANN) for detecting plant diseases (Kranth et al., 2018; Kranthi and Ahmed, 2018). In addition, other investigators also applied the use of multispectral images classification scheme for diseases in beet leaves (Bauer et al., 2009). The use of machine vision and fuzzy logic for grading diseased leaves was also applied by Sannakki and colleagues (Sannakki et al., 2011). A previous review conducted on machine learning for the detection and classification of plant leaf diseases was also affirmed by Annabel and group that such models can be applied (Annabel et al., 2019). Joshi et al. (2016) applied one of the image processing procedures to monitor/control diseases in rice. A testable procedure also performed was the image feature analysis to detect diseases in some crop species. Sun et al. (2017) and Wang et al. (2017) proposed and also applied deep learning models on image-based plant to identify and detect plant-related problems.

Recent global research interest has been directed toward machine learning methods as a required state-of-the-art approach using computer-generated tasks, as challenge of plant disease detection continues to increase. This is made effective by deep neural network training, which is associated with classified plant disease identification, and recognition procedures using remote devices and images of plant parts (Atabay, 2017; Brahimi et al., 2017). Machine learning encompasses the assessment of large amount of data, employing basic knowledge of algorithm development and high power of computer to process graphical data in the graphics processing units (GPUs). These features make it possible to assess data via the deep neural networks and enforce the parallelism in data computing (Nazki et al., 2019). Comparing machine learning with shallow learning methods, including support vector machines (SVM), Naïve Bayes and decision trees, its models have a potential of handling more data bypassing input data through numerous non-linearity functions in other to produce robust descriptive features and/or performance of recognized functions based on its features. Another specific advantage of using machine learning is its capacity to reveal relevant features of a plant and disease without any human-based labor. Although the challenge of coping with limited data of annotated plant specimen exists, a supervised application of machine learning algorithm would remove such concern. The collection of diseased plant data is one complex and cost-effective procedure that requires a collaborative effort of various investigators from different fields at each stage, although investigators may be faced with the problem of class imbalance. Using expert manipulated with classical and augmented data sets may encourage assessment and class balancing as reported in various literatures (Perez et al., 2017; Wong et al., 2016). Such manipulated image (by translation, rotation, scaling and flipping) motivates synthetic data formation, and variable assessment with process accuracy and improved recognition. Other researchers have also suggested the use of other approach which has the potential of eliminating the need for data duplication or image duplication and development of synthetic data. One of such system that uses image–image translation of representative data is the Generative Adversarial Networks (GANs) (Nazki et al., 2019; Isola et al., 2017; Zhu et al.,

2017; Goodfellow et al., 2014). The GANs were first introduced by Goodfellow and colleagues with an aim of generating synthetic images of plant specimen (Goodfellow et al., 2014). It encourages an improved quality of images while preserving the structures of a scene and translating images to synthetic but viable output of limited data. Today, research interest continues to arise with the need for machine learning application, as it possess the potential of growing agricultural improvement as well as expansion even in the next decade.

6.11 INTEGRATED IoTs FOR AGRO-EXPANSION

IoTs have been applied in improve plant disease management and control by collaborative models, which consisted a framework of network. The network explores live connection of agricultural nexus with sensory remote device and a monitor at a location, which is manipulated by an expert (Mangla et al., 2020; Nazki et al., 2019; Mahdavinejad et al., 2017). The device acquires data at the farm location, communicates to the reader node of the device and transfers data to the concerned location. This resource is monitored at a remote location while specifications based on the observations are taken as required. One major advantage of the model is the connectivity of its entities to a single network, as the data remains transparent to the entities via intelligent applicative tools. The application of IoT would both encourage smart farming and also predict the growth rate of plants, stage development of crops, disease infection, application of nutrient and/or fertilizers, weed control, monitoring of invading plant predators and marauders, as well as management or control of diseases in any location. The real-time update of occurrences in the farmland would be revealed to farmers early enough. In a post assessment of predicted situations, farmers may find it easy to design annual agricultural plan for cultivation (Vasisht et al., 2017). The application of such IoT approach in agricultural improvement and intelligent tracking tags is referred to as IoT-Agro collaborative model (Gill et al., 2017). It is also important to note that post-monitoring of such farmlands would result in specific actions, such as productivity monitoring, pesticide-level monitoring, growth rate monitoring, minimum wastage of resource, and control of cultivars (Ganesh, 2017). The model would also support various interest developments during natural disaster situation. Utilizing the resources effectively in a farm land with non-governmental and governmental funding plan for the farmer would also be creditworthy, if interest is directed or generated (Pachayappan et al., 2020).

6.12 DIVERSITY OF MACHINE LEARNING LANGUAGES

Machine learning has been supported by diverse languages that are specific to integrated library supports. Some of these languages are Weka, PyTorch, TensorFlow, ML.net, etc. The Weka-type machine learning language is a machine learning library type, which focuses on deep learning and neural networks. It is a library type that is available for various languages users for usability. Its useful languages includes R-language, Python language and Java [atUoW], etc. The PyTorch maching learning library also supports diverse language areas and aspects. It focuses on easy usability of library and fast evolving communities of computer vision with reinforcement learning. PyTorch mainly applies Python programming, although the C++ [PyT] may also be used. The GitHub community is another language type that supports and distributes the PyTorch extension for.NET [STA]. The Tensor Flow machine learning library type is the language learning type that focuses on a whole process of building and deploying machine learning models. It utilizes a high abstraction tool that is fortified with the keras API feature to easily initialize projects and models for a quick start with machine learning [Tenb]. It provides good information on how to get started and encourages application of integrated languages such as Python, Swift, IOS and JavaScript. It was initially developed for Python programmers, making Python the optimal language of use in library. Another applied language type is the ML.NET, which is designed for .NET users. The ML.NET machine learning library allows the use of different aspects of machine learning languages, such as object acquisition, detection, image classification and prediction or forecasting. ML.NET, in addition, utilizes the TensorFlow libraries and integrates it for other solutions.

6.13 FACTORS AFFECTING MACHINE LEARNING CHOICE

Although the choice of machine learning languages in the management of diseases and control of pathogen infection, including detection and identification of pathogens, has shown recongnizable advantages and promise for agricultural improvement, applying the strategy is also greeted with so anomalies. It is important to the most researchers and experts who would want to apply the strategy be well informed on the demerits and limiting factors in others to adequately apply it effectively. The following listed below are some of such and any suggestive step to avoid such factors:

- Data overfitting with specified Model learning language, which may be resolved by applying a regularized technique reduce data overfitting
- Class imbalance in Model learning type on small sample classes or under sampled class by building of more comprehensive datasets
- Covariate shift issues on Model learning type by applying a domain adaptation technique
- Poor consistencies in reference annotations of Model learning images, which is performed by some practitioners
- Datasets does not contain relevant and comprehensive Model learning Data for sharing; use in social network and scientific research environment (Barbedo, 2020)

6.14 APPLICATION OF IoT IN PLANT DISEASE DETECTION, CHARACTERIZATION AND MANAGEMENT

The various fallouts in the characterization of plant diseases using the image segmentation, the diversity of disease causing biotic agents and the ubiquitous nature of pathogen have informed the application of IoT-based technology in plant disease detection, characterization and management. According to numerous investigators, detection of plant diseases is an attempt to distinguish specific pathogens of a disease symptoms expressed by a plant part while observing the produced image from any artifact in the farm environment. This observation is conducted by experts where binary classification (absence or presence) of image segment is done. Of important note is that results from detection aids the definition of disease severity and/or outbreak. Whereas classification entails the various scientific-based methods employed to identify or differentiate various pathogenic strain and the type of pathogen either bacteria, virus, or fungus, it is viewed as a multiclass or repeated strategy to specify the detected pathogen type (Barbedo, 2020). Management and control are a strategy employed to nip the emerging disease situation before it affects the entire farmland. Some of such strategy include application of biocides or fungicides at an appropriate amount without cross-contaminating or cross-infecting the plants further. According to Meineke and his group, applying IoT and machine learning strategy in the investigation of plant disease and monitoring management/control of plant-associated diseases possess potential for advancement of agricultural production (Meineke et al., 2020). In addition, both plant disease detection and characterization have similar peculiarities, which are often guided by some choice of applicable techniques used in their algorithms. Applying IoT systems in plant disease classification and identification using generated images, image processing and machine learning strategy from artificial neural network encourages farmers to produce quality plant and agricultural products with increased profit and environmental wellness. It would also enhance real-time plant disease management/control with quality farm produce (Thakur and Mitta, 2020).

6.15   FUTURE PROSPECTS

While emphasizing on the need for taking images of plant part and its related disease without contact with farm, the use of the budding trio (data–IoTs–bio-robotics) becomes a necessity in the detection, characterization, and management and/or monitoring of plant diseases. The application of big data–IoT-based bio-robotics in diverse systems has proven relevant potential for real-time monitoring and analyzing plant parts. Such instant analysis would result early detection of any looming plant diseases with post-implementation of appropriate action for control. The application of IoT-based system would also remove issues associated with farm laborers and prevent the problem of cross-contamination of farm land by environmental pathogens. In the future, the inclusion of robots or drone to the framework or architectures of the IoT device would also enhance model efficiency, higher accuracy, and a reduced complexity of workability. In addition, the analysis of captured images could also be speedily assessed by other embedded applications, such as segmentation and convolutional neural network (SCNN) with appropriateness of disease detection, characterization, monitoring, and management or control. This system can also be connected to smartphones and cameras for handy evaluation of captured images by farmers without physically visiting farmlands. Probing of relevant disease pathogen for differentiation of diseases with similar symptoms on captured images but different pathogen type would also be encouraged. The appropriate implementation of such would find significant use with the application of the budding trio (data–IoTs–bio-robotics) in disease characterization and management or control.

6.16   CONCLUSION

An overview of the application of the budding trio (data–IoTs–bio-robotics) in plant disease detection, characterization, classification, monitoring, management and control was discussed in the forgoing. The necessity of image capturing, segmentation and sections of plant parts, duplication, convolutional neural network (CNN) and processing were described. It also emphasizes the various plant diseases, pathogens types, machine learning language types to apply, structural framework or architecture, step, and the model by various investigators or researchers. Other matrices may be included by various interest-based researchers with a view to maximize the relevance of big data–IoTs–bio-robotics in plant disease management and control. The detection and characterization of plant-related diseases at the early developmental stage would enhance appropriate control measure and prevent spread of such diseases. Automating and making the plant disease detection and identification strategies faster using diverse research-based and testable ideas attributable to computer technology remains a future for improved agricultural practices. Notwithstanding, the role of big data, robotics and drones in the improve application of IoT-based system in disease management and control cannot be disregarded, as it possesses potential for smarter farming and improved agricultural processes.

ACKNOWLEDGMENT

The authors appreciate the postgraduate students at Biotechnology and Emerging Environmental Infections Pathogens Research Group (BEEIPREG), Department of Microbiology and Biotechnology, Western Delta University, Oghara, Delta State, Nigeria, for the provision of both an enabling academic environment and platform for this research. The study did not receive any funding.

CONFLICT OF INTEREST

None was declared.

REFERENCES

Ancarani, A., Di Mauro, C., and Mascali, F. "Backshoring strategy and the adoption of Industry 4.0: Evidence from Europe." *Journal of World Business* 54 no. (4) (2019): 360–371. https://doi.org/10.1016/j.jwb.2019.04.003

Angadi, S., and Venkata Siva Reddy, R. "Enhanced framework for sentiment analysis in text using distance based classification scheme." In *2018 Second International Conference on Advances in Electronics, Computers and Communications (ICAECC)*, (2018), pp. 1–6. IEEE.

Angadi, R. "Introduction to Smart City and Agricultural Revolution: Big Data and Internet of Things (IoT)." In *Smart Cities and Smart Spaces: Concepts, Methodologies, Tools, and Applications*, (2019) pp. 135–176. IGI Global.

Annabel, L., Sherly, P., Annapoorani, T. and Deepalakshmi. P. "Machine Learning for Plant Leaf Disease Detection and Classification–A Review." In *2019 International Conference on Communication and Signal Processing (ICCSP)*, (2019), pp. 0538–0542. IEEE.

Atabay, D. "An open-source model for optimal design and operation of industrial energy systems." *Energy* 121 (2017): 803–821.

Atzori, L., Iera, A., and Morabito. G. "The internet of things: A survey." *Computer networks* 54, no. 15 (2010): 2787–2805.

Badage, A. "Crop disease detection using machine learning: Indian agriculture." *International Research Jornal of Engineering and Technology* 5, no. 9 (2018): 866–869.

Baker, K., Ward, S., and Turner, B. "Co-producing research with academics and industry to create a more resilient UK water sector." *Research for All* 4, no. 2 (2020): 150–168.

Barbedo, J. G. A. "Data fusion in agriculture: Resolving ambiguities and closing data gaps." *Sensors* 22, no. 6 (2022): 2285.

Bauer, S. D., Korc, F., Förstner, W., Van Henten, E. J., Goense, D. and Lokhorst, C. "Investigation into the classification of diseases of sugar beet leaves using multispectral images." *Precision agriculture* 9 (2009): 229–238.

Bergougnoux, V., The history of tomato: from domestication to biopharming. Biotechnology advances, 32, no. (1) (2014): 170–189.

Borah, M., and Binoy K. "Systematic construction of high dimensional fractional-order hyperchaotic systems." *Chaos, Solitons & Fractals* 131 (2020): 109539.

Brahimi, M., Boukhalfa, K. and Moussaoui, A. "Deep learning for tomato diseases: classification and symptoms visualization." *Applied Artificial Intelligence* 31, no. 4 (2017): 299–315.

Brunke, L., Melissa, G., Adam W. H. "Safe learning in robotics: From learning-based control to safe reinforcement learning." *Annual Review of Control, Robotics, and Autonomous Systems* 5 (2022): 411–444.

Chandra, S., Soumya R., and Goswami, R. T. "Big data security in healthcare: Survey on frameworks and algorithms." In *2017 IEEE 7th International Advance Computing Conference (IACC)*, (2017) pp. 89–94. IEEE.

De Mauro, A. "Defining Big Data." In *Digital Phenotyping and Mobile Sensing*, (2023) pp. 443–446. Springer.

Demetris, V., Christofi, M., Vijay, P. "Artificial intelligence, robotics, advanced technologies and human resource management: a systematic review." *The International Journal of Human Resource Management* 33, no. 6 (2022): 1237–1266.

Dixit, A., and Sumit N. "Wheat leaf disease detection using machine learning method-a review." *International Journal of Computational Science* 7, no. 5 (2018): 124–129.

Elgendy, N., and Elragal, A. Big data analytics: a literature review paper. In *Industrial conference on data mining* (2014) pp. 214–227. Springer.

Garcia, E., Maria A. J., Pablo, G., and Manuel A. "The evolution of robotics research." *IEEE Robotics & Automation Magazine* 14, no. 1 (2007): 90–103.

Ganesh, E. N. "Development of Smart City Using IOT and Big Data." *International Journal of Computational Technology* 4, no. 1 (2017): 36–37.

Gill, S. S., Inderveer, C., and Rajkumar, B. "IoT based agriculture as a cloud and big data service: the beginning of digital India." *Journal of Organizational and End User Computing (JOEUC)* 29, no. 4 (2017): 1–23.

Goodfellow, I. J., Vinyals, O., & Saxe, A. M. (2014). Qualitatively characterizing neural network optimization problems. arXiv preprint arXiv:1412.6544.

Graetz, G., and Michaels, G. "Robots at work." *Review of Economics and Statistics* 100, no. 5 (2018): 753–768.

Gruber, D. F., and Wood, R. J. "Advances and future outlooks in soft robotics for minimally invasive marine biology." *Science Robotics* 7, no. 66 (2022): 6807.

Hey, A. J. G., Tansley, S., and Tolle, K. *The Fourth Paradigm – Data-Intensive Scientific Discovery.* Redmond, WA: Microsoft Research, 2009.

Igere, B. E., Peter, W. O., Beshiru, A. "Distribution/spread of superbug and potential ESKAPE-B pathogens amongst domestic and environmental activities: A public health concern." *Discovery*, 58. no. 313, (2022,) 1–20

Igere, B. E., Ehwarieme A. D., Olubunmi A. "Molecular detection of *Laribacter hongkongensis* in fresh fruits cocktail collected from public market: An environmental and public health concern." *Discovery*, 57, no. 308 (2021a) 621–631

Igere, B. E., Igolukumo, B. B., Eduamodu, C., and Odjadjare, E. O. "Multi-drug resistant Aeromonas species in Annelida: An evidence of pathogen harbouring leech in recreation water nexus of Oghara Nigeria environs." *Scientia Africana* 20, no. 2 (2021b): 145–166.

Isola, P., Jun-Yan, Z., Tinghui, Z., and Alexei A. "Image-to-image translation with conditional adversarial networks." In *Proceedings of the IEEE conference on computer vision and pattern recognition*, (2017) pp. 1125–1134.

Joshi, A. A., and Jadhav. B. D. "Monitoring and controlling rice diseases using Image processing techniques." In *2016 International Conference on Computing, Analytics and Security Trends (CAST)*, (2016) pp. 471–476. IEEE.

Joshi, E., Deep Singh, S., Neelam, S., and Namrata, C. "Diseases of Groundnut and Their Control Measures." *Biotica Research Today* 2, no. 5 Spl. (2020): 232–237.

Kranth, G. P. R., Lalitha, M. H., Basava, L., & Mathur, A. (2018). Plant disease prediction using machine learning algorithms. *International Journal of Computer Applications*, 18(2), 0975–8887.

Kranthi, A. K., and Asraar Ahmed, K. A. "Determinants of smartwatch adoption among IT professionals-an extended UTAUT2 model for smartwatch enterprise." *International Journal of Enterprise Network Management* 9, no. 3–4 (2018): 294–316.

Kubick, W. R. "Big data, information and meaning." *Applied Clinical Trials* 21, no. 2 (2012): 26.

Larivière, B., David, B., Andreassen, T. W., Werner, K., Nancy, J. S., Voss, C. Nancy. V. W., and De Keyser, A. ""Service Encounter 2.0": An investigation into the roles of technology, employees and customers." *Journal of business research* 79 (2017): 238–246. https://doi.org/10.1016/j.jbusres.2017.03.008

Lindgren, P. "Multi business model innovation in a world of smart cities with future wireless technologies." *Wireless Personal Communications* 113, no. 3 (2020): 1423–1435.

Mahdavinejad, M. S., and Mohammadreza, R. "Machine learning for internet of things data analysis: A survey." *Digital Communications and Networks* 4, no. 3 (2018): 161–175.

Mangla, M., Deepika, P., and Shilpa Sethi, A. Review paper on techniques to identify plant diseases. *International journal of Engineering* (2020) 18: 2.

Meineke, E. K., Tomasi, C., Yuan, S., and Pryer, K. M. Applying machine learning to investigate long-term insect-plant interactions preserved on digitized herbarium specimens. *Applications in Plant Sciences* 8, no. 6 (2020): e11369.

Mora, C., Tittensor, D. P., Adl, S., Simpson, A. G. B., and Worm, B. How many species are there on earth and in the ocean? PLoS One. 9, (2011): e1001127.

Mubin, O., Catherine, J. S., Shahid, S., Abdullah, A. M, and Jian-Jie, D. "A review of the applicability of robots in education." *Journal of Technology in Education and Learning* 1, no. 209 (2013): 13.

Nazki, H., Lee, J., Yoon, S., and Sun Park, D. "Image-to-image translation with GAN for synthetic data augmentation in plant disease datasets." *Smart Media Journal* 8, no. 2 (2019): 46–57.

Nutter, F. W., Esker, P. D., and Netto, R. A. C. Disease assessment concepts and the advancements made in improving the accuracy and precision of plant disease data. *European Journal of Plant Pathology* 115(1), (2006) pp.95–103.

Pachayappan, M., Ganeshkumar, C., Narayanasamy, S. Technological implication and its impact in agricultural sector: An IoT Based Collaboration framework. *Procedia Computer Science* 171 (2020): 1166–1173.

Pantazi, X. E., Moshou, D., and Tamouridou, A. A. "Automated leaf disease detection in different crop species through image features analysis and One Class Classifiers," *Computers and Electronics in Agriculture* 156 (2019): 96–104.

Patil Suyassh, S., and Thorat, S. A. "Early detection of grapes diseases using machine learning and IoT", In *Second International Conference on Cognitive Computing and Information Processing*, (2016). IEEE Xplore.

Pérez-Expósito, J. P., Fernández-Caramés, T. M., Fraga-Lamas, P., and Castedo, L. "An IoT monitoring system for precision viticulture." In *2017 IEEE International Conference on Internet of Things (iThings) and IEEE Green Computing and Communications (GreenCom) and IEEE Cyber, Physical and Social Computing (CPSCom) and IEEE Smart Data (SmartData)*, (2017) pp. 662–669. IEEE.

Ruan, J., Jiang, H., Li, X., Shi, Y. Felix, T. S., and Weizhen, R. "A granular GA-SVM predictor for big data in agricultural cyber-physical systems." *IEEE Transactions on Industrial Informatics* 15, no. 12 (2019): 6510–6521.

Russom, P. "Big data analytics." *TDWI Best Practices Report, Fourth Quarter* 19, no. 4 (2011): 1–34.

Šabanović, S. "Robots in society, society in robots." *International Journal of Social Robotics* 2, no. 4 (2010): 439–450.

Sannakki, S. S., Rajpurohit, V. S., Nargund, V. B., and Yallur, P. S. "Leaf disease grading by machine vision and fuzzy logic." *International Journal of Social Robotics* 2, no. 5 (2011): 1709–1716.

Sarangdhar, A. A., and Pawar, V. R. "Machine learning regression technique for cotton leaf disease detection and controlling using IoT." In *2017 International conference of Electronics, Communication and Aerospace Technology (ICECA)* (2017), pp. 449–454. IEEE.

Sarma, A. C., and Girão, J. "Identities in the future internet of things." *Wireless Personal Communications* 49, no. 3 (2009): 353–363.

Shreyas Madhav, A. V., Raghav Rajaraman, S. H., and Kiliroor, C. C. "Application of artificial intelligence to enhance collection of E-waste: A potential solution for household WEEE collection and segregation in India." *Waste Management & Research* 40, no. 7 (2022): 1047–1053.

Srikant R. P. Innovative examples of big data usage in India, Dataquest (August 20, 2016).

Sun, Y., Liu, Y., Wang, G., and Zhang, H. "Deep learning for plant identification in natural environment." *Computational intelligence and neuroscience*, Hindawi, 2017 (2017): 1–6, Article ID 7361042.

Tanmayee, P. "Rice crop monitoring system—A lot based machine vision approach." In *2017 International Conference on Nextgen Electronic Technologies: Silicon to Software (ICNETS2)*, (2017) pp. 26–29. IEEE.

Thakur, T. B., and Amit Kumar, M. "Real time IoT application for classification of crop diseases using machine learning in cloud environment." *International Journal of Innovative Science and Modern Engineering* 6 (2020): 2319–6386.

Vashishth, V., Chhabra, A., and Sood, A., "A predictive approach to task scheduling for Big Data in cloud environments using classification algorithms." In *2017 7th International Conference on Cloud Computing, Data Science & Engineering-Confluence*, (2017) pp. 188–192. IEEE.

Verma, S., Chug, A., and Amit Prakash, S. "Prediction models for identification and diagnosis of tomato plant diseases." In *2018 International Conference on advances in computing, communications and informatics (ICACCI)*, (2018) pp. 1557–1563. IEEE.

Vidya, V., Archana, M., Bindhu Shree, N., and Tanuja, R. "Spamdoop-A privacy preserving big data platform for collaborative spam detection." 3(3) (March-2020).

Wang, G., Sun, Y., and Wang, J. "Automatic image-based plant disease severity estimation using deep learning." *Computational intelligence and neuroscience* 2017 (2017): 8.

Ward, J. S., and Barker, A. "Undefined by data: a survey of big data definitions." 5821 (2013), Cornell Press.

Wong, M. Y., Zhou, Y., and Xu, H. "Big data in fashion industry: Color cycle mining from runway data." Association for Information Systems, AMCIS 2016: Surfing the IT Innovation Wave - 22nd Americas Conference on Information Systems.

Zhang, Y., Chen, M., Mao, S., Hu, L., and Victor, C. M. "CAP: Community activity prediction based on big data analysis." *Ieee Network* 28, no. 4 (2014): 52–57.

Zhu, J. Y., Park, T., Isola, P., & Efros, A. A. (2017). Unpaired image-to-image translation using cycle-consistent adversarial networks. In *Proceedings of the IEEE international conference on computer vision* (pp. 2223–2232).

7 Big Data and Healthcare

Analysing the Utility, Challenges and Legal Framework in Health Industry in India

Rajesh Kumar, Dr. Hardik Daga, and Latika Choudhary
University of Petroleum & Energy Studies

CONTENTS

DOI: 10.1201/9781003330875-7

7.1   INTRODUCTION

The world today is expanding at an unfathomable speed. Technology today has advanced to such unbelievable leaps and bounds that nothing is unreachable for man today. We are the creatures of the 21st century, an era that has witnessed wondrous phenomena of the best of sports cars, skyscrapers, environmental degradation and technology boom. While some see technology as a boon, making their lives convenient and better, others regard it as an untamable servant bound to go out of control. In today's time, the technology is not only widely available and ready for use but is also seen to be insistently promoted in the society. It is also seen to be a miscreant that creates problems for us, particularly beginning with the decline of general social behaviour.

Technology has accelerated our ability and capacity to do more and ensure better results. Artificial Intelligence, Internet of Things and Big Data all work together for the creation of programs that can be utilised in various fields. Internet of Things have been defined by Chui et al. (2010) as 'sensors and actuators embedded in physical objects—from roadways to pacemakers—[that] are linked through wired and wireless networks, often using the same Internet Protocol (IP) that connects the Internet'. Internet of Things is able to capture data that can be organised by artificial intelligence and turned into Big Data.

While technology is deemed to makes lives convenient, economists have also drawn a significant connection between inventions and growth. In the words of Paul Krugman for many economists, 'Productivity isn't everything, but in the long run it's almost everything'. One may ask, as a natural response to this statement, why? The answer is that 'A country's ability to improve its standard of living over time depends almost entirely on its ability to raise its output per worker', or in simpler words the amount of time of labour that is required for production of anything. Many nations do not have an extensive wealth of minerals or oil and therefore cannot become rich by exporting the same. Thus, the only plausible solution for such countries to get wealthy is to improve the quality of living for the people. Thus, innovation is the only way to ensure productivity growth.

'Big data' is not a novel concept, but its definition continues to shift as new technologies emerge. Big data has been defined in a variety of ways, but the most common definition is that it is a set of datasets that, due to their volume, velocity, type, or complexity, necessitate the creation of novel hardware and/or software tools for their storage, analysis, and visualisation (Da Silva et al., 2008). Many healthcare systems, health insurers, researchers, governmental organisations, and other institutions share this information. Although healthcare data is inherently complex, there is significant potential and numerous advantages in developing and implementing

Big Data solutions in this domain. If the analysis of McKinsey Global Institute is to be believed, the healthcare infrastructure of the United States is capable of generating more than $300 billion annually, provided it uses. Two-thirds of the value might well be attributed to Big Data's innovative use in slashing healthcare expenses in the US (Manyika et al., 2011). Traditional medical studies have restricted their focus to determine whether a patient is sick by evaluating one specific data source, such as a patient's vital signs (Borckardt et al., 2008). Despite the necessity of this method for comprehending disease, research at this level obscures the variety and interdependence that defines the true underlying medical mechanisms (Data & Unit, 2010). The medical industry has been a technology laggard for decades, but it is now starting to adapt to the age of Big Data. With the aid of recent technologies, a substantial amount of information may be collected on each patient over a longer period of time. The possibility to provide a better characterisation of diseases, therapies, and the effectiveness of pharmaceutical goods in various healthcare systems is made possible by the growing volume and complexity of data that is currently being collected across several settings and devices. These data sources—often referred to as 'big data'—are often sizable, amass quickly, and contain a variety of data types and formats.

7.1.1 BACKGROUND OF THE STUDY

Big data is a term not only used to describe a collection of data volumes that are challenging to store, handle, and analyse but are also effective even with basic database technology (Hashem et al., 2015). The demand for data storage is expanding, as more and more systems transition to using data storage as their primary store. Currently, certain systems can only store a certain amount of data on their hard drives, but as data storage grows, additional storage space and Big Data technology as a solution become necessary. Modern data centres house Big Data and the analysis system that uses it. Some examples of data used to create large data sets include: online transactions, emails, images, audio/video files, medical records, social media interactions, scientific data, log data, postings, search queries, sensor readings, telephones, and their applications (Zikopoulos et al., n.d.). All the collected data is kept in databases that expand rapidly and become challenging to gather, form, store, manage, distribute, analyse, and visualise using specialised database software (Shobana & Kumar, 2015). Big data usage has started to permeate many facets of human existence, such as health services, where it is used. There are numerous medical imaging techniques available in the context of health to learn about specific structures or what is within the human body. For instance, Magnetic Resonance Imaging (MRI), Computed Tomography (CT), Ultrasound, and Photoacoustic Imaging can be used to visualise the anatomy of blood arteries (Gessner et al., 2013). A lot of storage space is needed for the scanning process. For instance, 66 TB of storage space is needed for high-resolution microscopic scanning of human brains (Scholl et al., 2011). That much data storage will not be supported by standard storage systems. In order to satisfy the needs of storage in the health sector, Big Data technology is crucial.

Big Data development necessitates that developing nations should be ready in terms of their architectural designs, communication networks, suitable hardware, and construction prices. In a number of instances, emerging nations have struggled to advance their technology, particularly in the information sector. One example is the South African health information system, which has been a financial failure due to either high data costs or low user acceptance (Dada, 2006). Because the current system and the one that will be built in the future are frequently incompatible, system development in developing nations frequently encounters difficulties. Additionally, due to differences in the cultural, economic, and systemic contexts of software designers, system development in underdeveloped nations is frequently hampered (Dada, 2006; Heeks, 2002). But, in the process, development must have advanced.

7.1.2 Adoption and Various Big Data Application

Big Data Lake is a contemporary, massive collection of data that is dispersed across all industries. Big Data was first used by carrier businesses, who effectively tapped this integrated data by extracting, processing, and loading client information. In actuality, e-commerce behemoths and forwarders like Amazon, which obsesses over consumer numbers, are responsible for popularising the word. Each online client click generates data that is stored in these enormous lakes. The outcome is then achieved by integrating the matter. In addition to speeding up the process, it has given clients confidence in their consigners.

Big Data is 'very huge data sets that can be processed computationally to identify patterns, trends, and correlations'. Conventional database systems are unable to properly process this sort of data, given the complexity that comes with it. The quantity of data is substantial; it changes at a rapid rate, or it does not correspond to the organisation's chosen database systems. In order to derive value from these data, an alternate approach will need to be conceived up and investigated (Dumbill, 2013). By utilising Big Data from a variety of sources, departments within an organisation can make progress towards their goals more quickly and with less of an impact on the natural world (Etzion & Aragon-Correa, 2016). Availability and exchange of data, data protection, human resource management, issues with statistics, and technological difficulties are all examples of Big Data issues that already exist (Satyanarayana & Venkata, 2015). There is something that may be considered to as the 'evil side' of Big Data, despite the fact that the list of benefits and prospects afforded by Big Data is literally limitless.

The downfall of Big Data includes its potential for abuse, as well as problems with imprecise Big Data tools, flawed modelling, online analytical, repressive employee management, and low prices (Picciotto, 2020). Organisations shall be required to choose the best service they intend to leverage, taking into account factors like advantages against drawbacks and open innovation, in order to maximise the prospective benefits for the organisation while limiting the negatives.

Big Data is almost always present. Big data analytics could be used in any industry, including those related to health or basic living standards. Given that this enormous amount of data can be exploited to one's advantage, Big Data is a field that can be used to any industry. Big Data has several uses, including in banking, finance, energy-efficient buildings, transportation, healthcare, and agriculture, but the focus of this study will be healthcare sector.

7.2 BIG DATA 101: THE HEALTH INDUSTRY

Data by itself is not regarded as 'big data'. What, though, makes Big Data so huge? In essence, it has to deal with many characteristics a dataset might have. There are five 'Vs' in the data science sector (Figure 7.1), which may be used to define Big Data.

- **Volume:** The amount of data produced by the many healthcare industry players is referred to as volume. Typically, healthcare data is long-term, massive, complex, noisy, heterogeneous, and loud (Sun & Reddy, 2013). For instance, in 2011, the American healthcare system's data volume was approximately 150 Exabytes (Cottle et al., 2013). The volume of digital healthcare data worldwide was estimated to be 500 petabytes in 2012, and 25,000 petabytes is expected by 2020 (Sun & Reddy, 2013).
- **Variety:** Healthcare information comes from a wide range of sources, some of which are more organised than others. Multimedia files, social media posts, blog entries, online server logs, and monetary transactions are only some of the sources of healthcare data. Furthermore, healthcare providers' data may come from a wide range of locations, and it may reside in a wide range of legacy and application systems, including transaction processing systems and various databases.
- **Velocity:** This is the rate or speed with which healthcare providers create, store, analyse, visualise, and exchange data. For successful and efficient patient care, the healthcare system needs the interchange of health information to be seamless, secure, and meaningful. This is due to the fact that

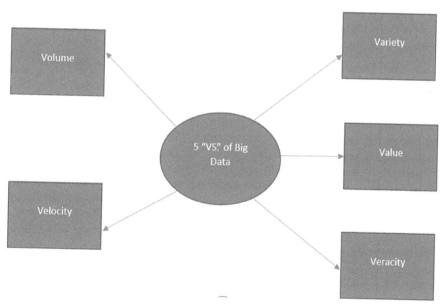

FIGURE 7.1 Various dimensions and contributions of Big Data in terms of variety, value, volume, velocity and veracity. It significantly increases the value of data.

patients frequently receive care from a variety of healthcare providers in various geographic regions. Healthcare professionals must have real-time access to this data in order to make judgements (Iroju et al., 2013). A patient may pass away too soon as a result of a mistake or omission during this process. Therefore, speed is necessary in healthcare, since it enables providers to exchange and use data quickly.

- **Veracity:** The level of data production is referred to as veracity. The accuracy of the data generated by the healthcare system has been a significant source of worry (*Big Data in Healthcare Hype and Hope – DocsLib*, n.d.). Unstructured data, for instance, contains a variety of grammatical patterns, statements expressed in a variety of natural languages, and the use of a single notion to signify a number of concepts. As a result, the healthcare system is marked by ambiguity, which has a negative impact on affordability and error rates. However, the accuracy of information and high-quality healthcare data are crucial for enabling healthcare providers to make important judgements at the appropriate moment when decisions that could mean the difference between life and death are at stake. Therefore, healthcare data needs to be accurate, dependable, and relevant.
- **Value:** Value is data pace, format, structure, and semantics. Flat files, relational tables, photos, and texts include healthcare system data. Healthcare terminology can have numerous interpretations. For example, in a radiological report of the chest, 'mass' refers to a lung mass, not a breast mass (Liu et al., 2011). The medical field makes extensive use of the same set of abbreviations to represent different ideas. Allophycocyanin, antibody-producing cells, activated protein C, and advanced pancreatic cancer are all possible alternatives (Reading Turchioe et al., 2022).

7.2.1 Big Data Application in Healthcare Sector: Detailed Analysis

Big Data in Healthcare is a field that has a significant impact on a nation. Big Data has evolved in the healthcare sector, with examples including the switch from a manual to a digital record-keeping system in hospitals (Zikopoulos et al., n.d.). With the help of Big Data, healthcare data is easier to identify, gather, and store (Bendre et al., 2016). There are three main types of 'Big Data' in the healthcare industry: 'traditional' medical data from the healthcare system (such as personal and family health histories, medical histories, laboratory reports, and pathology results), 'omics' data from the biological and molecular disciplines (such as genomics, microbiomics, proteomics, and metabolomics), and 'social media' data (Bendre et al., 2016).

The future of healthcare systems is unsustainable, according to the WHO report Health 2020 (*Health 2020: A European Policy Framework and Strategy for the 21st Century*, n.d.). Maximising health at all phases of life is essential, since it is a resource and a source of social and economic stability. A global capital resource, good health can no longer be considered the product of a single industry. Numerous elements from all facets of life tagged along with coordinated efforts from all facets of the community we are living in to contribute to sustainable health. New perspectives for researchers as well as the policy-making bodies are required to advance towards a better knowledge of health determinants, diseases' causes, and creative prevention and treatment techniques. Data-driven decision making and science are two of the most promising ways to accomplish this (Manyika et al., 2011). It has already shown to have a major influence on healthcare providers' actions (Vinker et al., 2015). The term 'The Data Deluge' is first mentioned in 'The Economist's' February 2010 issue (*The Data Deluge | The Economist*, n.d.). Data are largely under-utilised, since the ensuing exponential growth in data amounts far outpaces human capacity to deal. Nearly all facets of human activity, including cell phone use, transportation, financial aspects, supply and demand chains, etc. are subject to this. Electronic medical records, the quarantined individuals, bioinformatics and genome sequencing, photos, etc. all fall under this category of patient- and citizen-related health data. It holds true for all human knowledge, but it is particularly true for medical knowledge. Big Data is anticipated to have a tremendous impact on people's lives, such as in personalised medicine, but care systems will also need to make use of the vast amounts of complex, massively multivariate data that are supposed to be frequently collected and preserved across each person's life about all aspects of health determinants, patient care, and outcomes.

The Institute of Medicine (IOM) established the notion of Learning Healthcare System in 2005 as a confrontation to its findings in *To Err is Human* (America et al., 2000) and Crossing the Quality Chasm (*Improving the 21st-Century Health Care System – Crossing the Quality Chasm – NCBI Bookshelf*, n.d.). With this concept in mind, researchers developed the concept of a 'learning health system', an ecosystem in which all players may safely and efficiently contribute to share and use data to generate knowledge and support excellent decision making, leading to better health outcomes. With the advent of modern pharmacogenomics, for example, more and more citizens and patients are able to receive individualised care (Martin & Kroetz, 2014).

Through the use of individual- and population-level statistical health models, personalised medicine has the potential to vastly improve health and treatment results. Data integration across spatial dimensions, from the molecular to the community level, and across temporal scales, from genetics to lifestyle, is a major barrier to effectively utilise these massive, heterogeneous datasets in the field of health. The definition and reality of Big Data remains a central topic of discussion and debate. The concept 'Big Data' is used to describe huge, complicated datasets that are difficult to analyse using traditional methods. Data management encompasses the entire process, from gathering information to storing it, transferring it, making it accessible to others, and sharing it; from ensuring its quality through curation and quality management to analysing and learning from it through visualisation and human interaction; and from interpreting and making decisions based on the information gleaned from all of this (which includes reliability and accuracy).

Big data analytics are currently being adopted by a wide range of healthcare organisations, from multi-provider associations and single-run clinics to huge hospital networks. This growth is attributable to the service's many useful features, such as its ability to analyse clinical studies and health history rapidly and effectively, and to identify healthcare deception. The forecast for Big Data analytics services market for the year 2025 is very high across the globe (growth of 1500%) (*Health Big Data Analytics Services Market by Application 2025 Global Forecast | Statista*, n.d.).

7.2.2   How Big Data Aids Healthcare

Electronic medical records are now being used more often in the healthcare system than ever before to enhance the standard of patient care. However, due to the enormous growth in the amount of healthcare data, standard data processing systems are finding it challenging to analyse health-related data properly. Understanding the significance of Big Data in healthcare is necessary to efficiently extract values from healthcare data. As a result, this section explores the requirement for advanced tools and technologies to analyse large data in healthcare.

7.2.2.1   Evidenced-Based Care

Evidence-based healthcare is replacing more sporadic and subjective decision making in accepted medical practice (Savage, 2012). Evidence-based medicine is a practice in which the majority of patient care is guided by the best available scientific data. By combining data sets from many sources, Big Data offers evidence-based care. The trends and patterns in the data will offer sufficient proof for making diagnoses and administering treatments to patients. Smaller data sets might not provide enough proof to establish whether there are statistical differences in the data sets (Savage, 2012).

7.2.2.2   Reduced Cost of Healthcare

Rise in costs is one of the most crucial challenges that the health industry is confronted with. For cost, growth is one of the biggest issues the healthcare sector is dealing with. For instance, in the United States of America, the expense of healthcare accounted for around 16.9% of GDP in 2012 (*OECD Health Statistics 2014 – Frequently Requested Data – OECD*, n.d.). However, a recent study conducted by a Health Research Institute found that making information more accessible could lower the cost of healthcare (*How Big Data Impacts Healthcare – SPONSORED CONTENT FROM SAP*, n.d.). The survey also found that if non-traditional healthcare options were less expensive, patients would probably choose them, such as at-home urine tests using a gadget connected to a smartphone. As a result, Priyanka and Kulennavar (Saranya & Asha, 2019) predicted that using cutting-edge tools and methodologies to analyse data will save the United States of America $300 billion annually. This healthcare cost decrease represents around 8% of total national healthcare spending (Saranya & Asha, 2019).

7.2.2.3   Increases Patient Engagement

Big data makes ensuring that the information available to patients is reliable and current. The patients will be able to make decisions about their care, understand their options, and alter their lifestyle to prevent chronic diseases as a result.

7.2.2.4   Reduces Mortality Rate

Big data guarantees the early identification, diagnosis, and detection of diseases. This ensures that the appropriate decisions on a certain disease's treatment are made in an efficient and timely manner. This lowers the morbidity and mortality of the patients.

7.2.2.5 Enhances Provider–Patient Communication

Effective communication between healthcare professionals and patients is improved by Big Data. For instance, people with comparable health issues and medical professionals with comparable specialties from around the world can exchange ideas on the prevention and treatment of a certain disease via social media. This procedure makes healthcare organisations more interoperable.

7.2.2.6 Early Detection of Healthcare Security and Fraud

Big data can be utilised to quickly find trends and anomalies that point to security issues and healthcare fraud.

7.2.2.7 Enhances Care

By ensuring that decisions are based on substantial amounts of pertinent and current data, Big Data enhances the quality of care provided to patients. Big data has unquestionably good effects on the healthcare sector. However, the biggest issue facing Big Data in healthcare is not a shortage of data but rather a lack of information to help planning, strategy, and decision making (Dachis, 2012). Therefore, in order to derive value from health-related data, information must be evaluated, processed, and integrated. Therefore, the difficulties with Big Data in healthcare are described in this section.

7.3 ISSUES AND CHALLENGES FACED BY BIG DATA

The sample size of the databases that are utilised by businesses nowadays is increasing daily at a fast pace (Patel et al., 2012). However, if we intend to gain some benefits from such data collection, the generated and gathered information shall be both credible and accessible (Fuller et al., 2013). Nearly 95% of company data is now unused, and the requirement to process and analyse enormous volumes of data has also expanded. Numerous procedures, including tagging, highlighting, indexing, searching, and others are included in the data processing (Patel et al., 2012). Unfortunately, handling this information with current computational techniques exhibits serious constraints (Khan et al., 2014). Scalability, unstructured data, accessibility, real-time analytics, fault tolerance, and other problems are among the challenges (Patel et al., 2012), whereas, on the other hand, the restrictions on the usage include a shortage of standardised formats, interfaces to data, inconsistent biological entity identifiers, inadequate support for data-exchange frameworks, and a lack of visibility (Fuller et al., 2013). Big Data collections cannot be stored or processed by one or a few machines in a finite amount of time (Patel et al., 2012). The 'Big Data Problem' that is reflecting evidently in the society is now becoming a crucial aspect of our daily lives. In addition to the challenges of managing these data, handling errors may result in major financial losses and have a detrimental effect on the public image of the organisation (Meeker & Hong, 2014). The utilisation of such data mountains also raises a number of ethical concerns. For instance, if the words of Kord and Doug are to be believed, Big Data has a compelling power that instigates us to think about important moral questions, such as whether the applications of Big Data indeed is an infringement of fundamental, social, political, civil, and legal rights (Shaer et al., 2013). The security and privacy of the personal data of persons is another issue (Costa, 2014). According to Gosting, the tension between the interests of the individual and the interests of the community can be seen in the relationship between privacy and freedom (Savulescu et al., n.d.). It has also been noted by Boyd and Crawford that Big Data is sort of a socio-technical practice that inspires language that is both utopian and apocalyptic (Boyd & Crawford, 2012). Big Data handling may not only be useful for addressing issues like climate change, cancer research and environmental issues, but it also poses a risk of invasion of privacy and a reduction in human liberties. The US National Institutes of Health raised the issue in 2013, and the Data-Enabled Life Science Alliance (DELSA) is primarily interested in it (Trifonova et al., 2013).

7.3.1 Technology Issues and Challenges Posed by Big Data in Healthcare

Most modern, cutting-edge technologies are referred to as 'dual-use technologies' for their key feature of being used for both good and bad reasons (Pustovit & Williams, 2010). Boyd and Crawford claim that although technology is 'neither a boon nor a curse; nor it is neutral' (Boyd & Crawford, 2012a), it is the interaction of technology with society that may have adverse effects on the environment, society, and people. The application of science and technology to the field of healthcare presents many difficulties, and the moral climate is getting increasingly complicated. The ethics are at the heart of any organisation and business, particularly those involving Big Data (Zwitter, 2014). Big Data as a whole may not be a particular technology, but managing and analysing it requires cutting-edge technology. Some academics claim that while Big Data is morally neutral, efforts to connect organisational behaviour with social ideals lead to ethical problems (Mateosian, 2013). Exploring the emerging challenges and ethical dilemmas is crucial, but it is also a difficult task as the full understanding of ethical implications is still lacking (Boyd & Crawford, 2012a). Eventually, a certain number of such problems are applicable to data in a hard copy format, they are even more troublesome and important in the field of electronic Big Data, because enormous amounts of data are processed there (Paper et al., 2012).

Generally speaking, it has been stated that technologies can be classified based on how they affect people and society (Stylianou & Talias, 2015). There are three types of individuals who are significantly impacted by the usage of Big Data, which are further listed: those who generate, gather, and evaluate the data (Attribution-noncommercial-noderivatives et al., 2012). Additionally, we can pinpoint another group of people that stand to gain from Big Data analysis. Users, citizens/patients, and researchers are the categories used to classify the people in this instance of healthcare. Users could be the staff of healthcare organisations that provide medical care who are in charge of creating or maintaining such records and information, while researchers are those individuals who analyse the collection of such records. In this scenario, the community here refers to the common populace that healthcare data may indirectly affect. For each of these obstacles, such as data quality, identifying the ethical questions and concerns and covering and debating them will give us an idea of potential ramifications that could affect the general public, research-ers, citizens, and users, among other groups. As a result, this strategy enables us to research all pertinent topics for all potential affected parties.

7.3.1.1 Data Quality

The community here refers to the general populace that healthcare data may indirectly affect. For each of these obstacles, such as data quality, identifying the ethical questions and concerns and covering and debating them will give us an idea of potential ramifica-tions that could affect the general public, researchers, citizens, and users, among other groups. As a result, this strategy enables us to research all pertinent topics for all poten-tial affected parties (Fuller et al., 2013). More importantly, many of the data are full with flaws or errors. For instance, busy doctors may type fast and reverse numbers, click on the wrong menu choices, or simply just copy and paste the narrative from the records of the earlier visits without carefully correcting it in the electronic health records (EHRs) (Abrahão et al., 2017; Paper et al., 2012). Additionally, many times, EHRs lack infor-mation after patients receive a medication and are fragmented in other circumstances (Hoffman & Podgurski, 2013). Furthermore, health-related data are frequently very fragmented (Bill Hamilton, n.d.). Furthermore, if certain data are encoded properly, they can be regarded as bad. Many doctors and nurses don't use the latest version of the International Classification of Diseases (ICD-10), and there is minimal to no integration across different kinds of health records (Kayyali & Knott, n.d.). Therefore, it is impos-sible to transmit information for additional analysis. Additionally, Big Data and its tools and services utilised to examine them must communicate with one another (V, 2013). Moreover, many digital services continue to use a bureaucratic data processing para-digm (Keen, 2014). New innovations are emerging in order to replace this antiquated strategy, such as open data and telehealth, which will centralise the data collection and its linkage. Considering the advent of open data strategies, various healthcare providers now publish information that was previously unavailable for examination by outside individuals who might require such data for R&D (Keen, 2014).

7.3.1.2 Analysis

The challenge of handling data is not a new task in the healthcare industry. Leber asserts that the solution has always been quite straightforward: 'get health records dig-italised and keep them private, but make them available to individual doctors, insur-ers, billing departments, and patients when they need them' (Leber, n.d.). Objective to 'keep them private' does not diminish the problem. However, even if Big Data are perfect in and of itself, analysing them is still a very difficult undertaking (Hoffman & Podgurski, 2013). The primary problems (or pathologies, as the author referred to them) in the field of Big Data, according to Jacobs, are those that are related to the analysis of Big Data sets (Jacobs, 2009). When Big Data is analysed, numerous important questions come up, including: What does all this data mean? Which ana-lytic methods? How can results be visualised? How can data be made meaningful? Who has access to which information? How is data analysis used and for what pur-poses? How should these large data sets be handled? Are these data analyses biased in any way? So forth (Boyd & Crawford, 2012a; Mitchell et al., 2021). Big Data activities can be broken down into two main categories: (i) when data are gathered in real time and must be analysed right away, and (ii) when there is a massive amount of accumulated data that needs to be processed (Trifonova et al., 2013). In the first instance, real-time Big Data analysis in healthcare gives rise to new possibilities. Within a few minutes of the patient's data being collected, interactive medical data analysis can produce a tentative diagnostic (Trifonova et al., 2013). Additionally, the real-time Big Data analysis in hospitals pave the way for fresh insights into how to identify, treat, and prevent diseases on a larger scale of public health (Leber, n.d.). Despite the importance of this need, Leber claims that there isn't even a hospital-specific search engine for all of its data (Leber, n.d.). It is intriguing that despite the availability of numerous techniques and technologies for the analysis of Big Data, they are not used to thoroughly examine healthcare data. It is uncommon for hospitals to have both the requisite infrastructure (such as a supercomputer) and staff members who are capable of using such equipment or handling vast amounts of data. On the other hand, we have a vast amount of data that has already been gathered and is available for analysis. Unfortunately, these data are typically of limited value in their original form (Mitchell et al., 2021). For instance, the data in EHR are primarily observational information and not the outcome of trials. As a result, they could be very susceptible to systematic biases (Hoffman & Podgurski, 2013). This means that in order to finally discover their true value, the already available data (such as those in massive databases) must first be translated into a format that is open to study. As a result, there is a lot of demand from numerous new studies using Big Data that weren't initially gathered for study (Ioannidis, 2013). Measurement bias and mistakes, as well as selection, confounding, and consent, might affect the findings of such investigations. The final recommendations are not suitable for health policies as a result (Boyd & Crawford, 2012b; Ioannidis, 2013). The need for the development of tools that are characterised by stability and longevity is putting great pressure on the technology required to handle Big Data, as too many software tools crash far too frequently when working with Big Data (V, 2013). Additionally, large-scale genome research investigations have highlighted the need for new computational tools that enable insightful analyses (Shaer et al., 2013), and genomic research has the potential to change clinical practice (Haase et al., 2015). Furthermore, in order to collect and analyse data from large databases, Big Data analysts require unique analytical techniques. Additionally, improvements in artificial intelligence (such as machine learning and natural language processing) are anticipated to make a substantial contribution to the development of tools for the management of disorders (Costa, 2014). Large-scale project data storage requirements have prompted the emergence of novel computational approaches like cloud-based computing (Costa, 2014). Despite the usage of cloud solutions from many vendors, there are still a number of issues, especially with regard to the security and privacy of personal data.

7.3.1.3 Privacy

As personal healthcare information and many nations have a vast amount of data maintained at the national level, the tremendous volume of healthcare data is a rising reality in our time (Egan, 2013). Because of the immeasurable advantages that Big Data in healthcare can provide, more and more users are in need of direct access to the data, either from their offices or from distant locations via smart devices (Mitchell et al., 2021; Martínez-Pérez et al., 2015). On the one side, there are the patients who demand immediate access to their medical records. On the other side, there are indirect users that require this information, such as researchers, decision-makers in the medical field, physicians, insurers, etc. As a result, questions about the security and privacy of personal information about persons are raised, including: Who has access to it? What are its uses? Where is it used? Under what restrictions? (Boyd & Crawford, 2012a). Many ethical discussions that are pertinent to these issues centre on the concepts of identity, privacy, ownership, and reputation (Mateosian, 2013). Limitations and ethical issues are raised by these inquiries. For instance, citizens might not want to disclose private information because of privacy concerns (Bill Hamilton, n.d.). As a result, if a sizeable portion of the target population refuses to provide access to their personal data, researchers and policy makers cannot have a good picture of a particular target group. In order to safeguard citizens, security and privacy guarantees must be established (Bill Hamilton, n.d.). Significant difficulties also arise when Big Data is connected to poorer health outcomes, or higher expenses for minority groups and individuals (Egan, 2013). Additionally, a lack of data sets leads to the development of new digital divisions (Boyd & Crawford, 2012a). Since there are frequently tight regulations governing patient privacy, and, as a result, clinicians are reluctant to use such data, there are regrettably a number of restrictions on the access to Big Data from hospitals (Leber, n.d.). However, when we have access to large amounts of data, privacy concerns are equally important. It is not necessarily moral just because something is available (Boyd & Crawford, 2012a). The EHR is one of the most contentious sources of concerns about privacy in healthcare (Hoffman & Podgurski, 2013; Lee & Gostin, 2009). It is anticipated that the methodical study of the Big Data included in EHRs will considerably advance targeted medicines and personalised therapies. Although the potential rewards are immeasurable, a variety of ethical, legal, and technical concerns and obstacles prevent a thorough investigation of EHRs' Big Data (Costa, 2014). Many people use their own computer or mobile device to access or store their personal data, but this comes with a number of difficulties, because the Internet is inherently unsafe and fraught with danger (Bill Hamilton, n.d.; Levy & Strombeck, 2002). However, there is a noticeable trend on the Internet where people share comprehensive health information using online tools (such as Patients like Me) (Costa, 2014). Since the patients make their personal information available to the public, these data may be a novel and distinctive data source for Big Data analysis without privacy concerns, but the researchers will once again have to deal with issues with data quality, as they may be characterised by errors, ambiguities, and biases. Private data protection has historically been the discloser responsibility. The citizens/patients made the decision as to whether or not they wanted their private information public, and if they did not want their information published, they withheld some information (Zwitter, 2014). The privacy considerations are more complicated in the digital age. Up to this point, the emphasis has been on controlling personally identifiable information, but this is insufficient because secondary users of personal data sets can undo privacy, confidentiality, and identity breaches (Costa, 2014; Richards & King, 2014). Modern privacy concerns necessitate the development of new encryption and secure transmission solutions to address local hardware and cloud computing security problems (V, 2013). The citizens/patients made the decision as to whether or not they wanted their private information public, and if they did not want their information published, they withheld some information (Zwitter, 2014). The privacy considerations are more complicated in the digital age. Up to this point, the emphasis has been on controlling personally identifiable records; however, this is insufficient, since the secondary users of personal data can undo privacy and identity breaches (Costa, 2014). Modern privacy concerns necessitate the development of new encryption and secure transmission solutions to address local hardware and cloud computing security problems (V, 2013).

7.3.1.4   Economic

The employment market and insurance providers will both be significantly impacted by all the aforementioned problems. Additionally, the healthcare sector will lose a substantial sum of money in sales and earnings, if it does not acquire and employ the instruments needed to handle massive amounts of data properly (Raghupathi, 2012). Healthcare organisations need new methods to manage their limited healthcare resources as demand rises (Cornelissen et al., 2014), and Big Data could provide a step in that direction. Improving patient outcomes and care quality while cutting costs is crucial for all parties involved in healthcare (Costa, 2014). Healthcare funders need technically competent systems that 'can identify cost overruns that can constitute fraud, abuse, waste, and errors', in order to develop reliable comparable standards by which to judge the quality of care actually delivered (Srinivasan & Arunasalam, 2013). Healthcare businesses can effectively address the numerous cost challenges they confront by using appropriate and cutting-edge software applications (Charles, n.d.). The need for such investments is urgent, given the increasing cost pressures. With the right strategy, healthcare organisations can decrease unnecessary readmissions and reimbursement (Charles, n.d.).

7.4   BIG DATA AND LEGAL PROTECTION IN INDIA IN THE HEALTHCARE SECTOR

Electronic medical records (EMRs) are becoming a more popular way for hospitals in India to store patient data. In reality, the Healthcare Establishments Act stipulates that 'holding and provision of EMR for every patient' is necessary for the registration and continuous operation of any clinical facility under the Registration and Regulation, Act 2010, *The Clinical Establishments*, *Registration and Regulation*, *Act, 2010* and *National Health Portal Of India*, n.d., Guidelines published on May 23, 2012.

There has been a worldwide trend towards EMRs. The US approved a rule requiring the use of EMRs by all healthcare organisations by 2015 in order to receive federal funding, and the UK's National Health Service has pledged to have patient data 'mostly paperless' by 2020. The growth of EMRs has been rapid, even among the other BRICS nations.

7.4.1   Inadequacy of Current Legal Framework in India

The general basis for the protection of personal information in India is provided by sections 72 (*Section 72: Breach of Confidentiality and Privacy - Info. Technology*

Law, n.d.) and 43(a) (*Section 43A of Information Technology Act: Compensation for Failure to Protect Data*, n.d.) of the Information Technology Act. 'Section 43(a) and the sensitive personal information rules' detail the obligations that must be met by any business that accumulates retail chains or is otherwise in agreement with records that can be used to identify an individual, such as a passcode, credit card number, social security number, health record, or biometric information. Section 72 also protects personal information. It's important to remember that section 43(a) only applies to 'bodies corporate', which are described as 'firms, sole proprietorships, or other associations of individuals engaged in commercial or professional activities.'

Public hospitals and medical facilities are always more heavily utilised, because the majority of folks in India cannot afford private healthcare. If public hospitals or non-profit organisations do to uphold reasonable security practices, there are little remedies available, leaving a significant amount of personal data exposed. In India, the current framework for regulating EMRs is the draught Electronic Health Record Standards published by the Ministry of Health and Family Welfare (MoHFW). Information security standards for health records are laid forth here, including the technical, administrative, and physical safeguards that must be in place. Moreover, doctors are obligated to maintain patient confidentiality throughout the entire process, ensuring that all aspects of information provided by the patient, including their private and domestic life, align with the regulations set forth by the Indian Medical Council (Professional Conduct, Etiquette and Ethics) Regulations, 2002 (Code of Medical Ethics Regulations, 2002 | NMC, 2002) (MCI code of ethics).

There are a number of problems with the EMR standards, including a vague definition of 'personal health information', a lack of clarity concerning coverage, a lack of specifics regarding when patients would have access to their records, and the failure to label URLs and IP addresses as confidential information. In contrast, the Medical Council of India's code of ethics provides only general guidelines without any mechanisms for enforcing compliance. Because of this, it is no longer necessary to obtain consent before disclosing an individual's medical records, even if those records have been de-identified.

There are essentially no rules dictating how this information should be used or preserved in the absence of a suitable framework, raising the danger of medical data being misappropriated and commercialised. Most of the health records connected to the Aadhaar number wherever possible, and as recent investigations have shown, the legal structure controlling the use of Aadhaar is also hazy, adding another level of ambiguous privacy consequences.

In India, hospitals are not required by law to report security breaches. For instance, the HIPAA (*Health Insurance Portability and Accountability Act of 1996 (HIPAA) | CDC*, n.d.) (Health Insurance Portability and Accountability Act, 1996) mandates that hospitals notify breaches that harm more over 500 patients (*HHS HIPAA Breach Settlement Involving Less than 500 Patients | HHS.Gov*, n.d.). As a result, there is no established structure governing EMRs, and how they are acquired and utilised. Additionally, there are no available remedies for data breaches brought on by public hospitals' negligence.

7.4.2 THE INDIAN CONSTITUTION AND RIGHT TO PRIVACY

According to Article 21 (*Article 21 in The Constitution Of India 1949*, n.d.) of the Indian Constitution, the right to privacy was first recognised in Justice K.S. Puttaswamy v. Union of India (*Justice K.S.Puttaswamy(Retd) vs Union Of India on 26 September, 2018*, n.d.) and then confirmed in Puttaswamy. However, unlike other fundamental rights, the right to privacy is not absolute under the Indian Constitution; and, as such, it may be restricted by the state in accordance with the Constitution.

Even in the Aadhaar case (*The Aadhar Case*, n.d.), three requirements were set forth to determine if an Act violating any rights was acceptable. The first need is that the activity be authorised by law (lawfulness). The activity must also be necessary for a valid point to be made (need). Third, the activity (invading privacy) must be appropriate, given the need for it.

The judgement in *Puttaswamy* (*Justice K.S. Puttaswamy (Retd) vs Union Of India on 26 September, 2018*, n.d.) further stressed on the doctrine of proportionality by articulating four sub-parts:

1. There must be a reasonable objective in order for a measure to restrict a right.
2. It should be an appropriate means of working towards this objective.
3. There cannot be any option that is not only less limiting but also productive.
4. The measures can't have an unfairly significant effect on the person who has the legal right.

7.4.3 PRIVACY CONCERNS ARISING FROM BIG DATA: THE PANDEMIC STRUGGLE

The government's application for 'Arogya Setu' has been the topic of discussion. According to the app's privacy statement (*Privacy Policy – Aarogya Setu*, n.d.), it gathers user's personal information and provides the government with the necessary information for 'carrying out medical and administrative interventions necessary regarding COVID-19'.

If a person's right to privacy must ever be restricted, it must be done by a legitimate law that has been approved by the legislature. According to a review of pertinent statutes, including The Epidemic Diseases Act of 1897 (*The Epidemic Diseases Act, 1897*, n.d.) and The National Disaster Management Act of 2005 (*The Disaster Management Act, 2005*, n.d.), there does not appear to be any legal requirement requiring the publication of a consumer's personal health information in a public database. Despite this initial illegality, the state's action fails to pass the 'proportionality' standard.

To pass the proportionality test, any action taken by the federal or state governments that breaches the fundamental rights of their citizens must not be 'excessive'. It means that no existing measures should be used, if they would be less effective with less invasion. This is the 'necessity stage,' according to Puttaswamy (*Justice K.S.Puttaswamy(Retd) vs Union Of India on 26 September, 2018*, n.d.). Some governments have adopted the practise of using permanent ink to stamp individuals who have been tested positive or who have been placed under quarantine. The release of an Internet database containing the COVID-19 patients' personal health information has a number of issues. Without a specific data protection law in the nation, which is ostensibly a continuous violation of the Supreme Court's order while upholding the constitutionality of the Aadhaar Act (*The Aadhaar Act, 2016*, n.d.), these individuals' personal information is disclosed to the public without their consent, and is, therefore, vulnerable to being misused and abused. States have a tendency to view civil freedoms as being essential during such crises, conflicts or emergencies. Some argue that it is morally correct to do so, and it might be argued that the Constitution acknowledges this by including the provisions of Articles 352–360, which imagine a completely different society in times of emergency.

7.4.4 TRENDS: SECTOR-SPECIFIC LAWS AND REGULATORY GUIDANCE

Information Technology Act 2000 supplemented with the Information Technology (Reasonable Security Practices and Procedures and Sensitive Personal Data or Information) Rules, 2011, governs the current legal scenario of e-health regime in India Rules, 2011. The Act along with the rules offers to a certain extent protection from disclosure and transfer of sensitive information covering within its ambit medical records and history.

The laws, however, have not been revised to reflect the rapid advancement of technology, leaving many issues unresolved. The government has responded by introducing DISHA (*Ministry of Home Affairs DISHA BILL*, n.d.) and the 2019 Personal Data Protection Bill ('PDP Bill'). Any personal information collected, disclosed, shared, or otherwise processed in India is subject to the PDP Bill, as is any personal information processed by the state, any Indian enterprise, any Indian citizen, or any person or body of individuals incorporated or constituted under Indian law. Companies outside of India that routinely supply products or services to data principals in Indian territory or that engage in profiling of data principals in Indian territory fall under the ambit of the law.

Additionally, EMRs and EHRs are becoming more and more popular in India among clinical facilities and healthcare practitioners as the preferred means of keeping patient data. In reality, the Clinical Establishments (Registration and Regulation) Act 2010 regulations stipulate that every clinical institution must 'maintain and provide an EMR for every patient', in order to register and remain in operation. The EHR Standards, a unified standard-based framework for the development and upkeep of EHRs by healthcare providers, were first announced by the MoHFW in 2013, and they were amended and made public in December 2016.

7.4.5 DISHA AND ITS FEATURES

The Digital Health Data (*Ministry of Home Affairs DISHA BILL*, n.d.) ('DHD') and related personally identifiable information are generated, collected, accessed, stored, transmitted, and used in accordance with the rules established by DISHA ('PII'). According to DISHA, health information, including physical and physiological characteristics, mental health status, sexual orientation, medical histories, and biometric data can exclusively belong to the person to whom it pertains.

The salient features of DISHA are as follows (*Ministry of Home Affairs DISHA BILL*, n.d.):

- Data held in a digital health record (DHD) comprises information around an individual's personal mental or physical well-being as well as their donation of any organs or biological substance, among other things.
- Information that may be used alone or in conjunction with other pieces of data to identify, contact or find a specific individual is considered personally identifiable information (PII). Personal data contains things like name, address, date of birth, vehicle number, bank account numbers, etc.
- To implement DISHA, the law establishes both a federal agency called the National Electronic Health Authority (NeHA) and a number of state agencies named State Electronic Health Authorities (SeHA).
- Hospitals, nursing homes, dispensaries, clinics, sanatoria, and pathology labs, as well as any other organisation that collects DHD, are all included.
- It has been proposed by DISHA to make stringent penalties for the offenders and defaulters in the form of imprisonment or fine, or both.

7.4.6 Challenges to Implementation of DISHA

How to gain informed consent from a data owner will be the most important problem with data collecting and dissemination. Effective DISHA enforcement will be a concern as well, given that clinical establishments may run out of resources due to the costs of adopting security measures.

Data that is stored electronically is susceptible to security lapses, necessitating the adoption of extensive and technologically advanced data security procedures. The foundation of DISHA will be sensitivity, preservation of individuals' right to privacy, and security of their data.

7.4.6.1 Link between DISHA and PDP Bill

Unlike DISHA, which prohibits the commercial use of Digital Health Data (DHD), the PDP Bill mandates explicit authorization from the individual whose sensitive personal data is involved in order to handle the data. As a result, it remains uncertain which law will govern the collection, use, and processing of DHD. Both the PDP Bill and DISHA have overriding clauses, which is an interesting parallel (Sections 96 and 52, respectively). As a result, this law supersedes all other laws whose provisions are in contradiction with it. Historically, it has been established that in the event of a conflict between the provisions of a special law (such as DISHA on the issue of DHD) and the provisions of a general law (such as the PDP Bill on the subject of DHD), the provisions of the special law (in this case, DISHA) shall take precedence.

It will be interesting to see how the government implements the DISHA and PDP legislation, neither of which has yet been enacted by the Parliament and is therefore awaiting action. By taking these steps, India would modify its approach to data protection, putting it in line with international standards. While existing law for the protection of health or personal data is broader in scope, the proposals place extra requirements on the data collector with severe fines and penalties for noncompliance. Assuming these measures become legislation, accurate accounting for these commitments is essential.

To improve its own electronic health and medical record governance, India should look into the methods used by countries further along the technological curve. The government should speed up the implementation of the Healthcare Data Privacy and Security Act so that all hospitals are covered, and the regulator can respond fast to occurrences of negligent security and exploitation of personal information. This is necessary because patient health records include sensitive information, and a data breach could have serious consequences.

7.5 CONCLUSION

The implementation and usage of Big Data is on the exponential rise and majorly in the healthcare sector in India. Discussion on Aadhaar and Aarogya Setu has fuelled demands of privacy protection and security of sensitive medical data. Since usage of Big Data in healthcare is indispensable, regulatory framework to govern the same is of paramount need. The DISHA and PDP remain to be in bill stage, and we, for now, cannot ascertain the form and shape it will be enacted (if enacted). The said bills aspire to transform the personal and health data protection scenario in India, and will bring it at par with global standards. The existing legal scenario is not sufficient to create any substantial and specific obligation for medical record collectors. Sanctioning noncompliance by imposing penalties and stringent fine will contribute to curb privacy concerns. For now, at this nascent (bill) stage, we cannot be assured of these bills resolving all our concerns surrounding Big Data in the Indian healthcare sector. We will have to sit back and look for gaps, if there are any, after they take form of law.

REFERENCES

Abrahão, M. T. F., Nobre, M. R. C., & Gutierrez, M. A. (2017). A method for cohort selection of cardiovascular disease records from an electronic health record system. *International Journal of Medical Informatics*, *102*, 138–149. https://doi.org/10.1016/J. IJMEDINF.2017.03.015

America, I., Kohn, L. T., Corrigan, J. M., & Donaldson, M. S. (2000). *Committee on Quality of Health Care in America.* https://www.ncbi.nlm.nih.gov/books/NBK225176/

Article 21 in The Constitution Of India 1949. (n.d.). Retrieved September 14, 2022, from https://indiankanoon.org/doc/1199182/

Attribution-noncommercial-noderivatives, C. C., License, I., & By-nc-nd, C. C. (2012). *No Title.* 2, 183–203.

Bendre, M. R., Thool, R. C., & Thool, V. R. (2016). Big data in precision agriculture: Weather forecasting for future farming. *Proceedings on 2015 1st International Conference on Next Generation Computing Technologies, NGCT 2015, September*, 744–750. https://doi.org/10.1109/NGCT.2015.7375220

Big Data in Healthcare Hype and Hope - DocsLib. (n.d.). Retrieved September 2, 2022, from https://docslib.org/doc/11844224/big-data-in-healthcare-hype-and-hope

Bill Hamilton. (n.d.). *Impacts of big data. Potential is huge, so are challenges - PubMed.* Retrieved September 15, 2022, from https://pubmed.ncbi.nlm.nih.gov/24015484/

Borckardt, J. J., Nash, M. R., Murphy, M. D., Moore, M., Shaw, D., & O'Neil, P. (2008). Clinical practice as natural laboratory for psychotherapy research: A guide to case-based time-series analysis. *American Psychologist*, *63*(2), 77–95. https://doi.org/10.1037/0003-066X.63.2.77

Boyd, D., & Crawford, K. (2012a). Critical questions for big data - Provaocations for a cultural, technological, and scholarly phenomenon. *Informacios Tarsadalom*, *2*, 7–23.

Boyd, D., & Crawford, K. (2012b). Critical questions for big data - Provocations for a cultural, technological, and scholarly phenomenon. *Informacios Tarsadalom*, *2*, 7–23.

Charles, D. S. (n.d.). *How hospitals can make big data pay big*. Retrieved September 15, 2022, from https://www.healthcareitnews.com/news/how-hospitals-can-make-big-data-pay-big

Code of Medical Ethics Regulations, 2002 | NMC. (2002). https://www.nmc.org.in/rules-regulations/code-of-medical-ethics-regulations-2002/

Cornelissen, E., Mitton, C., Davidson, A., Reid, C., Hole, R., Visockas, A. M., & Smith, N. (2014). Determining and broadening the definition of impact from implementing a rational priority setting approach in a healthcare organization. *Social Science & Medicine (1982)*, *114*, 1–9. https://doi.org/10.1016/J.SOCSCIMED.2014.05.027

Costa, F. F. (2014). Big data in biomedicine. *Drug Discovery Today*, *19*(4), 433–440. https://doi.org/10.1016/J.DRUDIS.2013.10.012

Cottle, M., Hoover, W., Kanwal, S., Kohn, M., Strome, T., & Treister, N. W. (2013). Transforming health care through big data: strategies for leveraging big data in the health care industry. *Institute for Health Technology Transformation - IHT*, 1–24.

da Silva, R. D. J., Labidi, S., Monteiro, M. S., & da Silva Farias, O. DEVELOPING OF AN INTELLIGENT SYSTEM FOR FUELS QUALITY CONTROL AND MONITORING. INTELLIGENT SYSTEMS AND AGENTS 2008, 177.

Dachis, J. (2012). Big data is the future of marketing. *Business Insider, September*, 1–7. http://www.businessinsider.com/big-data-is-the-future-of-marketing-2012-7

Dada, D. (2006). *The Failure of E-Government in Developing Countries: A Literature Review*. 1–10, Wiley Online Library

Data, B., & Unit, I. C. (2010). Big data in the intensive care unit. *American Journal of Respiratory Critical Care*, *187*(11), 1157–1166. https://doi.org/10.1164/rccm.201212-2311ED

Dumbill, E. (2013). Making sense of big data. *Big Data*, *1*(1), 1–2. https://doi.org/10.1089/BIG.2012.1503

Egan, B. M. (2013). Prediction of incident hypertension. Health implications of data mining in the "Big Data" era. *Journal of Hypertension*, *31*(11), 2123–2124. https://doi.org/10.1097/HJH.0b013e328365b932

Etzion, D., & Aragon-Correa, J. A. (2016). Big data, management, and sustainability: Strategic opportunities ahead. *Organization & Environment*, *29*(2), 147–155. https://doi.org/10.1177/1086026616650437

Fuller, J. C., Khoueiry, P., Dinkel, H., Forslund, K., Stamatakis, A., Barry, J., Budd, A., Soldatos, T. G., Linssen, K., & Rajput, A. M. (2013). Biggest challenges in bioinformatics. *EMBO Reports*, *14*(4), 302–304. https://doi.org/10.1038/EMBOR.2013.34

Fuller, J. C., Khoueiry, P., Dinkel, H., Forslund, K., Stamatakis, A., Barry, J., Budd, A., Soldatos, T. G., Linssen, K., Rajput, A. M., & Participants, H. U. B. (2013). Biggest challenges in bioinformatics. *Nature Publishing Group*, *14*(4), 302–304. https://doi.org/10.1038/embor.2013.34

Gessner RC, Frederick CB, Foster FS, Dayton PA. Acoustic angiography: a new imaging modality for assessing microvasculature architecture. Int J Biomed Imaging. 2013;2013:936593. doi: 10.1155/2013/936593. Epub 2013 Jul 17. PMID: 23997762; PMCID: PMC3730364.

Haase, R., Michie, M., & Skinner, D. (2015). Flexible positions, managed hopes: The promissory bioeconomy of a whole genome sequencing cancer study HHS public access. *Social Science Medicine*, *130*, 146–153. https://doi.org/10.1016/j.socscimed.2015.02.016

Hashem, I. A. T., Yaqoob, I., Anuar, N. B., Mokhtar, S., Gani, A., & Ullah Khan, S. (2015). The rise of "big data" on cloud computing: Review and open research issues. *Information Systems*, *47*(July), 98–115. https://doi.org/10.1016/j.is.2014.07.006

Health 2020: A European Policy Framework and Strategy for the 21st Century. (n.d.). Retrieved September 2, 2022, from https://apps.who.int/iris/handle/10665/326386

Health Big Data Analytics Services Market by Application 2025 Global Forecast | Statista. (n.d.). Retrieved September 1, 2022, from https://www-statista-com.eu1.proxy.openathens. net/statistics/909669/global-big-data-in-healthcare-analytics-market-size-by-application/

Health Insurance Portability and Accountability Act of 1996 (HIPAA) | CDC. (n.d.). Retrieved September 21, 2022, from https://www.cdc.gov/phlp/publications/topic/hipaa.html

Heeks, R. (2002). Information systems and developing countries: Failure, success, and local improvisations. *Information Society*, *18*(2), 101–112. https://doi.org/10.1080/01972240290075039

HHS HIPAA Breach Settlement Involving Less than 500 Patients | HHS.gov. (n.d.). Retrieved September 21, 2022, from https://www.hhs.gov/hipaa/for-professionals/compliance-enforcement/examples/honi/index.html

Hoffman, S., & Podgurski, A. (2013). Big bad data: law, public health, and biomedical databases. *The Journal of Law, Medicine & Ethics : A Journal of the American Society of Law, Medicine & Ethics*, *41*(Suppl. 1), 56–60. https://doi.org/10.1111/JLME.12040

How Big Data Impacts Healthcare - Sponsored Content FROM SAP. (n.d.). Retrieved September 2, 2022, from https://hbr.org/sponsored/2014/09/how-big-data-impacts-healthcare

Improving the 21st-century Health Care System - Crossing the Quality Chasm - NCBI Bookshelf. (n.d.). Retrieved September 2, 2022, from https://www.ncbi.nlm.nih.gov/books/NBK222265/

Ioannidis, J. P. A. (2013). Informed consent, big data, and the oxymoron of research that is not research. *The American Journal of Bioethics : AJOB*, *13*(4), 40–42. https://doi.org/10.1080/15265161.2013.768864

Iroju, O., Soriyan, A., Gambo, I., & Olaleke, J. (2013). Interoperability in healthcare: Benefits, challenges and resolutions. *International Journal of Innovation and Applied Studies*, *3*(1), 262–270. http://www.ijias.issr-journals.org/abstract.php?article=IJIAS-13-090-01

Jacobs, A. (2009). The pathologies of big data. *Communications of the ACM*, *52*(8), 36–44. https://doi.org/10.1145/1536616.1536632

Justice K.S.Puttaswamy(Retd) vs Union Of India on 26 September, 2018. (n.d.). Retrieved July 4, 2022, from https://indiankanoon.org/doc/127517806/

Kayyali, B., & Knott, D. (n.d.). *The big-data revolution in US health care: Accelerating value and innovation*. Retrieved September 15, 2022, from https://www.mckinsey.com/industries/healthcare-systems-and-services/our-insights/the-big-data-revolution-in-us-health-care

Keen, J. (2014). Digital health care: Cementing centralisation? *Health Informatics Journal*, *20*(3), 168–175. https://doi.org/10.1177/1460458213494033

Nawsher Khan, Ibrar Yaqoob, Ibrahim Abaker Targio Hashem, Zakira Inayat, Waleed Kamaleldin Mahmoud Ali, Muhammad Alam, Muhammad Shiraz, Abdullah Gani, "Big Data: Survey, Technologies, Opportunities, and Challenges", *The Scientific World Journal*, vol. 2014, Article ID 712826, 18 pages, 2014. https://doi.org/10.1155/2014/712826

Leber, J. (n.d.). *In The Hospital Of The Future, Big Data Is One Of Your Doctors*. Retrieved September 15, 2022, from https://www.fastcompany.com/3022050/in-the-hospital-of-the-future-big-data-is-one-of-your-doctors

Lee, L. M., & Gostin, L. O. (2009). Ethical collection, storage, and use of public health data: A proposal for a national privacy protection. *JAMA*, *302*(1), 82–84. https://doi.org/10.1001/JAMA.2009.958

Levy, J. A., & Strombeck, R. (2002). Health benefits and risks of the Internet. *Journal of Medical Systems*, *26*(6), 495–510. https://doi.org/10.1023/A:1020288508362

Liu, K., Hogan, W. R., & Crowley, R. S. (2011). Natural language processing methods and systems for biomedical ontology learning. *Journal of Biomedical Informatics*, *44*(1), 163–179. https://doi.org/10.1016/j.jbi.2010.07.006

Manyika, J., Chui Brown, M., Dobbs, R., Roxburgh, C., & Hung Byers, A. (2011). Big data: The next frontier for innovation, competition and productivity. *McKinsey Global Institute, June*, 156. https://bigdatawg.nist.gov/pdf/MGI_big_data_full_report.pdf

Martin, M. A., & Kroetz, D. L. (2014). Abacavir pharmacogenetics – From initial reports to standard of care. *33*(7), 765–775. https://doi.org/10.1002/phar.1278.Abacavir

Martínez-Pérez B, de la Torre-Díez I, López-Coronado M. Privacy and security in mobile health apps: a review and recommendations. *J Med Syst*. 2015 Jan;39(1):181. doi: 10.1007/s10916-014-0181-3. Epub 2014 Dec 7. PMID: 25486895.

Mateosian, R. (2013). Ethics of big data. *IEEE Micro, 33*(2), 60–61. https://doi.org/10.1109/mm.2013.35

Ministry of Home Affairs DISHA BILL. (n.d.). Retrieved September 21, 2022, from https://pib.gov.in/PressReleasePage.aspx?PRID=1739499

Mitchell, I., Locke, M., Wilson, M., & Fuller, A. (2021). *The White Boook of Big Data*. https://www.abebooks.com/9780956821621/White-Book-Big-Data-Definitive-0956821626/plp

OECD Health Statistics 2014- Frequently Requested Data - OECD. (n.d.). Retrieved September 2, 2022, from https://www.oecd.org/els/health-systems/oecd-health-statistics-2014-frequently-requested-data.htm

Hoffman S, Podgurski A. *Big bad data: law, public health, and biomedical databases. J Law Med Ethics*. 2013 Mar;41 Suppl 1:56–60. doi: 10.1111/jlme.12040. PMID: 23590742.

Patel, A. B., Birla, M., & Nair, U. (2012). Addressing big data problem using Hadoop and Map Reduce. *3rd Nirma University International Conference on Engineering, NUiCONE 2012*, 6–8. https://doi.org/10.1109/NUICONE.2012.6493198

Picciotto, R. (2020). Evaluation and the big data challenge. *American Journal of Evaluation, 41*(2), 166–181. https://doi.org/10.1177/1098214019850334/FORMAT/EPUB

Privacy Policy – Aarogya Setu. (n.d.). Retrieved September 14, 2022, from https://www.aarogyasetu.gov.in/privacy-policy/

Pustovit, S. V., & Williams, E. D. (2010). Philosophical aspects of dual use technologies. *Science and Engineering Ethics, 16*(1), 17–31. https://doi.org/10.1007/s11948-008-9086-1

Raghupathi, W. R. and V. (2012). Big data analytics in healthcare: Promise and potential. *Communications of the ACM, 55*(10), 11–13. https://doi.org/10.1145/2347736.2347741

Reading Turchioe, M., Volodarskiy, A., Pathak, J., Wright, D. N., Tcheng, J. E., & Slotwiner, D. (2022). Systematic review of current natural language processing methods and applications in cardiology. *Heart, 108*(12), 909–916. https://doi.org/10.1136/heartjnl-2021-319769

Richards, N. M., & King, J. H. (2014). *Big Data Ethics. 1881*(2013) https://papers.ssrn.com/sol3/papers.cfm?abstract_id=2384174

Saranya, P., & Asha, P. (2019). Survey on big data analytics in health care. *Proceedings of the 2nd International Conference on Smart Systems and Inventive Technology, ICSSIT 2019, Icssit*, 46–51. https://doi.org/10.1109/ICSSIT46314.2019.8987882

Satyanarayana, K., & Venkata, L. (2015). A survey on challenges and advantages in big data. *Ijcst, 6*(2), 115–119. http://www.ijcst.com/vol62/1/24-LENKA-VENKATA-SATYANARAYANA.pdf

Scholl, I., Aach, T., Deserno, T. M., & Kuhlen, T. (2011). Challenges of medical image processing. *Computer Science - Research and Development, 26*(1–2), 5–13. https://doi.org/10.1007/s00450-010-0146-9

Section 43A of Information Technology Act: Compensation for failure to protect data. (n.d.). Retrieved September 21, 2022, from https://www.itlaw.in/section-43a-compensation-for-failure-to-protect-data/

Section 72: Breach of Confidentiality and Privacy - Info. Technology Law. (n.d.). Retrieved September 21, 2022, from https://www.itlaw.in/section-72-breach-of-confidentiality-and-privacy/

Orit Shaer, Ali Mazalek, Brygg Ullmer, and Miriam Konkel. 2013. From big data to insights: opportunities and challenges for TEI in genomics. In *Proceedings of the 7th International Conference on Tangible, Embedded and Embodied Interaction* (TEI '13). Association for Computing Machinery, New York, NY, USA, 109–116. https://doi. org/10.1145/2460625.2460642

Shobana, V., & Kumar, N. (2015). Big data - A review. *International Journal of Applied Engineering Research, 10*(55), 1294–1298. https://doi.org/10.26634/jit.6.1.13507

Srinivasan, U., & Arunasalam, B. (2013). Leveraging big data analytics to reduce healthcare costs. *IT Professional, 15*(6), 21–28. https://doi.org/10.1109/MITP.2013.55

Stylianou, A., & Talias, M. A. (2015). The 'magic light': A discussion on laser ethics. *Science and Engineering Ethics, 4*, 979–998. https://doi.org/10.1007/s11948-014-9566-4

Jimeng Sun and Chandan K. Reddy. 2013. *Big data analytics for healthcar*e. In Proceedings of the 19th ACM SIGKDD international conference on Knowledge discovery and data mining (KDD '13). Association for Computing Machinery, New York, NY, USA, 1525. https://doi.org/10.1145/2487575.2506178

The Aadhaar Act, 2016. (n.d.). Retrieved September 14, 2022, from https://www.uidai.gov.in/ images/Aadhaar_Act_2016_as_amended.pdf

The Aadhar Case. (n.d.). Retrieved September 14, 2022, from https://www.ijalr.in/2020/11/ the-aadhar-case-ks-puttaswamy-v-union.html

The Clinical Establishments (Registration and Regulation) Act, 2010 | National Health Portal Of India. (n.d.). Retrieved September 21, 2022, from https://www.nhp.gov.in/ the-clinical-establishments-registration-and-regulation-act-2010_pg

The Data Deluge | The Economist. (n.d.). Retrieved September 2, 2022, from https://www. economist.com/leaders/2010/02/25/the-data-deluge

The Disaster Management Act, 2005. (n.d.). Retrieved September 14, 2022, from https://www. ndma.gov.in/sites/default/files/PDF/DM_act2005.pdf

The Epidemic Diseases Act, 1897. (n.d.). Retrieved September 14, 2022, from https://legisla- tive.gov.in/sites/default/files/A1897-03.pdf

Trifonova, O. P., Il'in, V. A., Kolker, E. V, & Lisitsa, A. V. (2013). Big data in biology and medicine: Based on material from a joint workshop with representatives of the interna- tional data-enabled life science alliance, July 4, 2013, Moscow, Russia. *Acta Naturae, 5*(3), 13–16. http://www.pubmedcentral.nih.gov/articlerender.fcgi?artid=3848064&tool =pmcentrez&rendertype=abstract

V, M. (2013). The big challenges of big data. *Nature, 498*, 255–260.

Vinker, S., Bitterman, H., Comaneshter, D., & Cohen, A. D. (2015). Physicians' behavior following changes in LDL cholesterol target goals. *Israel Journal of Health Policy Research, 4*(1). https://doi.org/10.1186/s13584-015-0016-9

Zikopoulos, P. C., Melnyk, R. B., Brown, B., & Coss, R. (n.d.). *Hadoop for Dummies.* John Wiley & Sons. www.dummies.com/cheatsheet/hadoop

Zwitter, A. (2014). Big data ethics. Big data & society, 1(2), 2053951714559253.

8 Big Data Analytics in Energy Management from Energy Generation to Consumption

Merve Er and Gökçen Bayram
Marmara University

CONTENTS

8.1 INTRODUCTION

Growing climate change problem and rising energy prices brought energy sector to the forefront of the global agenda. Effective management of energy production, transmission, storage and consumption stages is crucial to increase energy efficiency,

DOI: 10.1201/9781003330875-8

reduce operating and maintenance costs, and reduce Green House Gas (GHG) emissions. Nowadays, digital tools and technologies of the Fourth Industrial Revolution are transforming the energy sector. Installation of new measurement devices and technologies enable collection of massive amounts of data in energy networks (Zhou et al. 2016). Especially, use of IoT, cloud computing and smart sensors provides the opportunity to collect, store, analyse and share real-time energy data. As a result, traditional data analytics have become inadequate to cope with this growing stream of high-volume and complex data. Therefore, nowadays, 'big data analytics' play a critical role for making data-driven decisions in the energy sector (Zhang et al. 2018a; Marinakis et al. 2020).

Big data analytics is an important element of sustainable, efficient, and secure power and energy systems. These analytics are used in various stages of energy networks; make highly accurate demand forecasts (Pérez-Chacón et al. 2020), understand energy consumer behaviour and the factors influencing energy consumption (Zhou and Yang 2016; Kuo et al. 2018), segment consumers (Kwac et al. 2014), detect energy losses and electricity theft (Arif et al. 2022), predict maintenance requirements (Canizo et al. 2017), etc. Energy big data comes from various sources and in different forms. Energy big data include smart sensor data, load demand, operational performance, condition monitoring, failure and diagnostics data, maintenance records, energy price, meteorological data, carbon emission, etc. Big data analytics include advanced tools to gather real-time important insights from these diverse data sets (Kezunovic et al. 2020). These insights may be used to identify energy consumption trends, anomalies, maintenance requirements, operational effectiveness and energy losses. Big data analytics are also changing the renewable energy sector, which is the key for a clean energy future. These advanced tools provide accurate predictions for highly uncertain and volatile renewable energy sources (de Freitas Viscondi and Alves-Souza 2019; Xu et al. 2020; Mujeeb et al. 2019).

This chapter examines the energy big data concept and provides an overview of big data applications in the sector from multiple perspectives. The remainder of the chapter is structured as follows. Next section presents big data-driven energy management systems. Section 8.3 explains the importance of big data in understanding consumer behaviour and forecasting future energy demand. Section 8.4 summarises the role of big data analytics in the optimisation of power generation and transmission operations, and maintenance activities. Section 8.5 presents the importance big data for increasing the utilisation from renewable energy resources and gives some example applications from different renewable energy areas. Section 8.6 examines data-driven energy management approaches in energy-intensive industries. Section 8.7 examines the use of big data analytics in smart cities and buildings. Section 8.8 explains the benefits and challenges of big data analytics. Finally, the last chapter provides a discussion for the current and future state of the energy industry in today's digital era.

8.2   BIG DATA-DRIVEN SMART ENERGY MANAGEMENT

Energy is essential for human life and industrial growth. Energy consumption occurs due to many different activities such as lightning, cooking, heating, cooling,

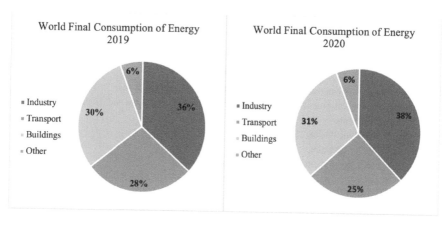

FIGURE 8.1 World final consumption of energy according to sectors 2019/2020. IEA 2021.

use of electronic appliances, and transportation or industrial processes. Industrial sector accounts for a significant portion of the global energy consumption. Figure 8.1 shows world final consumption of energy according to different sectors in 2019 and 2020. As it is seen from the figure, the share of industry increased from 36% to 38%. Share of buildings is also increased by 1%, and it is expected to grow in the future as a result of expansion of smart cities and buildings over the world. Energy management, efficiency and green transition is important in all industries. Various investments and projects have been done to reduce energy consumption and emissions.

Due to energy resource scarcity, increasing concentrations of greenhouse gases in the atmosphere, and climate change, energy efficiency and management is getting more importance in all areas. Energy management includes planning, operating, monitoring and controlling of energy production, consumption, storage and distribution units. Energy industry is under a huge digital revolution due to increasing adoption of advanced technologies, such as Internet of Things – IoT (Internet of Energy – IoE), smart sensors, cloud systems, and digital twins. Adoption of these technologies lead to interconnected energy systems and vast amounts of data load, which may be called as 'energy big data'.

Big data refers to the data sets that have high volume, high velocity and high variety. Big data has five key characteristics: volume, velocity, variety, veracity and value (Zhou and Yang 2016). Big data is too large, complex and unmanageable to be dealt with traditional methods. Therefore, advanced, and cost-effective techniques and technologies are required to acquire, store, manage and process big data. Akhavan-Hejazi and Mohsenian-Rad (2018) classified big data in power systems as domain data and off-domain data. Various types of data are collected from smart meters and other devices installed at different stages of power systems: power generation, transmission and distribution (Arif et al. 2022; Jaradat et al. 2015; Zhou et al. 2016; Marinakis et al. 2020). Supplementary data such as weather data, financial market data and social media data are also used to improve the accuracy and reliability of big data analytics. Example sources for energy big data are given in Table 8.1. As it

TABLE 8.1

Example Sources of Energy Big Data

Data from Power Systems

- Supervisory control and data acquisition (SCADA) and telemetry systems
- Operational data (real-time flows and energy parameters such as voltage and temperature)
- Utility measurements
- Intelligent electronic devices (IED)
- Anomalies during operations
- Advanced metering infrastructure (AMI) and smart sensors
- Condition monitoring and diagnostics systems of power plants (e.g. for wind turbines, solar panels, hydro turbines)
- Maintenance records
- Oscillographic and synchrophasor data
- Mobile power distribution terminal
- Meteorological data

Data about Consumers and their Operations

- Smart meters (e.g. energy consumption readings, power quality)
- Intelligent electronic devices (IED)
- Smart home appliances
- Additional data about household customer profile (such as GDP, physical attributes of properties, use of home appliances), and industrial and commercial customers

Supplementary Data

- Market price
- Meteorological data
- Geographic Information System (GIS)
- Social media

seen from the table, energy systems include various types of different data: operational performance, maintenance records, consumption data, diagnostics systems data, etc. Energy big data is growing with the use of new and advanced technologies and transition from analog to digital devices.

Lifecycle of energy big data consists of the following steps (Akerkar and Hong 2021): (i) data collection, (ii) data pre-processing, (iii) data storage, (iv) data analytics, (v) data visualisation, and (vi) decision making. Big data analytics offer a wide range of solutions in many different business areas. Big data analytics is about uncovering hidden, meaningful and important patterns and insights from large and complex data sets. There are four types of big data analytics: descriptive, predictive, prescriptive and diagnostic. Descriptive analytics focus on the analysis of current and past data to better understand 'what has happened'. Predictive analytics use big data to make predictions about future. Prescriptive analytics provide recommendations for optimal course of actions. Diagnostic analytics are used to find the causes of patterns, variations and abnormalities.

Energy networks are highly complex and include many planning and optimisation problems, including energy planning, power generation cost minimisation, load scheduling, optimisation of energy consumption, improvement of energy efficiency, etc.

Big data analytics may provide solutions and important insights in various planning, optimisation and management problems within energy networks. Some of these areas are listed in the following:

- Optimisation of energy production operations
- Data-driven supply/demand decisions and planning
- Data-driven capacity management and investment decisions
- Understanding the energy consumption behaviour (Zhou and Yang 2016; Kuo et al. 2018) and predict future consumption (Pérez-Chacón et al. 2020)
- Energy consumption analysis/customer behaviour analysis
- Discovering abnormal usage patterns (anomaly detection) in energy grids
- Improving customer satisfaction
- Setting energy pricing
- Power quality monitoring
- Load analysis
- Power outages
- Prediction of maintenance requirements
- Improving emergency responses
- Fault analysis in energy grids
- Detection of technical and non-technical energy losses, such as energy theft (consumption without billing) (Arif et al. 2022)
- Improving the access electricity and energy efficiency (Razmjoo et al. 2022)
- Optimisation of renewable energy sources (Hannan et al. 2021)
- Prediction of renewable energy output (Mujeeb et al. 2019; de Freitas Viscondi and Alves-Souza 2019)
- Interactive communication with smart grids (Hannan et al. 2021)

Big data may also be used to eliminate energy waste. Energy wastage occurs when energy is produced and transferred to the grid, but not consumed. Therefore, balancing supply and demand is a critical problem that needs to be solved to prevent this energy loss. Big data analytics utilise from energy consumption data from distributed resources and provide highly accurate forecasts (Zhou and Yang 2016; Rashid 2018). These forecasts have an important role in energy supply planning.

A general framework is presented for big data-based energy management systems in Figure 8.2. Energy data is the core point of big data-driven energy management. Various big data tools and platforms are available. The most suitable one is selected by considering the target problem type and available data. Big data and relevant technologies are utilised to solve different energy planning, optimisation and management problems, as it is seen in the third box of Figure 8.2. Energy data visualisation is also important to assist decision makers in understanding the analytical results more efficiently.

Increase in the available data provided by digitalisation technologies and the analysis power of big data tools increase the accuracy and speed of energy demand forecasts and renewable energy supply. Additionally, optimised planning and management of energy utilities increase the energy efficiency and decrease maintenance costs; hence, these developments may reduce operational costs in power plants and

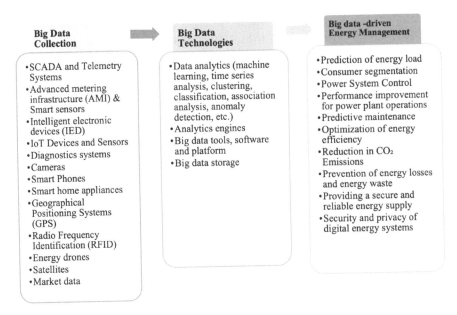

FIGURE 8.2 A general framework for big, data-based energy management.

transmission lines. These advances may create a positive impact on unit prices that end users spend for energy in the future. Failures that may occur in power plants and distribution channels may also be prevented by using real-time big data monitoring. Prevention of power cuts help to provide more reliable and uninterrupted service for customers. Lastly, occupational accidents may also be predicted and prevented using big data analytics.

8.3 ENERGY DEMAND ANALYSIS AND FORECASTING

Big data analytics may be used to predict energy consumption, analyse consumption behaviour, identify peak times and set energy prices. Smart meters provide real-time monitoring of energy usage data. Energy providers use big data analytics to forecast power demand fluctuations, and respond to these changes to ensure reliable and stable power.

8.3.1 UNDERSTAND ENERGY CONSUMER BEHAVIOUR

Various factors are considered to increase accuracy of energy demand forecasts, such as historical consumption data, real-time smart meter data, weather forecasts and social factors (Akerkar and Hong 2021). Zhou and Yang (2016) analysed household energy consumption behaviour from different dimensions, including time, user and spatial dimensions, and discussed the use of energy big data analytics to understand consumption behaviour. Many different factors may have an impact on household energy usage: income level, household characteristics, electrical appliances, energy price, weather conditions, etc. (Zhou and Yang 2016). Therefore, social and economical factors may be considered to increase the accuracy of energy consumption prediction. Big data analytics are very helpful in developing accurate forecasts and customer segmentation based on energy big data and supplementary data. Kuo et al. (2018) used big data analysis and machine learning to analyse energy consumption of Taiwan's convenience stores and the impact of five classes of influencing factors, including architectural space and geographical conditions, management type, business equipment, local climatic conditions and service area socioeconomic conditions.

8.3.2 Forecasting Future Energy Consumption

Time series models are frequently used to forecast energy consumption. Different researchers have adapted time series methods to analyse big data time series. Pérez-Chacón et al. (2020) proposed a novel algorithm, called big PSF, to forecast Uruguay electricity demand based on the Pattern Sequence-based Forecasting (PSF) algorithm. PSF algorithm is based on the analysis of pattern sequences in the time series data. Clustering is performed to transform the time series, pattern sequences are extracted and future behaviour of time series is forecasted based on the similarity of pattern sequences. Pérez-Chacón et al. (2020) transformed the PSF algorithm to deal with the big data time series by making some improvements.

Smart meter market has grown rapidly all over the world and countries need to manage millions of readings coming from these smart meters. Rashid (2018) explored the electricity consumption time series data of a set of commercial buildings and applied different forecasting methods on this data set. Results of big data analytics may be used for planning future power consumption and load, assessing new investments and ensuring reliability of supply.

8.3.3 Consumer Segmentation

Smart meter installation is growing rapidly, and it is expected that the rise in the global smart meter market will continue to grow. Smart meters are helping utilities to expand their electricity consumption and load management programs. These devices provide individual level and aggregated data from households with high time resolution. The energy consumption data generated by smart meters provide valuable information about usage characteristics and patterns. Clustering and classification methods can be used to identify consumer profiles, and develop competitive marketing strategies and personalised offers based on this information.

Households use energy for various purposes, including space heating, water heating, cooling, lightning, cooking and use of different home appliances. Various factors have direct and indirect impacts on household energy consumption. Some of these factors are listed in the following:

- Demographic and socioeconomic factors
  - Location of the house
  - Number of individuals in a household
  - Family composition (e.g. age)

- - Total household income
  - Education level of households
  - Employment
- Lifestyle
  - Social differences (e.g. time spent outside)
  - Technology use routine (use of electrical home appliances)
- Physical building characteristics
  - Type of house (e.g. apartment)
  - Total floor area
  - Construction date
  - Number of windows
  - Type of heating or cooling system
- Weather
  - Climate zone
  - Meteorological data
- Energy price

Hence, household energy consumption varies significantly among different household groups in terms of load size and timing. Segmentation can be helpful to better define and understand these different groups.

Big data-driven customer segmentation may be used to derive important insights about energy consumers in the energy sector: (i) understand households' energy consumption behaviour and patterns (e.g. energy usage volume, daily usage patterns, peak times such as dinner time), and (ii) identify target customers that have the highest potential. The results of the analysis may be used for marketing strategies, differential pricing for different consumer segments, quality improvement for power services and energy-efficiency initiatives.

Kwac et al. (2014) proposed a segmentation framework to understand household's energy use lifestyle and classify households according to different features. They identified representative load shapes by using adaptive K-Means algorithm, and then applied hierarchical clustering to summarise the load shape dictionary generated in the previous stage. Their analysis was based on hourly electricity consumption data of 229 K residential customers.

8.3.4 Detection of Energy Losses Based on Energy Consumption Data

Energy consumption data is also used to detect energy losses. Energy losses can be categorised as technical and non-technical losses (Arif et al. 2022). Technical losses may occur due to power dissipation from cables, conductors, lines, transformers and other equipment used in transmission and distribution networks. Non-technical losses may occur because of electricity theft, installation errors, unbilled accounts, and errors in reading and billing systems. Arif et al. (2022) proposed two novel methods for electricity theft detection using electricity consumption records and auxiliary data. They used a new classification method combining Temporal Convolutional Network (TCN) and Enhanced Multi-Layer Perceptron (EMLP) to classify customers as honest and fraudulent. One of the strengths of their model is the use of additional attributes of households, including number and distribution of residents in a house, existence of air conditioner and other appliances and physical properties of the property (total area, floor, build year, roof height, type of connection, ceiling insulation and number and description of rooms) (Arif et al. 2022).

8.3.5 PRICING

There are many factors that affect the demand and supply side of electricity, and, thus, impact price of electricity. Big data analytics help to make better pricing decision and develop differential pricing models. Some of the variables that may be used in big data-driven pricing decisions are as follows: electricity consumption, total supply in the country, renewable energy production, GDP, seasonal variations, etc.

8.4 BIG DATA ANALYTICS TO IMPROVE OPERATIONS AND MAINTENANCE IN ENERGY NETWORKS

Data measurement and collection in power systems is developing with growing installation of smart meters, sensors and control devices on different stages of power systems: power generation, transmission and distribution.

8.4.1 ELECTRIC POWER SECTOR

Energy consumption is growing across all countries due to increasing population and growing digitalisation trend. Electrical energy is the most convenient and versatile form of energy. Distribution grids are the backbone of the energy transition process. Performance and maintenance of electricity transmission and distribution lines are crucial to ensure a smooth, sustainable and reliable electricity flow. Countries are making significant amounts of investments on smart energy grids. Big data analytics play a significant role in the smart grid environment. Smart grids may include millions of smart meters generating data (Rashid 2018). Big data analytics provide successful solutions to analyse the energy data in smart grids. Daki et al. (2017) categorised big data analytics used in smart grids under five headings as follows:

- Signal Analytics
- Event Analytics
- State Analytics
- Engineering Operations Analytics
- Customer Analytics

Engineering operations cover effectiveness, performance and forecasting studies.

Smart grids are electricity grids that are based on digital technology. These networks automatically monitor energy flows, control energy distribution processes and allow two-way data flow between utilities and customers. Management of the whole process from the generation of electrical energy to distribution and transportation to the end consumer is performed automatically in these smart networks. The benefits of smart grids can be listed as improving existing services, increasing reliability, energy savings and low cost (Jaradat et al. 2015). Electricity consumption is measured and monitored in shorter intervals instead of long time periods with the help of smart meters. Deployment of measurement devices and measurement synchronisation result in more reliable data, which can be used in the optimisation of electricity generation, distribution and consumption.

In a conventional network, consumption data is read once a month. In this case, it is very difficult to reach the sufficient data required for an efficient energy management. On the other hand, in smart grids, real-time and short-term consumption data of the consumer can be accessed with smart meters and sensors located on the electricity distribution network. If millions of smart meters installed in the network send data at regular intervals, for example, in 20-minute periods, data is sent 72 times a day from a smart meter in one day. If we talk about 1 million meters, 72 million data points will be collected per day (Daki et al. 2017). The use of smart grids is very valuable for an effective energy management.

When an effective energy management cannot be achieved, production and consumption cannot be balanced, and when the demand is higher than the amount of production, energy constraints and interruptions are encountered. One of the most important benefits of smart networks is that it balances demand and production capacity thanks to full-time and high-volume data.

When electricity production is examined from environmental and economic dimensions, the importance of big data is better understood. From the environmental perspective, fossil fuels are the largest sources of electricity generation. They result in high amounts of GHG emissions and therefore contribute to climate change. From the economic perspective, fossil energy sources will be exhausted within a few centuries. There are fluctuations in the prices of these resources that decrease day by day. Countries may face energy supply problems due to natural disasters, wars and political events. These events also may impact the energy price in the current location and other regions too. In summary, electricity price is adversely affected by fuel prices and problems experienced in the supply of fuels (Wang et al. 2017). However, electricity consumption is growing all over the world due to increased digitalisation and urbanisation. Smart networks and solutions help to increase the utilisation from energy sources and reduce energy losses.

Renewable energy is another solution for the aforementioned problems. However, renewable energy sources are highly volatile and uncertain. These energy sources are sensitive to geographical and climatic conditions. Big data analytics are used to create accurate forecasts for renewable energy supply, and these analytics are also used in providing accurate future forecasts for electricity consumption; so, they help to balance electricity demand and supply. Renewable energy sources also generally serve at national level, hence they are not affected from political issues or transportation price fluctuations caused by crisis.

Big data analytics are also used for fault detection (Marinakis 2020) and predictive maintenance in power systems (Canizo et al. 2017). Maintenance management aims to reduce failures and breakdowns, plan maintenance and reduce maintenance costs. Predictive maintenance focuses on prediction of equipment failure and preventing its occurrence by performing maintenance. Therefore, it increases the operational safety of the system. Use of big data analytics improves the transparency and visibility of the health of the system, and provides data-based decision making to identify the best maintenance policy.

8.5 BIG DATA ANALYTICS IN RENEWABLE ENERGY SYSTEMS

Renewable energy is the key to fight against climate change. Renewable energy provides clean and low-cost electricity with zero or very little carbon emission. Solar, wind, geothermal, hydroelectric, bioenergy, and tidal and wave energies are the main types of renewable energy. The most important difference of renewable energy from fossil energy sources is that they are constantly present in nature and do not face the risk of depletion like fossil energy sources, because as long as nature exists, energy types such as solar energy, wind and waves will continue to exist. Today, energy security and global warming problems lead countries towards the use of renewable energy sources. The fact that carbon emissions are negligible has increased the share of renewable energy sources in electricity generation, heating and cooling processes, and transportation sectors. Governments make huge investments, and offer financing and funding programs for renewable energy systems. Figure 8.3 shows electricity generation by energy source in 2020 and 2021. The dependency to fossil fuels is still very high. The use of coal, which was 35.1% in 2020, increased to 36% in 2021, and it is seen that coal is heavily preferred in electricity generation worldwide. Natural gas and hydroelectricity follow coal in electricity generation. In terms of renewable energy (excluding hydroelectricity), there is an increase in 2021 compared to 2020.

Energy-related carbon emissions have increased significantly over the past decade. However, the need for electricity is also growing. Therefore, renewable energy sources have a crucial importance for the sustainability of earth. Figure 8.4 represents renewable energy generation by source. Especially, there is a huge growth in the number of wind farms and solar systems. Renewable energy supply is highly volatile and uncertain, especially due to the dependence of renewable energy sources to climate-related factors, such as wind speed, air density, weather temperature and

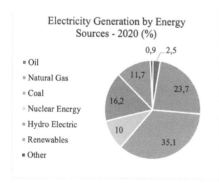
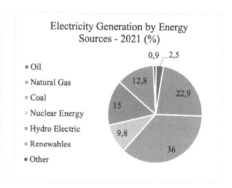

FIGURE 8.3 Electricity generation by energy sources in 2020 and 2021. bp Statistical Review of World Energy 2022.

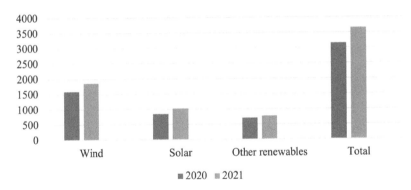

FIGURE 8.4   Renewable energy: Generation by source (Terawatt-hours). bp Statistical Review of World Energy 2022.

precipitation. Due to the fluctuating and intermittent characteristics of renewable energy sources, production will not be continuous, and it may not be able to meet demand in some periods. Problems such as unstable generation, voltage instability and frequency fluctuation may also occur (Zhou et al. 2017). Uncertainty in renewable energy sources also affects the planning and scheduling processes in smart grids. As smart grids integrate different distributed energy sources, the fluctuating nature of renewable energy systems makes it very difficult to provide stability in the systems.

Big data analytics may unlock the predictability of renewable energy resources (Mostafa et al. 2022). As renewable energy resources are highly dependent on nature, big data analytics provide important insights by including huge amounts of weather data and other factors in predictive analytics. These analytics support planning, optimisation and control of renewable energy resources. Renewable energy investors can use big data analytics to get more value from renewable energy sources and power plants. Big data-driven analytics may be used in the following areas:

- Assessment of renewable energy potential and selection of optimal site for renewable energy investments
- Identification of the key factors affecting renewable energy generation
- Forecasting renewable energy supply (Zhou et al. 2017; de Freitas Viscondi and Alves-Souza 2019; Mujeeb et al. 2019; Xu et al. 2020)
- Predicting productive weather conditions
- Predicting the renewable energy amount that will contribute to the power grid
- Keeping energy supply and demand in balance
- Large-scale renewable energy monitoring
- Fault detection and diagnosis for renewable energy power systems
- Preventing system failures caused by outages
- Online assessment of voltage stability
- Predictive maintenance of renewable energy systems (Canizo et al. 2017)
- Avoiding delays and system shutdowns

Big data is the key component in developing efficient, stable and reliable renewable energy systems. More accurate forecasts may be done for the output of these power plants, considering meteorological and geospatial data. Historical production data coupled with additional information helps producers to match supply and demand, and ensure a smooth power production. Various pre-determined physical, economical, environmental and process-related indicators may also be used for developing early warning systems. Effective management of renewable energy also required performing risk analysis, failure event analysis, asset condition and maintenance monitoring. All of the aforementioned functions and analytics require utilisation of various types of data sets. Table 8.2 summarises some of the big data types used in renewable energy analytics.

8.6 DATA-DRIVEN ENERGY MANAGEMENT IN ENERGY-INTENSIVE INDUSTRIES

Energy-intensive industries include the sectors that use high amounts of energy. Some of these industries are cement, refineries, iron and steel, chemicals manufacturing, pulp and paper, food and beverages, etc. A better use of energy and digitalisation in

---

TABLE 8.2
Examples of Big Renewable Energy Data

Solar Energy	Wind Energy	Geothermal Energy
• Weather observations, such as solar irradiation, sunshine duration, air temperature	• Wind turbine power output	• Geological data set
	• Weather observations, such as wind speed, wind direction, air density, atmospheric pressure, weather temperature	• Geothermal heat pump data
• Generation and transmission line data		• Thermal observations
		• Geothermal source temperature
• Solar sensor data (e.g. sun trackers, battery voltage sensor, solar current sensor)	• Wind turbine sensor data (e.g. data on speed, vibration, temperature)	• Thermal radiation
		• Amount of power generation
• Time series data of solar power generation	• Statistical data on wind velocity	• Sale price to grid
		• Spatial distribution of hot springs and geothermal wells
• Topographic data	• Variation of current output	
• Satellite data	• Wind turbine performance and health-monitoring data (e.g. turbine vibrations)	

Hydroelectricity	Tidal and Wave Energy
• Change in hydropower generation	• Tidal power generation
• Rainfall data	• Current data
• Quantity of water available	• Wave steepness, height, length and period
• Geological data	• Gravitational effects of sun and moon
• Water pollution analysis	
• Turbine rotor vibrations	

these industries helps to decrease energy intensity and increase the sustainability of the planet. Energy data is used to predict future energy consumption and trends, provide visibility for energy usage, losses and abnormal consumption, generate alerts, and provide insights for reducing energy wastage and increasing energy efficiency. Data-driven energy management and optimisation may provide the following benefits for industrial organisations: reduce energy consumption without effecting performance, discover and solve energy losses, decrease energy costs, decrease emissions and environmental impact of energy use, and improve brand reputation.

Energy big data analytics may be a hard process due to the complex production structure in manufacturing and tough working environment. Zhang et al. (2018b) proposed a new, big data-driven framework for energy efficiency and emission reduction in energy-intensive manufacturing industries. They proposed the use of IoT devices and sensors as energy control points at different levels in production. One of the layers of their framework includes big data mining model, including association, regression, classification, clustering, prediction and diagnosis to make energy-efficient decisions.

There may be some barriers in developing data-driven energy management programs: (i) difficulty in collecting data, (ii) cost of developing energy management system (EMS) that automatically collects and analyses data, (iii) high complexity of production processes, and (iv) lack of expertise or confusion about data analytics. Energy measurement data may be collected manually or automatically. Digital devices play a significant role especially in data acquisition in tough work environments, e.g. high temperature and pressure.

8.7   BIG DATA ANALYTICS FOR ENERGY MANAGEMENT IN SMART CITIES AND BUILDINGS

Smart building market grows exponentially with the advances in technologies such as IoT. Buildings account a huge portion of the entire energy consumption and greenhouse gas emissions. Therefore, nowadays, energy efficiency and cost saving are very critical topics due to growing world population, increasing energy consumption due to technological devices, scarcity of energy resources and environmental concerns regarding energy-related carbon emissions. Smart city is another trend that is growing in popularity. Many countries have adopted smart city solutions. For a city to be defined as a smart city, there must be eight technological solutions. These are, respectively: (i) smart management in which the participation of the public is ensured in the management of the city by using information technologies, (ii) smart citizenship in which technological solutions are applied to the problems of the citizens about the smart city, (iii) smart health that enables the citizens to access health services more easily thanks to technology, (iv) smart and efficient energy systems and clean energy by providing the energy needed by the city from renewable energy sources, (v) smart buildings that are environment friendly and safe structures, (vi) smart transportation that develops solutions to traffic problems, (vii) smart security where city security is ensured by technology, and (viii) smart infrastructure where all digital data used for the city is stored and transformed into information (Kocaman 2020). As can be seen from these components, big data and energy play an active role for a city to be a smart city and for this city to be sustainable. Energy planning and efficiency are prior tasks in smart cities. Smart cities rely on data to optimise energy utilisation and provide opportunities for energy-efficiency improvement. Big data analytics are also used to detect anomalies and electricity theft in energy networks. Arif et al. (2022) proposed a novel classification method to detect electricity theft in smart cities. They used various data on electricity consumption, residents in a house, and physical attributes of the property to classify customers as honest and fraudulent.

The concept of smart energy is aimed to monitor the energy production, transmission, distribution and consumption in smart cities, and to provide uninterrupted and fault-free energy to consumers. In addition, the prevention of air pollution caused by energy production and consumption can be achieved with smart energy application. In the development of smart cities, it is important that there is an uninterrupted flow of energy from the electrical networks and that there are no problems and wastes in the production and distribution stages of electrical energy. Relevant data should be collected during the production, transmission, distribution and consumption of energy, and necessary information should be obtained from this data. The concept of big data is important for achieving these goals.

Reducing carbon emissions from energy production and consumption is one of the main goals of smart cities. In these cities, energy is used extensively for heating and cooling of buildings. Fossil fuel-based energy types are also used in transportation. In line with the concept of smart energy, energy sources are used in electrical energy production, energy sources used in transportation and buildings are being reviewed, and there is a demand for environmentally friendly renewable energy sources. Figure 8.5 conceptually summarises the relationship between energy and big data in smart cities. Big data provides important insights for efficient management of all components of smart cities.

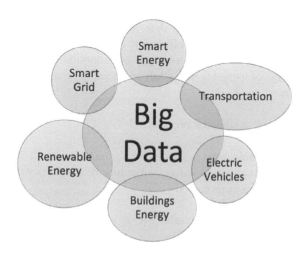

FIGURE 8.5   Energy and big data relationship in smart cities.

A total of 235 cities around the world were examined by the Eden Strategy Institute in line with the smart city criteria, and top 50 smart city governments were listed in the 2020/21 report (Eden Strategy Institute 2021). According to the report, top five smart city governments are as follows: Singapore, Seoul, London, Barcelona and Helsinki. Barcelona, Helsinki, New York, Melbourne, Amsterdam, Dubai and Vienna aim to meet their energy needs from renewable energy sources in the context of clean energy. Amsterdam and Dubai are developing smart grid technology. New York City uses data in the field of energy (Hilburg 2018). The city of Barcelona has achieved 30% saving in energy by using smart LED lamps supported by sensors, detecting motion and burning accordingly (Adler 2016). In the city of Vienna, 1.5 million data is produced every day with the smart grid system containing 6000 inhabitants, and the energy planning of the city is made with the help of analysed data. Smart meters and smart grids are new and key technologies in providing smart and sustainable energy for smart cities. Smart grids tools are effective to integrate and manage various different energy types, increase energy efficiency and decrease energy costs (Razmjoo et al. 2022).

Smart building data is usually held in a variety of raw or processed forms; they are heterogeneous and held in different positions (Marinakis 2020). Marinakis et al. (2017) claim that data are collected from five different areas. They are listed as buildings' energy profiles that include data about energy consumption, weather conditions, occupants' feedback where the data come through Thermal Comfort Validator or social media, energy production data from renewable energy production such as wind turbines and energy prices data from energy market. This data is meaningless without analysis. Therefore, big data expertise has a critical importance to apply appropriate pre-processing and select the best analytic based on the aim of the analysis.

8.8 BENEFITS, CHALLENGES AND BARRIERS OF BIG ENERGY DATA ANALYTICS

Big data analytics help us to convert data into value for better decision making. Available data is used to increase efficiency, resilience and robustness of energy operations (generation, storage, distribution, consumption) and the entire system. Some of the benefits of using big data analytics in energy management systems may be listed as follows:

- Optimise energy production processes
- Enhance planning
- Reduce operational costs
- Prevent accidents, improve safety and reduce down times with the help of prediction of maintenance needs
- Increase energy efficiency
- Provide cost benefits for renewable energy production and distribution

There are several challenges regarding the complexity of energy networks, diversity of energy data sources, huge investments for hardware and software, data security and privacy issues, decision on how to store and analyse the collected data, and difficulty to find data scientists with enough skills in big data analytics.

8.8.1 DIFFICULTY IN COLLECTING ENERGY DATA

Data is the key point for creating effective energy management systems. However, energy consumption may be a difficult challenge due to lack of automised technologies to collect data, difficulty of calculation, etc. Additionally, big data analytics may require data from different areas, e.g. weather data, GPS data, and consumer information. This distributed structure necessitates integrating data from multiple sources, which is a complex task. New digital technologies (e.g. sensors, IoT, cloud systems) are providing opportunities to collect, share, store and analyse energy-related data. There may be also legislative issues that may provide a barrier for collecting and sharing energy-related data.

8.8.2 DECISION ON BIG DATA TOOL AND PRE-PROCESSING OF DATA

Power plants accumulate vast amounts of data coming from various sources, such as different plant operations, suppliers, etc. It is not an easy work to plan how to convert this data load into values for the facility. Big data analytics provide useful solutions; however, choosing the right big data technology is a critical and difficult decision point. Power companies need to consider different criteria for this decision: current data types, aim of the analysis, data processing speed, and compatibility. Multi-criteria decision-making tools can also be used to select the right analytic (Daki et al. 2017).

Additionally, data comes from many different sources and departments, which brings heterogeneity, inconsistency and data redundancy problems. Therefore, data pre-processing may require a huge amount of time and effort. These problems provide a challenge for the analysis of the data and developing an integrated data management system.

8.8.3 DATA SECURITY AND PRIVACY ISSUES

Smart grid systems and smart meters include personal information about customers and their habits. This sensitive consumer data also needs to be protected under legal regulations. Therefore, data security, privacy and access management are important concerns (Akerkar and Hong 2021). Critical energy infrastructures are highly vulnerable to cyber-attacks. Unfortunately, many energy companies in the world have been targeted by hackers. Some of these attacks were resulted in energy shortages and shut down of services. Moreover, the amount of energy provided by nuclear power plants is increasing, and nuclear power plants started to incorporate digital systems rather than analog systems in their process control and also nuclear reactor systems.

8.9   DISCUSSION

Industry 4.0 technologies such as IoT, cloud computing and smart sensors are transforming the energy sector. These technologies generate and transmit huge amounts of data that cannot be processed and stored with traditional data analytics. Big data analytics help to get insights such as hidden patterns, correlations and outliers from huge data resources. In the energy industry, big data analytics can be used to improve operational efficiency and performance, establish predictive maintenance programs, optimise energy use and make better data-driven decisions in various stages of energy networks. Many countries are making significant investments to advanced technologies: digital energy infrastructure, IoT enabled devices, advanced metering structure, smart grids, etc. All of these devices and technologies generate and share vast amounts of data, and data are meaningless without data analysis. Therefore, big data application is growing very fast in the energy sector. Nowadays, energy drone applications are also growing in popularity. Drones fly over the utility sites and provide inspection data about the condition of the power lines, turbines, solar farms, etc. Images gathered by drones are used to identify any defects and damages.

Energy sector is in a rapid revolution both in terms of digitalisation and green energy transition. Governments are making huge investments to clean and renewable energy technologies, including solar, wind, hydropower, geothermal, biomass and wave power. These technologies are highly nature dependent; hence, there is a huge variability and uncertainty in renewable energy sources. Therefore, data is a critical component in these energy networks. Big data analytics are especially important to accurately predict power output of renewable energy sites, considering many different parameters, e.g. air temperature, wind speed and direction, humidity, and solar radiation.

Increasing digitalisation of all sectors bring some threats and risks as well as opportunities. Critical digital energy infrastructures are attractive targets for cyber-attacks. Energy networks serve millions of people; a disruption in these infrastructures may lead to significant losses and create negative cascading economic, business and societal effects. A cyber-attack may result in disruption of energy facility operations, interruption of services to customers, disruption of businesses and cities/regions, and theft of sensitive customer and employee data. Actors in the energy industry need to incorporate cyber-security safeguards and develop cyber-resilient energy systems to protect critical infrastructure, and eliminate threats against data and access.

REFERENCES

Akerkar, R. & Hong, M. *Big Data in Electric Power Industry: Opportunities and Challenges for Sogn og Fjordane Region.* Vestlandsforsking: Western Norway Research Institute; (2021).

Akhavan-Hejazi, H., Mohsenian-Rad, H. "Power systems big data analytics: An assessment of paradigm shift barriers and prospects." *Energy Reports* 4(2018): 91–100.

Arif, A., Alghamdi, T.A., Khan, Z.A., Javaid, N. "Towards efficient energy utilization using big data analytics in smart cities for electricity theft detection." *Big Data Research* 27(2022): 100285.

bp Statistical Review of World Energy. (2022), 71st edition. https://www.bp.com/content/dam/bp/business-sites/en/global/corporate/pdfs/energy-economics/statistical-review/bp-stats-review-2022-full-report.pdf (Access date: 26.09.2022)

Canizo, M., Onieva, E., Conde, A., Charramendieta, S., Trujillo, S. "Real-time predictive maintenance for wind turbines using big data frameworks." *2017 IEEE International Conference on Prognostics and Health Management (ICPHM)* (2017), IEEE Xplore.

Daki, H., Hannani, A.E., Aqqal, A., Haidine, A., Dahbi, A. "Big data management in smart grid: Concepts, requirements and implementation." *Journal of Big Data* 4(2017): 13.

de Freitas Viscondi, G., Alves-Souza, S.N. "A systematic literature review on big data for solar photovoltaic electricity generation forecasting." *Sustainable Energy Technologies and Assessments* 31(2019): 54–63.

Eden Strategy Institute. "Top 50 Smart City Governments 2021" (2021). http://www.eden-strategyinstitute.com

Hannan, M.A., Al-Shetwi, A., Ker, P.J., Begum, R.A., Mansor, M., Rahman, S.A., Dong, Z.Y., Tiong, S.K., Mahlia, T.M.I, Muttaqi, K.M. "Impact of renewable energy utilization and artificial intelligence in achieving sustainable development goals." *Energy Reports* 7(2021): 5359–5373.

IEA. "World Energy Outlook 2021" (2021), https://www.iea.org/reports/world-energy-outlook-2021.

Jaradat, M., Jarrah, M., Bousselham, A., Jararweh, Y., Al-Ayyoub, M. "The internet of energy: smart sensor networks and big data management for smart grid." *Procedia Computer Science* 56(2015): 592–597.

Kezunovic, M., Pinson, P., Obradovic, Z., Grijalva, S., Hong, T., Bessa, R. "Big data analytics for future electricity grids." *Electric Power Systems Research* 189(2020): 106788.

Kocaman, E.G. "Akıllı ve Sakin Şehirler İçin Enerji Çözümleri." İstanbul Sabahattin Zaim Üniversitesi Fen Bilimleri Enstitüsü Dergisi 2(2020): 40–47.

Kuo, C.F.J., Lin, C.H., Lee, M.H. "Analyze the energy consumption characteristics and affecting factors of Taiwan's convenience stores-using the big data mining approach." *Energy & Buildings* 168(2018): 120–136.

Kwac, J., Flora, J., Rajagopal, R. "Household energy consumption segmentation using hourly data." *IEEE Transactions on Smart Grid* 5(2014): 1.

Marinakis, V. "Big data for energy management and energy-efficient buildings." *Energies* 13(2020): 1555.

Marinakis, V., Doukas, H., Tsapelas, J., Mouzakitis, S., Sicilia, A., Madrazo, L., Sgouridis, S. "From big data to smart energy services: An application for intelligent energy management." *Future Generation Computer Systems* 110(2020): 572–586.

Mostafa, N., Ramadan, H.S.M., Elfarouk, O. "Renewable energy management in smart grids by using big data analytics and machine learning." *Machine Learning with Applications* 9(2022): 100363.

Mujeeb, S., Alghamdi, T.A., Ullah, S., Fatima, A., Javaid, N., Saba, T. "Exploiting deep learning for wind power forecasting based on big data analytics." *Applied Sciences* 9(2019): 4417.

Nambiar, R., Shroff, R., Handy, S. "Smart cities: challenges and opportunities." *10th International Conference on Communication Systems & Networks (COMSNETS)* (2018), DOI:10.1109/COMSNETS.2018.8328204Corpus ID: 4556518

Pérez-Chacón, R., Asencio-Cortés, G., Martínez-Álvarez, F., Troncoso, A. "Big data time series forecasting based on pattern sequence similarity and its application to the electricity demand." *Information Sciences* 540(2020): 160–174.

Rashid, M.H. "AMI smart meter big data analytics for time series of electricity consumption." *2018 17th IEEE International Conference on Trust, Security and Privacy in Computing And Communications/12th IEEE International Conference on Big Data Science and Engineering, IEEE* (2018), IEEE Explore.

Razmjoo, A., Gandomi, A.H., Pazhoohesh, M., Mirjalili, S., Rezaei, M. "The key role of clean energy and technology in smart cities development." *Energy Strategy Reviews* 44(2022): 100943.

Villessuzanne, C.C., Weigel, R., Blain, J. "Clustering of European smart cities to understand the cities' sustainability strategies." *Sustainability* 13(2021): 513.

Wang, K., Xu, C., Zhang, Y., Guo, S., Zomaya, A.Y. "Robust big data analytics for electricity price forecasting in the smart grid." *IEEE Transactions on Big Data* 5(2017): 126.

Xu, Y., Liu, H., Long, Z. "A distributed computing framework for wind speed big data forecasting on Apache Spark." *Sustainable Energy Technologies and Assessments* 37(2020):100582.

Zhang, Y., Huang, T., Bompard, E.F. "Big data analytics in smart grids: A review." *Energy Informatics* 1(2018a): 8.

Zhang, Y., Ma, S., Yang, H., Lv, J., Liu, Y. "A big data driven analytical framework for energy-intensive manufacturing industries." *Journal of Cleaner Production* 197(2018b): 57–72.

Zhou, K., Fu, C., Yang, S. "Big data driven smart energy management: From big data to big insights." *Renewable and Sustainable Energy Reviews* 56(2016): 215–225.

Zhou, K., Yang, S. "Understanding household energy consumption behavior: The contribution of energy big data analytics." *Renewable and Sustainable Energy Reviews* 56(2016): 810–819.

Zhou, Z., Xiong, F., Huang, B., Xu, C., Jiao, R., Liao, B., Yin, Z., Li, J. "Game-theoretical energy management for energy internet with big data-based renewable power forecasting." *IEEE Access* 5(2017): 5731–5746.

9 Artificial Intelligence (AI) at the Edge for Smart Cities Applications

Anurag Mudgil, Anvit Negi, Armaan Dhanda, and Anukriti Kumar
Delhi Technological University

Surendrabikram Thapa
Virginia Tech

S. Indu
Delhi Technological University

CONTENTS

DOI: 10.1201/9781003330875-9

9.1 INTRODUCTION

The modern world around us is so centralized on computers. Most of the tasks we perform today need computers. Modern-day industries have become efficient with the inculcation of computers to perform daily activities. With the ever-increasing demand for better computers every day, there have been efforts to improve computers daily. Fueled by unprecedented innovation in electronics and computing, modern-day computers have become very powerful with a massive increase in computation power [1]. As a result of such innovations, today's computers can complete the work in a fraction of the time that hundreds of computers took some years back. Computers have not only become advanced in terms of computing power but also have become highly portable. Massive heavyweight computers of the early days have become so portable that we can fit them in our pockets. Besides this, the increased development and innovation in nanotechnology have enabled computers to fit in small chips or even smaller devices at the atomic level. Due to this portability and availability, computers are used in almost all fields.

Lately, in the past fifty years or so, artificial intelligence has become a fascinating phenomenon. Artificial Intelligence (AI) has powered computers with the ability to perform work independently and make independent yet knowledgeable decisions [2]. The research in artificial intelligence has sky-rocketed in the recent years due to massive improvements in computer architectures, mainly parallel computing. Deep learning algorithms have many components that need enormous computation power. Hence, we need Graphics Processing Units (GPUs) to tackle high computation power requirements problems. GPUs can facilitate the task of parallel computation and make algorithms perform heavy tasks with ease. Artificial Intelligence, often called the fourth industrial revolution, has been used in many sectors [3]. Businesses harness the power of AI-based business analytics to find out solutions for many of their problems. Clinicians and doctors often use AI to build intelligent models that can help to diagnose the disease.

Similarly, engineers use AI to optimize various functions, build different simulation models, build adversaries, and many more topics. Recently, AI was even used to discover possible vaccines against the COVID-19 pandemic [4]. This shows how important AI has been to accelerating research, development, and knowledge discovery [5]. Modern-day AI disrupts every sector. With privileges provided by computers, robots, and modern machines, people have started to live a life with more space for technology. Electronics devices like phones, televisions, surveillance cameras, etc., have become a part of human life. Even the mechanical and electrical devices we use in our homes have gained some level of autonomy with the help of intelligent sensors embedded in them [6]. Most of today's devices are connected to the Internet, and much data is shared every second. This information processed by various physical devices can be used to serve some of our purposes. Aggregated information from different physical devices would give much information. Thus, creating a network of such physical devices is needed. In order to make devices perform tasks more intelligently, they are connected over the Internet, which allows them to share data in more convenient ways. This network of physical objects or things connected over the Internet is often called the Internet of Things (IoT). The devices share everything over the cloud. A cloud is where data can be stored and accessed remotely according to our needs. Cloud computing has made IoT reach its good potential [7]. IoT is slowly and progressively changing research areas like precision healthcare, business analytics, smart homes, and the industry. The concept of a smart city has only become possible because of the IoT. A smart city is an urban area where various electronic devices and cognitive sensors are used to collect information. The valuable insights deciphered from the data are used to manage the resources, home appliances, services, etc. The city's operations are heavily improved with the help of such smart IoT devices [8].

However, data sharing has never been so easy. There is latency, privacy issues, etc., when it comes to IoT. Edge AI eliminates such problems by reducing costs and latency to give users a seamless experience [9]. Also, privacy is taken care of by locally processing most of the data rather than sharing it over a centralized cloud [10]. This chapter will discuss Edge AI, its advantages, and its use cases. Similarly, the chapter also points down the limitations of Edge AI and the conclusion that discusses future possibilities of Edge AI in smart city applications.

9.2 EDGE ARTIFICIAL INTELLIGENCE: FUTURE OF ARTIFICIAL INTELLIGENCE AND THE INTERNET

Wireless technology had massive growth in the last few years, resulting in a drastic increase in the number of devices that can transfer or collect data through a wireless network, i.e., IoT devices. A report estimates that this number can go as high as 25 billion, with close to 3.9–11.1 trillion dollars of economic impact annually by 2025 [11]. IoT devices have revolutionized technology and are helpful in various fields like industrial automation. However, having limited computational power and little memory has been one of the most significant limitations of IoT devices.

With the growth in IoT devices, one other field that has seen tremendous growth is Deep Neural networks (DNNs). They are used in various domains, from speech detection, image detection, analysis of big data, and much more. The only drawback with these DNNs is their computational requirements and the amount of data required for their functioning. To use DNNs and support their resource demand, many data centers are built for their computational requirements.

DNNs use this data for functioning; where does this data come from? This data is often generated from IoT devices like sensors, microphones, smart cars, etc., which are later transported to a cloud data center. This leads to an increase in the overall cost because of the cost of communication and also an increase in the response time. Sometimes critical data is at risk of vulnerability, so the concept of Edge AI was introduced to overcome these problems. Edge AI uses the principle that rather than doing these computations at a cloud data center, we do them close to the source of data, i.e., making the data source intelligent and decreasing the traffic to the cloud. This is achieved by installing edge-computing devices near the data source, as shown in Figure 9.1. These edge devices have both computational powers and can

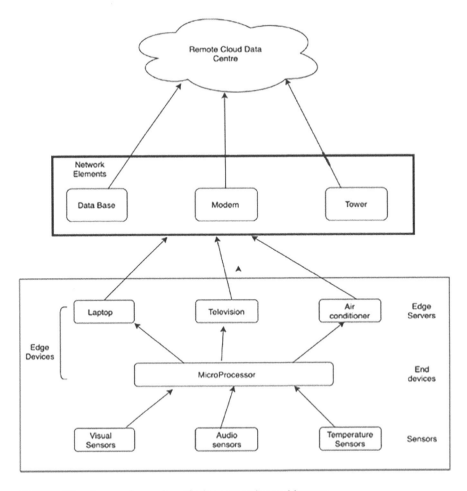

FIGURE 9.1   A general overview of edge computing architecture.

communicate with the data center. Jetson NANO (Nvidia) is an Edge AI hardware with a microprocessor and AI chip that can help you do machine learning (ML) tasks faster and near the source of data. To summarize, Edge AI means we try to do our ML tasks as close to the machine as possible.

9.2.1 PROBLEMS SOLVED BY ARTIFICIAL INTELLIGENCE AT THE EDGE

In the previous section, we discussed how the concept of Edge AI was introduced, which provides computational capabilities to the data source, thus preventing the repeated transfer of data from the data source to a data center. This makes Edge AI a beneficial device and provides many benefits over traditional systems.

Consider a self-driving car that is traveling on the road. Here, it acts as a data source where the objects in front of it are the data. If this car travels to a remote location where Internet connectivity is low, and if it were to send this data to remote cloud data centers every time for computation because of low bandwidth, there would be a time lag in the response, which may lead to an accident. So, in this case, Edge AI can help to tackle the problems of systems having latency. Another example where Edge AI proves much better is an automated machine checking whether a given product is faulty or not, passing on a belt. If it took much time to decide, then a faulty object may get passed before it is removed from the belt because of any connectivity issue. Thus, Edge AI provides more responsiveness, and decisions are taken within milliseconds. Thus, it is excellent for devices that require feedback in real time.

Transferring data through a connection is always prone to intercept; the more significant the distance, the more the chances for interception. So, Edge AI reduces the risk of intercepting data and increases privacy. Even for the data where the computation must be done remotely, the Edge AI can detect and discard sensitive information before transferring the data, thus improving safety.

Also, by using Edge AI companies can detect and solve issues related to maintenance or repair. It will also allow them to make predictions that prevent redundant servicing of the machine by optimizing the maintenance schedule. Also, since most of the data is now computed locally, it saves money on Internet bandwidth and cloud storage. The clouds can now be used to analyze already processed data. AI at the edge creates a decentralized architecture, making the system more robust and providing constant services even in the case of network failure or if there is any cyber-attack [12].

Processing data locally also reduces power consumption and helps cut energy costs, since it is not required for the data source always to be connected to the remote repository to exchange the data. It is also used to better manage IoT devices by improving the data processing field, and expanding the network of IoT devices can be done quickly without building additional infrastructure. Due to all these advantages, AI is now heading toward Edge AI. Many AI companies, the defense sector, and even open source have been investing significantly in Edge AI.

9.2.2 WORKING OF EDGE ARTIFICIAL INTELLIGENCE

Edge AI means performing the computation on data as close to the device as possible, keeping the data computing power away from a centralized system. In edge computing, the cloud takes information from the previous datasets, and end devices such as sensors and mobile phones.

The gadgets serve as clients as well as creators of data. As a result, rather than only unidirectional requests, the networks are now bidirectional. To minimize congestion from systems to the cloud, nodes at the network edge perform a variety of computational activities, which include the processing of data, storing, node management, and protection. Data from the cloud also perform computer functions on data transferred to and from the cloud, such as processing, storage, caching, and load balancing. The edge must be well designed to do such activities quickly, reliably, safely, and securely while maintaining privacy. As a result, it must be able to provide features like differentiation, extensibility, isolation, and dependability.

Usually, multiple network nodes run Edge AI, which minimizes the distances between the location where data gets collected and the location where data is processed, reducing bottlenecks and making the application faster. At the edge of networks, more than a billion IoT devices use embedded processors that are well-suited for some basic applications like video.

These devices need to stay connected to the Internet to transfer the data they have collected. However, edge computing enables the device to make decisions without transferring the data to a central system and receiving the decisions from there. Consider a robot that has an Edge AI-based application associated with it. Now, this application can process data fed to it by the robot, generate the results, and store them locally. When it gets connected to the network again, it can transfer this application to a server to store or maybe be processed further. However, if it was not using edge computing, it had to continuously send this data to the server and obtain the results from that server [12].

9.3   A GLANCE AT EDGE DEVICES

Edge devices are things in the IoT environment, connecting to centralized computer systems via various networks. In edge computing, the data processing will take place at the network edge, unlike traditional computing, which is entirely in the cloud and has been fueled by the IoT and comprehensive web-based solutions.

Even though computational capability has increased dramatically, the bandwidth becomes a drawback, since the capacity of the network has been limited. As a result of the increased data generated by edge devices, the network is getting more complex—the bottleneck in cloud computing. For instance, a camera in an autonomous car collects a large volume of visual data, which the system must process to make appropriate driving judgments. The reaction time would be too long if the vehicle had to transmit this extensive data to the cloud for processing, which could cause accidents. Information processing at the network edge would result in faster response times, more efficient processing, and reduced network load.

Lately, the focus of research has been shifted to the microdata center to optimize the performance, specifically the network time performance of the system. Edge computing, which can be seen in Figure 9.1, describes the processes that enable computations to take place at the network edge close to data sources. It works downstream and upstream of data on behalf of the cloud network. Any resource between the data point and the cloud center capable of computing is an edge device.

9.3.1 NEED FOR EDGE COMPUTING

Within a decade, it is estimated that more than 100 billion active devices, including sensors and various smart devices, would provide a continuous stream of information that needs a proper framework for management. These devices are used for various applications, from monitoring to collecting data, from reasoning to performing a task. These kinds of processes require vast computational ability in real time. Edge computing analyses data closer to its source, which results in lower latency. In a literal sense, latency can be defined as the time data takes to travel from source to destination. These improved computational abilities enable real-time actions and provide better insights to the decision maker.

With an increase in data usage of these tedious algorithms from a computational perspective, these algorithms demand much higher efficiency and speed in data gathering and analysis, which again points out the need for an edge-computing system that can handle such vast amounts of data in real-life scenarios. The cost reductions can be the businesses' sole purpose in adopting an edge-computing architecture. Companies that migrated several apps to the cloud may have realized that bandwidth expenses were more significant than planned. Hence, a viable solution like edge computing is needed.

The capacity to process, store, and churn data faster and efficiently, allowing for more feasible real-time tasks crucial to businesses, is becoming the essential advantage of edge computing. Before this, much time was required by a smartphone to operate a facial recognition feature via a cloud-based service. Given the rising capability of intelligent devices, the proposed edge architectures will allow an application to run locally or on an edge server, reducing latency multiple times. In addition, advanced technologies such as the 5G networks, expected to be at least ten times faster than the present network, will expand the potential for AI-enabled applications, demanding even more edge-computing acceleration.

9.3.2 ROLE OF FIELD PROGRAMMABLE GATE ARRAY (FPGA) IN EDGE DEVICE NETWORK

The AI hardware industry has constantly proliferated, with a market value of $7.6 billion in 2020 and is expected to rise to 57.8 billion by 2026. General-purpose computing in traditional processing units comprises the basic architecture, which dictates that a fetching command and an operation on data cannot take place simultaneously, leading to sequentially directed work. The multiprocessor system, however, tries to avoid this sequential process by using various protocols, such as snooping protocol, although it does need additional data exchange between cores and adds latency. This coded parallelism must divide the burden across processing parts as efficiently as possible. Otherwise, a computational load and communication imbalance might arise. System on Chips (SOCs) is intrinsically superior to GPUs in terms of latency, power, parallel computing, and extensibility. The FPGAs can make custom-made hardware according to the algorithm, leading to extensive computational advantage, and more straightforward and efficient design [13]. Moreover, this unique quality allows the board to be operated on low power compared to traditional processing units [14].

Application-specific integrated circuits (ASICs) have grabbed the front regarding popular AI chipsets, followed by FPGAs. However, ASICs miss the mark following the main characteristics of intelligent computing at the Edge. This is also true in terms of cost. IoT installations may range from tens to hundreds of thousands of nodes. These application-specific circuits are challenging to design, have a long design time, and may require extensive research and a significant capital investment of tens of millions of dollars to manufacture.

Moreover, this cost is justified only when a large quantity of units is produced. Furthermore, AI is constantly evolving, with thousands of different topological changes and various new implementations. This necessitates the development of a low-cost, adaptable, reconfigurable platform that can be prototyped and deployed quickly. The FPGA serves this purpose and hence is a promising device in edge device implementation [14]. Figure 9.2 depicts a trade-off between the cost and computational power of the system, and FPGAs have provided an optimal solution to this multivariable problem of concern.

9.3.3 Developer Kits

9.3.3.1 Jetson Nano

Aimed at contemporary algorithms that possess significant computational demand, the Jetson Nano has 472 Giga Floating Point Operations per second (GFLOPs). It is used in potential applications ranging from Network Video Recorders (NVRs) to intelligent gateways. It operates multiple neural networks concurrently, incorporating parallelism, and analyses multiple high-resolution sensors simultaneously. With the increasing power demands of today's hardware, the Jetson Nano stands out, operating at a power of nearly 5–10 W. This tremendous low-power device that encompasses pipelining principles to its core can be one of the most suited hardware platforms for running various edge algorithms in specific scenarios.

		Reconfigurability/ Flexibility	Power Consumption	Size	Speed (Latency + Parallel Processing)	Cost
Popular AI Chipsets	Custom-specific solution (E.g., ASIC, SoC)	Medium to High	Low	Small	High	High
	CPU	Low	Low	Small	Low	Low
	GPU	Medium	High	Small	Medium to High	Medium
	Traditional FPGA Solution	High	High	Large	High	Medium

FIGURE 9.2 AI chipsets and their ability to meet edge application needs.

This device is the latest gadget to join its manufacturer's portfolio of edge-computing platforms. All the platforms are optimized in a certain sense with various applications ranging from low-cost to edge ML for the Jetson Nano. The Jetson family of computing devices is very versatile regarding ML frameworks [15].

9.3.3.2 Intel Movidius Vision Processing Units (VPUs)

It is capable of efficient and faster performance in terms of power and speed, respectively. This unit is majorly used for computer vision and artificial intelligence workloads. The remarkable feature of these devices is parallel programmability and load-specific acceleration; in other words, smart hardware acceleration for deep neural nets and OpenCV applications majorly relate to VR and smart cameras. These omnipresent properties of Movidius make it ideal for edge-computing applications. The smart hardware acceleration according to the workload makes the device ideally suited for edge computational devices with various applications [16].

9.4   EDGE ARTIFICIAL INTELLIGENCE FOR SMART MOBILITY AND EFFICIENT TRANSPORTATION

Smart mobility refers to optimizing transport and communications to consolidate new sustainability standards, efficiency, safety, and air quality by using alternative forms of transportation, in addition to a gas-powered automobile. The following are some examples of smart mobility: intelligent cars, real-time traffic monitoring, pedestrian detection, ridesharing, car sharing, public transit, etc. [17]. Increased traffic congestion and its associated side effects, such as pollution, deaths caused by accidents, and lost time and money, are a few reasons for the need for smart mobility. The following concepts underpin smart mobility:

- **Flexibility:** Travelers may pick from various means of transportation depending on their needs.
- **Efficiency:** The journey takes the traveler to their destination with a minor interruption and is feasible in the shortest amount of time.
- **Integration:** Regardless of whether types of transportation are employed, the whole route is planned door to door.
- Transportation advances away from polluting automobiles and toward zero-emission automobiles.
- **Safety:** The number of deaths and injuries can be dramatically decreased.
- Accessibility and social benefit are two different characteristics of intelligent mobility, which implies that it should be inexpensive for everyone and contribute to a higher quality of life.

Intelligent electric cars are an excellent example of how technology can help to reduce human effort, and help us to save fuel and time at the same time. Intelligent cars are autonomous vehicles with little or no human help [18]. It does so with the help of using various sensors, actuators, complicated algorithms, ML systems, and powerful processors. The possibilities for improving ease and quality of life are endless. It is a boon for elderly and disabled people who face difficulties with classic cars and transportation systems [19]. However, the true promise of self-driving automobiles is their ability to reduce CO_2 emissions drastically. Experts highlighted three trends in new research that, if implemented simultaneously, would unleash the full potential of autonomous vehicles: vehicle automation, vehicle electrification, and carpooling. By 2050, these could:

- Reduce traffic congestion and save time (30% fewer automobiles).
- Costs of commuting have been reduced by 40%.
- Improve the walkability and livability of your neighborhood.
- Free up parking spaces that can be used for other purposes like schools, playgrounds, etc.
- Would help reduce greenhouse gas emissions in cities by about 70% around the globe.

9.4.1 Smart Cars

For more than a century, the automobile industry has been a vital economic sector, and it is now moving toward connected and automated automobiles. Vehicles are growing more sophisticated, and they are becoming less dependent on human control. Vehicle-to-vehicle and linked vehicle-to-everything communications, in which data from sensors and other sources is sent across high-bandwidth, low-latency, and high-reliability channels, are laying the foundation for entirely autonomous driving. When people are behind the wheel, they conduct calculations on the go. All the information we get from our senses of voice, sight, motion, and other senses is analyzed to give us a feel of the surroundings and what we need to do to keep the vehicle on track [20]. Sensors in autonomous cars absorb this data, which must be analyzed on the go. This data needs to be cleaned, pre-processed, and then processed once again. The processed data needs to be converted into a format that an AI model can understand. Ordering to do all this with all the data that is being generated every second by various sensors is a very tedious task. Using cloud computing and current networks to process it leads to latency, which is not feasible for automated vehicles, because we need a response within split seconds. To solve this problem, we require more storage and computational capacity, and more AI to be brought to the Edge.

In Edge-based AI, we do the computation locally instead of using the cloud. The benefits of doing so are as follows:

- Edge-based AI is more responsive and closer to real time than the traditional centralized IoT architecture. Insights are provided and analyzed instantly, usually on the same hardware or devices.
- Edge-based AI ensures greater security. Even if no one is aware, sending data back and forth with Internet-connected devices exposes data to manipulation and exposure. Processing at the Edge reduces this danger, while also providing an additional benefit.
- Edge-based AI is very adaptable.
- The operation of Edge-based AI does not need an Engineer.

9.4.2 Edge Artificial Intelligence (AI) for High-Definition Real-Time Navigation and Traffic Monitoring

AI is essential for effective and efficient navigation and ensuring that the trip from point A to point B is as safe and enjoyable as possible. The most significant advantage of AI is its capacity to increase efficiency and finish complicated jobs that are difficult for humans to handle. Regarding navigation, this means analyzing real-time situations, and providing the best route to avoid traffic and other road mishaps. To get complex near-reality maps for navigation, we need an enormous amount of data. There is also a requirement for data on the same road in various environmental and meteorological situations to guarantee that the navigation system is responsive. The more the information available, the more precise the maps and the better the navigation. To collect this data, many cities have started upgrading their present city network, so that data from them can be processed locally and used for navigation. This data is then shared. An autonomous vehicle needs data to be processed quickly to detect cars, traffic signs, people, and routes [21]. Edge AI allows it to quickly locate and analyze all the information required by the central controller.

9.4.3 Edge Artificial Intelligence (AI) for Real-Time Traffic Monitoring for Safe Roads

Artificial Intelligence provides a massive scope in traffic monitoring and controlling. In most cities, no proper traffic monitoring or controlling systems are enabled. Currently, traffic lights can be considered primary controllers of traffic, but they still seem highly inefficient, as they do not consider real-time traffic monitoring.

Edge AI can prove to be highly effective for traffic control. The primary purpose of Edge AI would be to provide the fastest and most reliable traffic flow possible. They can also be used with traffic lights to re-calibrate traffic lights to ease congestion. It can help overcome the problems of conventional traffic monitoring systems in the following ways:

- **Getting rid of car crashes caused due to drivers' misjudgment:** Driver error is the most common cause of street automobile accidents [22]. The solution to such dangerous driver behavior is to hand over control of the vehicle to something that is not distracted, occupied, inebriated, or intoxicated while driving, as humans are. As a result, vehicle automation will be required.

  These sophisticated cars, for example, react to risks much faster. Furthermore, vehicle-to-vehicle communication might allow them to exchange data quickly and warn each other about nearby threats [23].
- **Identifying ideal routes:** Although AI-driven cars need petrol and energy, they are powered by data. Intelligent cars and trucks gather data regularly, which may be used to give helpful information via analytics. Transportation companies may use such insights to look at patterns to assess journey times, bottlenecks, fuel and charging station availability, popular destinations, etc., and thus determine the most suitable route for transportation in real time.

- **Traffic patterns streamlining:** Experts can use artificial intelligence and big data analytics to regulate vehicle traffic flow in different areas. Traffic managers will have the option of preventing urban congestion or limiting bottlenecks during peak hours. They would be even better at serving open-air suburbanites. Furthermore, AI is essential in anticipating the movements of vulnerable roadway users, such as walkers. AI-based traffic management may result in a wide range of flexible options, fewer crashes and fatalities, and a negligible greenhouse gas output.
- **Recognizing and responding to emergencies:** Some automobile types use artificial intelligence to make emergencies more manageable. Auto characteristics that have been brought out by technology include the ability to identify health situations such as a heart attack, the need for health services, and providing essential information such as car position [24]. These skills benefit cab drivers who operate in the evenings and at night.

  Identifying weaknesses in drivers, managers may evaluate driver performance in real time using AI and other advancements such as facial recognition [25]. This luxury will allow decision makers to dispatch relief drivers based on the scenario and reduce poor driving behaviors. Because such information is readily available, the transportation sector and organizations can give better training to the majority of drivers.

9.5   ENTERING A DATA-DRIVEN HEALTHCARE DECADE WITH EDGE

AI is, without a doubt, a data-dense and computationally complex technology. It is widely used in a lot of medical applications [26–28]. Concerns about bandwidth, latency, security, and cost are significant roadblocks for most healthcare enterprises, especially when seconds may make or break a patient's result. By assisting AI in overcoming these technical difficulties, edge helps AI [29].

One of the more apparent reasons for edge computing's acceptance in a sector where seconds may mean the difference between life and death is the decreased latency that comes with processing data at the edge. However, with the advent of telemedicine, the delay will inevitably develop as technology, and services become increasingly disseminated throughout a healthcare organization's network. Latency must be maintained to the minimum in situations when real-time crucial decision making and actions are needed to save lives. Edge computing can bring quicker and more responsive AI-based services to facilitate quicker decision making by placing important processing jobs closer to end-users.

Many medical technology businesses recognize that Edge AI is the next wave of AI in healthcare. Patient data is kept and processed locally on a device rather than transferred to the cloud using Edge-based AI. Only the least time-consuming data sets should be moved to the cloud; the remainder should be kept on-site. Healthcare firms and patients will benefit from increased security, if sensitive patient data is sent less often between devices and the cloud.

Finally, as healthcare moves into the data-driven decade, there is a pressing demand for data storage and computing on the device. Other benefits like speed, privacy, and security allow physicians to make quicker, more educated judgments while remaining secure.

9.5.1 Autonomous Monitoring of Patients

The ability to automate processes is one of AI's distinctive selling points. AI algorithms may gather data from various sensors and evaluate it to choose the best course of action. Edge AI will help to take this to the next level. It provides unsupervised surveillance of hospital rooms and patients using image processing and input from other sensors [30].

Consider the case of fall detection. With an accelerometer and gyroscope, wearables can detect whether a person falls unexpectedly. These gadgets' Edge AI can be taught to detect falls in real time and even notify caretakers. In most circumstances, this can save a person's life. The fall detection function on Apple Watch is one example of this.

Monitoring vital indicators is another area where Edge AI may be useful. Medical equipment that captures data such as heart rate, temperature, respiration rate, blood pressure, and other parameters may use AI to identify any anomaly in real time [31]. The gadgets may then alert hospital personnel, who could subsequently act. This is not only important for the patient, but it also enhances their whole experience.

9.5.2 Transforming the Rate of Biomedical Discovery with Artificial Intelligence

During this coronavirus situation, when thousands of people died, the healthcare sector could not rely on traditional methods to learn more about the virus to make a vaccine for the greater good. Hence, it has to take the help of AI to fasten this process and uncover as much information as possible about the virus to produce effective antiviral treatments [32].

AI is used to create a biomedical research discovery tool that enables anybody to do deep searches and uncover solutions to challenging research topics that would have taken weeks or months to locate using specific keyword searches. Additionally, AI can process data to make the vaccine and speed up drug development. AI applications have traditionally been powered by data centers and cloud computing [27]. Of course, big data will always be processed on the cloud.

Conversely, AI has come closer to the user over time, making its way into software, IoMT endpoints, and other medical devices. Wearable health monitors, such as ECG and blood pressure monitors, may collect and analyze data locally, which patients may then share with their doctor for a quick health check. As a result, more AI-focused healthcare firms see the advantages of edge computing.

9.5.3 New Applications in Radiology

Digital Imaging and Communications pictures in radiology are huge. As a result, sending these photos to the cloud for processing and receiving ML inference may be very expensive and time consuming. Edge AI, on the other hand, allows the analysis to take place locally, resulting in a considerably quicker diagnosis and cheaper [33].

- **Detecting Covid**: Using Natural image processing on the X-rays of the lungs of patients can be used to diagnose Covid in patients and get results in seconds. It can be helpful before results come from the blood tests, which can take time.
- **Detection of cardiovascular abnormalities**: Using Advanced Imaging Applications in the Healthcare Industry, the automation of cardiovascular problems in routine imaging tests, such as chest X-rays, may result in speedier decision making and fewer diagnostic mistakes.
- **Detecting cancer**: The application of artificial intelligence to the notion of imaging data may also aid in the detection of significant issues such as the development of cancer cells by monitoring changes in tissue mass in the body.
- **Fracture and other musculoskeletal injuries detection**: Using artificial intelligence to identify hairline fractures, soft tissue injuries, and dislocations may help surgeons feel more confident about their treatment options.
- **Assisting with the diagnosis of neurological disorders**: Algorithms may help diagnose neurological diseases by highlighting photos with questionable findings and providing risk ratios that the pictures include evidence of PLS or ALS.

9.5.4 An Edge Computing-Based Smart Healthcare

With the COVID-19 outbreak, virtual medical consultations have become both a popular and necessary alternative [4]. Healthcare consultations have changed dramatically to IoT-based digitized healthcare systems due to the Internet's vast expertise in medical things [34]. Several attempts have been made in this field to develop an easy and dependable architecture for healthcare and monitoring systems derived from IoT [35]. Medical systems have been progressively improving, thanks to the introduction of wearable devices, which are both smart and portable in the biomedical industry. Most of these types of equipment are used in medical examinations at the preliminary stage to collect data related to EEG, Spo2 level, body temperature, respiratory rate, motion activity, and glucose recognition. They are primarily concerned with health preservation by providing early examinations to determine the chances of other complications. This design is also energy efficient, since it does not always turn on all the sensors. The system's algorithm will control how the sensors are used, and their cost and longevity. The AI technology addresses the issue of remote patient monitoring, while also providing necessary treatments via hospital doctors.

9.5.5 Providing Quality Healthcare to Remote Rural Regions

Providing good-quality medical services in rural and remote areas is still a huge problem, especially in developing and underdeveloped countries. The accessibility and size of medical services in a conventional way could not fulfill the requirements of patients. In the healthcare business, even though there has been enhancement in video conferencing that can be interactive and help doctors diagnose from far away, intelligent devices help to share other vitals for further assistance. Nevertheless, still, doctors have struggled to provide quality care to those who live far from hospitals because of connection limitations [36]. This problem can be solved using IoT medical devices and edge-computing applications. IoT Healthcare devices may expand the reach of existing networks, enabling medical personnel to access critical patient data even in areas where the connection is limited. The new healthcare platforms have the potential to make medical procedures more time efficient and portable, allowing them to be used even in remote places. This is an example of an Edge AI computing use case that can potentially expand the variety of health services available dramatically.

9.6 SECURED SMART CITIES WITH EDGE ARTIFICIAL INTELLIGENCE

As we are advancing in the field of artificial intelligence, the vision once seen of building smart cities is close to being accomplished, and Edge AI has provided a significant breakthrough in this. Smart cities improve people's quality of life, create a safer, greener, and cleaner environment, and a much better place to live in, and increase life expectancy. Edge AI is helpful in many areas, from building smart cities to safety and surveillance; it makes the devices much more efficient and decreases latency, improving the system's real-world performance.

9.6.1 EDGE-BASED ARTIFICIAL INTELLIGENCE (AI) FOR SMART HOMES

Since the advent of smartphones, there has been much research in the field of not only inventing new devices but also making the existing devices easier to use or making them "smart." Today we are surrounded by many electric devices in our homes like television, microwave, and air conditioner, but to use these devices more efficiently, we currently want our devices to be intelligent and more connected. We want them to recognize our video and audio gestures and make decisions based on the situation. We also want them to understand these and make decisions with significantly less response time. We want to make them smart [37].

The boom in Edge AI has opened research in this field. The possibility of embedding ML algorithms, i.e., neural networks on the device itself, has enabled the machine to take decisions in a short response time.

Some scenarios in intelligent homes where Edge AI proves to be very helpful are:

1. We could install speech and image-recognizing door locks in our homes, and Edge AI ensures that all this private and sensitive data is safe because the processing will be done at the edge, so data will not be transferred, and chances of interception are pretty much reduced.
2. Health-related smart devices like fitness trackers use Edge AI to ensure that sensitive data is well protected.
3. Edge AI increases the robustness of smart devices, because now, even in the case of a network outage, these devices will still work and thus reducing the chances of failure.

9.6.2 EDGE AI-BASED INTERNET OF THINGS (IoT) FOR DATA ENCRYPTION, STORAGE, AND SECURITY

The protection of personal data is the biggest concern nowadays while using smart devices. Users are becoming more aware of the importance of protecting personal data. Edge AI also finds its use in data encryption by combining it with blockchain technology [38].

Combining blockchain with Edge AI opens up many new paradigms in the applications that work with sensitive and personal data. Combining a distributed ledger with Edge AI creates a secure database, which cannot be used without the owner's permission. Because of Edge AI, the devices use Ethereum smart contracts to analyze, process, and share their data, and they are not required to share this data continuously to a blockchain cloud.

We currently have many methods that enhance security on everyday smart devices by encrypting the data, e.g., anonymization, cryptographic methods, data obfuscation methods, etc. However, these require extensive calculations, making it difficult to use an Edge AI-based IoT.

So, instead of using these traditional methods, we use distributed ML (DMLs), where Edge nodes pass the parameters to the other edge nodes for cooperative learning after each training, and the actual data is not passed, thus making it even more secure and reducing the chances of data leakage even further, and also reduces the data burden [39].

With so many distributed architectures being deployed and data becoming increasingly sensitive, the cloud usually has a multilayer of encryption. With the advancement of Edge AI, edge nodes can determine which security mechanism works best for AI-enabled devices like robots, phones, and tablets. As we have already discussed, since the computations on the data are performed on edge, the device does not need to send the data back to the central system, so the chances of interception get reduced to a significant amount, making our data much more secure.

9.6.3 EDGE ARTIFICIAL INTELLIGENCE-BASED INTERNET OF THINGS (IoT) FOR SAFETY AND SURVEILLANCE APPLICATIONS

Edge AI can also be combined with computer vision and solves many problems. One of the usages of Edge AI combined with computer vision is surveillance cameras installed in public and private places. Before the development of artificial intelligence, the video camera was used to record the feed and send them to a centralized system where an operator was sitting who used to analyze the stream. This was very cumbersome and prone to error. Then, as the computer vision field grew, these video cameras were replaced by smart video systems. These devices not only capture the video feed but also perform the processing on this feed, and analyze and extract information in real time from the feed; but they also had to send this data to a centralized place where all the processing used to occur, and information was extracted at one single location. This caused lots of communication costs. With the rise in the field of Edge AI now, the processing is done on the video camera itself, and only a few alerts or small-sized mini clips are sent to a centralized system [40]. This size specification helped in saving money on Internet bandwidth. Also, cloud storage is not required to store all the video feeds, and can be reserved for some alerts or controversial video clips. These surveillance cameras can also be used for safety in parking lots and offices.

9.6.4 FURTHER APPLICATIONS OF EDGE ARTIFICIAL INTELLIGENCE FOR SECURITY APPLICATIONS

Edge AI also found its usage in many security systems. Doors with smart locks that lock and unlock based on image recognition make use of Edge AI, which prevents sensitive data from hackers and increases their robustness. Also, speed and security cameras installed on the roads to detect overspeeding cars use Edge AI [41]. Fire alarms are another example where Edge AI is of extreme importance, because if there is a network breakdown in case of a fire, then fire alarms sharing information to a centralized system will fail; thus, computations at the edge are exceptionally crucial for them.

There are many more examples where Edge AI is used in building smart cities [13]. We will soon find more and more devices that use edge-computing techniques in the future. Research in this field is growing at a rapid pace. Some people might feel that Edge AI will soon replace the cloud; but this is far stretched, because, for most processes, some centralized system is always required. Edge AI is a way of covering the shortcomings of a cloud. Cloudlet is a new technology that combines the benefits of both Edge AI and the cloud. It is a small-scale cloud data center located at the edge of the Internet. It helps increase the resiliency at a device's level [42].

This provides the various aspects of the Edge AI-based network. It discusses applications and provides a brief scope of improvisation, for example, the concept of distributed systems concerning neural net training. The added layer of security with efficient resource management and applications from a software point of view has been discussed. In the following parts, hardware-level optimizations and applications have been discussed.

9.7 RESOURCE UTILIZATION OF SMART CITIES WITH EDGE ARTIFICIAL INTELLIGENCE

All the devices, from personal computers to supercomputers, have some form of integrated electronics. The rapid change in the semiconductor industry has helped transform the IoT capabilities of a network. The semiconductor aspect of the IoT system includes energy-efficient and computationally capable devices.

Because of the lowering cost of implementing these IoT devices and rising demand, the IoT paradigm has significantly influenced both consumers' lives and corporate models. The tendency is anticipated to accelerate, but hardware resources are one of the bottlenecks the current system faces.

Presently, sensors and actuators form the backbone of IoT networks. The sensors and actuators are fundamentally analogous; therefore, their hardware utilization is comparable. The aspect of this hardware statement regarding IoT networks is energy utilization.

Most IoT devices are battery powered or work on externally supplied energy from energy harvesters. Considering their restricted energy budget, the electricity that can be used will require intelligent resource utilization, requiring hardware engineers to develop ultra-low-power solutions to minimize load and maximize the nodes present in the network for the same energy budget. Several parts of the design are energy hungry, like wireless transmitters, which are severely limited by power. Hence, the designer must use low-power cutting-edge technologies, such as ultra-wideband or UWB [43], increasing the network's energy budget.

Many believe that the edge-computing paradigm is more ecologically friendly than cloud computing, since it may limit the amount of data that must be transported, lowering energy costs. As previously stated, several studies have focused on the decentralization of workload. The goal is to decrease latency by outsourcing specific processes to nearby servers [44]. In reality, such infrastructure may be used to improve performance in urban contexts. However, to effectively manage the workload, it is often necessary to divide it evenly and synchronize the various responsibilities.

When we look at energy management, two kinds of optimization can be used to increase efficiency: one is the optimization on the software level, and the other is energy-efficient hardware implementation. Software optimization can be used to synchronize all workloads [45]. The complete operating system should be employed rather than the incomplete embedded firmware, since a complete operating system grows into a prevailing instrument for complicated and complex tasks. For multiple remote users and while considering a variety of scenarios that are often required for IoT systems, the main OS can be a virtual operating system that is an emulated OS on the device, or it can let the users have more than one instance of the operating system running simultaneously, sharing the kernels with intelligent resource allocation [43].

The hardware optimization is rather intriguing. Hardware optimization is preferred over software one, since, with an exponential increase in the number of IoT devices, software optimization cannot fulfill the purpose in the long run. Hence, a hardware overhauling is necessary. Here, hardware-specific changes have been discussed to revamp the software-based myopic view of the problem mentioned above.

9.7.1 Application-Specific Integrated Processors (ASIP) Architecture

These processors use more power than ASICs but can adapt to changing standards without re-designing and producing a new integrated circuit, a key cost barrier for the IoT network expansion. IoT hardware should ideally be optimized while not being very application-specific to reduce nonrecurring manufacturing costs by mass producing millions of tiny, inexpensive integrated circuits. These limits force IoT manufacturers to use older silicon technology methods, such as those between 200 and 130 nm. These nodes are particularly useful in this industry, since they have been demonstrated to be mature, inexpensive, mixed-signal competent, embedded-flash competent, and low power, making them a low-risk alternative. Smaller technical nodes are still necessary for high-performance applications that demand lightning-fast execution [46].

The dedicated hardware approach is not helpful in the IoT world. The IoT ecosystem requires versatile hardware that can be updated with a technological shift or increased workload. Traditional ASICs (shown in Figure 9.3) are unchangeable, and hence there is a loss of flexibility. As shown in Figure 9.4, the ASIP architecture removes this drawback of ASICs by incorporating a programmable control unit rather than a hard-coded FSM machine. This way, the circuit can be reused or modified according to the demand of the designer [46]. Lately, addressing the voltage scaling and power gating, the data stored in a flip flop is retained, since they use an NVFF which stands for the

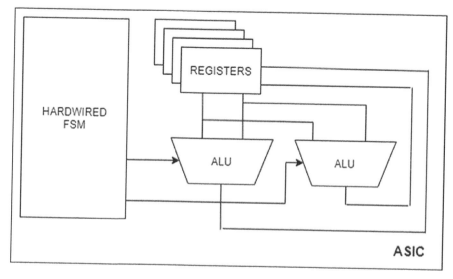

FIGURE 9.3 Architecture of ASIC architecture.

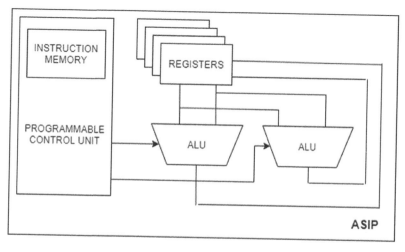

FIGURE 9.4 Architecture of ASIP architecture.

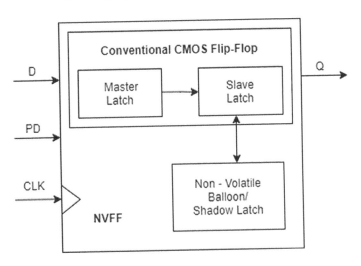

FIGURE 9.5   Basic structure of nonvolatile flip flop.

nonvolatile flip flop. This technology minimizes any power loss; hence, the flop can theoretically hold data forever. The minimization is achieved by including a shadow latch, also called a balloon latch, as shown in Figure 9.5. But this approach uses proper ground and power supply [47]. Although it works, it increases leakage concerning accurate nonvolatile memory.

CPUs incorporate a power management system that shuts down or switches to low-energy mode portions of the core, peripherals, or even memory hierarchy components [47].

These kinds of optimization are required, because:

- To remove modules that are not included in the current task and consume power while running in the background.
- To extend the battery's life and, as a result, the embedded system's life.
- To minimize the workload of the cooling system saving power.

Because most IoT nodes are portable, battery-powered devices, including an onboard component that can proactively manage energy usage, is quite valuable. Additionally, since processes and operations are carried out chronologically, not all of the units will be employed at the same time. As a result, turning off these components is necessary for the reasons stated above.

Nowadays, low-power microcontroller units are also used as nodes, as they offer low-cost and power-efficient solutions idle for the edge-computing environment. MCUs now have low-power features that halt the whole system, allowing peripherals to operate autonomously while the core performs no operations. Deep-sleep condition is the term used to describe this state. When no work has to be completed, MCUs may enter this state, and the wake-up signal is often generated by an internal timer (deep sleep for a set duration) or an external interrupt (event wake-up).

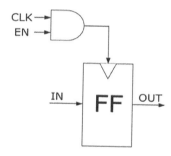

FIGURE 9.6 The clock gating method.

There are several more low-power solutions, such as clock gating, as shown in Figure 9.6, which involves turning off the clock in parts of the circuit that are not needed for the current operation. Additionally, clock gating preserves the state of the circuit, enabling normal functioning to be restored simply by reinserting the clock. The hardware overhead required to manage the clock signal is small, and this method proves to be quite successful due to its precise granularity.

Lastly, the IoT expansion should be looked at from the software and hardware levels. This might improve the myopic view of the software-oriented industry experts and ease the anticipated expansion of the network. Besides developing ultra-low-power circuits, retrofitting the present hardware capabilities is one of the challenging aspects of this whole ecosystem. The trade-off between cost and performance would determine this result.

9.8 FURTHER APPLICATIONS OF EDGE ARTIFICIAL INTELLIGENCE IN SMART CITIES

Until now, we discussed so many applications of Edge AI in building up smart cities. We have seen that Edge AI is beneficial in so many diverse areas. We are surrounded by devices where Edge AI can be applied for their more efficient usage. Here, we will discuss some more applications of edge computing.

9.8.1 INDUSTRY

In industry, there are many IoT-based devices. One example is a device that tells whether a final product is set to be sent for delivery. The biggest challenge these devices face is that they have short battery life and are resource constrained. They continuously monitor the events' information and send them to a remote server. The server then processes this information and tells the device what decision to make [48]. These devices can use Edge AI technology where the decisions are taken on the device itself, and, maybe later, it can send some alerts to the remote server for storage purposes. As the decision of whether the product is faulty or not is decided by the device itself, and it is not required to exchange information with the cloud continuously. This reduces the communication cost, and real-time responses fasten the production rate and benefit the industry. Many other IoT devices in a sector can use edge computing. Edge AI mechanisms for applications in an industry are essential for the entire world in solving many relevant issues at the global level and play a big part in industrialization.

9.8.2 DATA ANALYTICS

Data Analytics is one of the fields where ML is prevailing. Recommendation systems are a driving force for many applications like YouTube, Netflix, etc. Finance analytics also uses ML to make financial predictions, fraud detection, risk management, etc. In these models, the more data we have, the more accurate are the models [49]. However, as we increase the amount of data, we get accompanied by the problem of data piracy. Current models use encryption techniques to protect the data, make databases more secure, hide ML models, etc. However, this will always have limitations, and there always remains a possibility that this security mechanism can be breached. So, another good solution is using edge computing. We can deploy our ML services on edge devices, not only preventing privacy to a large extent but also cutting communication costs.

9.8.3 TRAFFIC SAFETY

Even after many advances in vehicle safety and the construction of better roads, we witness many road accidents around us. These accidents occur because of blind spots, poor visibility, and over speeding. Early warning systems can be introduced on the roads, improving road safety by alerting drivers about critical scenarios [50]. The current state-of-the-art solutions involve simple AI-based devices that generate an alert in these situations. The biggest problem with these devices is data latency. Getting real-time updates is crucial when traveling on the road; even a matter of milliseconds can prove essential. However, these devices usually send the data to the central, cloud-based data centers, typically located outside the city far away. So, this transfer of information takes time, depending on the network connection, which can prove very costly. Edge AI is the best solution in this situation, which prevents data latency and gives real-time results.

9.8.4 ENTERTAINMENT

There is a potential use of Edge AI in gaming and watching movies. By caching content, the edge can improve the latency. These applications are distributing the CDNs more and more widely onto the edge, making them more flexible; thus, customization can be done depending on user traffic demands. Cloud gaming is also one of the potential areas where edge computing may find its use soon. There are many latency-based issues while gaming, and a slow Internet connection can spoil the entire gaming experience. The gaming companies are trying to build edge servers that will be as close to gamers as possible to reduce the latency and provide a smooth gaming experience.

9.8.5 SMART GRID

Edge AI is one of the reasons for the rapid increase in the popularity and adoption of smart grids, which help industries manage their energy consumption better. The IoT devices connected to an edge network in factories, offices, etc., monitor energy use by watching their consumption in real time [51,52]. Doing these analyses can help industries to make better decisions. For example, they are finding areas where highly powered machines are run during off-peak times for electricity demands, thus striking new and better deals for the industry.

9.8.6 AUTONOMOUS VEHICLES

As already discussed, Edge AI is one of the most crucial technologies for autonomous vehicles. Autonomous vehicles need to detect objects in front of them to prevent accidents and what decisions to make. Suppose the car continuously shares data with a remote data center that instructs the vehicle. In that case, this will cause latency, proving very costly and life threatening later. So, to remove latency and take real-time decisions, edge computing is introduced in autonomous vehicles where the decisions are taken by the car itself. There are many applications of Edge AI, and it has many opportunities. It has revolutionized the field of artificial intelligence, and there is much research in this field. Many AI-based companies have started investing in Edge AI by observing its diverse applications.

9.9 CONCLUSION

Edge computing can enhance the existing cloud computing scenario's privacy, speed, and accessibility. The approach allows artificial intelligence to be used by many users, from influential organizations to individuals. Edge computing may be included in the present methods to safely tackle the data bandwidth issue. Edge computing may be used in various ways, depending on the sector. In other words, Edge AI may be used in specific industries.

Edge AI can analyze data without requiring a device connected to the Internet and make decisions in milliseconds. As a consequence, the cloud model's communication costs are significantly lowered. In other words, Edge AI transfers data and processing to the user's closest point of contact, whether a computer, an IoT device, or an Edge server. For example, Google, Alexa, and Apple Homepod speakers employ ML to learn words and phrases, and then store them locally on the device. Without an Edge network, the response time would be seconds; with Edge, the time is less than 500 ms. Edge AI tackles the privacy considerations that come with transmitting and storing large volumes of data in the cloud, and the bandwidth and latency limitations that limit data transfer. It has benefited driverless cars and will help reduce power consumption by extending battery life. It might be utilized with robots, surveillance systems, and other equipment. Edge AI will undoubtedly have a significant influence on our future. Companies and corporations are already using it to provide customers with an efficient and hassle-free experience.

Edge computing offers numerous benefits and is used in several applications, but it also has its security issues. These hazards are increased by design faults, improper configuration, and implementation difficulties in edge devices and servers. Furthermore, many edge devices lack full-featured user interfaces, making it difficult to discern between persistent and transpired threats. Although the impacts of a prospective attack are limited to a small region, including intelligence at the edge layer can also be dangerous because usually, the hardware used in this edge layer has weak security protocols, making it vulnerable to attacks. The problem is made worse by the carelessness of humans in command of the Edge. According to the research of 439 million households with Wi-Fi networks, over half of them were unsecured, while the remaining 80% had their routers set to default passwords. The situation is significantly worse with public Wi-Fi hotspots, with 89 percent being unsecured or improperly configured.

Additionally, updating or reconfiguring security software on edge devices is challenging, since obsolete devices may no longer be supported, or the device's low hardware resources may restrict the authentication techniques employed. Furthermore, the diversity of edge networks hinders the implementation of a single security policy. Finally, micro servers lack the hardware safety features seen on commodity servers in the edge-computing environment.

REFERENCES

1. Zawacki-Richter O, Latchem C (2018) Exploring four decades of research in computers & education. *Computers & Education* 122:136–152.
2. Ghimire A, Thapa S, Jha AK, Adhikari S, Kumar A (2020) Accelerating business growth with big data and artificial intelligence. In: *2020 Fourth International Conference on I-SMAC (IoT in Social, Mobile, Analytics, and Cloud) (I-SMAC)*. IEEE, pp. 441–448.
3. Ghimire A, Jha AK, Thapa S, Mishra S, Jha AM (2021) Machine learning approach based on hybrid features for detection of phishing URLs. In: *2021 11th International Conference on Cloud Computing, Data Science & Engineering (Confluence)*. IEEE, pp. 954–959.
4. Ghimire A, Thapa S, Jha AK, Kumar A, Kumar A, Adhikari S (2020) AI and IoT solutions for tackling COVID-19 pandemic. In: *2020 4th International Conference on Electronics, Communication and Aerospace Technology (ICECA)*. IEEE, pp. 1083–1092.
5. Kaiwartya O, Abdullah AH, Cao Y, Lloret J, Kumar S, Shah RR, Prasad M, Prakash S (2017) Virtualization in wireless sensor networks: Fault-tolerant embedding for internet of things. *IEEE Internet of Things Journal* 5 (2):571–580.
6. Jha AK, Ghimire A, Thapa S, Jha AM, Raj R A (2021) Review of AI for urban planning: towards building sustainable smart cities. In: *2021 6th International Conference on Inventive Computation Technologies (ICICT)*. IEEE, pp. 937–944.
7. El-Sayed H, Sankar S, Prasad M, Puthal D, Gupta A, Mohanty M, Lin C-T (2017) Edge of things: The big picture on the integration of edge, IoT and the cloud in a distributed computing environment. *IEEE Access* 6:1706–1717.
8. Gill SS, Tuli S, Xu M, Singh I, Singh KV, Lindsay D, Tuli S, Smirnova D, Singh M, Jain U (2019) Transformative effects of IoT, blockchain and artificial intelligence on cloud computing: Evolution, vision, trends and open challenges. *Internet of Things* 8:100118.

9. Elbamby MS, Perfecto C, Liu C-F, Park J, Samarakoon S, Chen X, Bennis M (2019) Wireless edge computing with latency and reliability guarantees. *Proceedings of the IEEE* 107 (8):1717–1737.
10. Rahman MS, Khalil I, Atiquzzaman M, Yi X (2020) Towards privacy-preserving AI based composition framework in edge networks using fully homomorphic encryption. *Engineering Applications of Artificial Intelligence* 94:103737.
11. What is Edge Computing? (2021) https://blogs.nvidia.com/blog/2019/10/22/what-is-edge-computing/.
12. Murshed M, Murphy C, Hou D, Khan N, Ananthanarayanan G, Hussain F (2019) Machine learning at the network edge: A survey. *arXiv preprint arXiv*:190800080, *ACM Computing Surveys* 54(8): Article 170.
13. Negi A, Raj S, Thapa S, Indu S (2021) Field programmable gate array (FPGA) based IoT for smart city applications, Data-Driven Mining, Learning and Analytics for Secured Smart Cities Advanced Sciences and Technologies for Security Applications, p. 135–158.
14. Biookaghazadeh S, Zhao M, Ren F (2018) Are FPGAs suitable for edge computing? In: *Workshop on Hot Topics in Edge Computing (HotEdge)*, Computing and Augmented Intelligence, School of IAFSE-SCAI.
15. Jetson Nano Developer Kit and Module. https://www.nvidia.com/en-in/autonomous-machines/embedded-systems/jetson-nano/product-development/.
16. Intel® Movidius™ Vision Processing Units (VPUs). https://www.intel.com/content/www/us/en/products/details/processors/movidius-vpu.html.
17. Benevolo C, Dameri RP, D'auria B (2016) Smart mobility in smart city Lecture Notes in Information Systems and Organization. In: Teresina Torre, Alessio Maria Braccini, Riccardo Spinelli (eds.), *Empowering Organizations*, edition 1, Springer, pp. 13–28.
18. Helmers E, Marx P (2012) Electric cars: Technical characteristics and environmental impacts. *Environmental Sciences Europe* 24 (1):1–15.
19. Choi I-K, Kim W-S, Lee D, Kwon D-S (2015) A weighted qfd-based usability evaluation method for elderly in smart cars. *International Journal of Human-Computer Interaction* 31 (10):703–716.
20. Kaiwartya O, Abdullah AH, Cao Y, Altameem A, Prasad M, Lin C-T, Liu X (2016) Internet of vehicles: Motivation, layered architecture, network model, challenges, and future aspects. *IEEE Access* 4:5356–5373.
21. Uddin MI, Alamgir MS, Rahman MM, Bhuiyan MS, Moral MA (2021) AI traffic control system based on deepstream and IoT using NVIDIA Jetson Nano. In: *2021 2nd International Conference on Robotics, Electrical and Signal Processing Techniques (ICREST)*. IEEE, pp. 115–119.
22. Bonyár A, Géczy A, Krammer O, Sántha H, Illés B, Kámán J, Szalay Z, Hanák P, Harsányi G (2017) A review on current eCall systems for autonomous car accident detection. In: *2017 40th International Spring Seminar on Electronics Technology (ISSE)*. IEEE, pp. 1–8.
23. Duffy SH, Hopkins JP (2013) Sit, stay, drive: The future of autonomous car liability. *SMU Science and Technical Review* 16:453.
24. Etzioni A, Etzioni O (2016) Designing AI systems that obey our laws and values. *Communications of the ACM* 59 (9):29–31.
25. Rezaei M, Klette R (2011) Simultaneous analysis of driver behavior and road condition for driver distraction detection. *International Journal of Image and Data Fusion* 2 (3):217–236.
26. Thapa S, Adhikari S, Naseem U, Singh P, Bharathy G, Prasad M (2020) Detecting Alzheimer's disease by exploiting linguistic information from Nepali transcript. In: *International Conference on Neural Information Processing*. Springer, pp. 176–184.

27. Yu K-H, Beam AL, Kohane IS (2018) Artificial intelligence in healthcare. *Nature Biomedical Engineering* 2 (10):719–731.

28. Thapa S, Singh P, Jain DK, Bharill N, Gupta A, Prasad M (2020) Data-driven approach based on feature selection technique for early diagnosis of Alzheimer's disease. In: *2020 International Joint Conference on Neural Networks (IJCNN)*. IEEE, pp. 1–8.

29. Thapa S, Adhikari S, Ghimire A, Aditya A (2020) Feature selection based twin-support vector machine for the diagnosis of Parkinson's disease. In: *2020 IEEE 8th R10 Humanitarian Technology Conference (R10-HTC)*, IEEE Xplore.

30. Gómez J, Oviedo B, Zhuma E (2016) Patient monitoring system based on internet of things. *Procedia Computer Science* 83:90–97.

31. Gupta D, Choudhury A, Gupta U, Singh P, Prasad M (2021) Computational approach to clinical diagnosis of diabetes disease: A comparative study. *Multimedia Tools and Applications*: 80(6), 1–26.

32. Liu J, Zhu Z, Zhou Y, Wang N, Dai G, Liu Q, Xiao J, Xie Y, Zhong Z, Liu H (2021) 4.5 Bi-oAIP: A reconfigurable biomedical AI processor with adaptive learning for versatile intelligent health monitoring. In: *2021 IEEE International Solid-State Circuits Conference (ISSCC)*. IEEE, pp. 62–64.

33. Mehrizi MHR, van Ooijen P, Homan M (2021) Applications of artificial intelligence (AI) in diagnostic radiology: A technography study. *European Radiology* 31 (4):1805–1811.

34. Pace P, Aloi G, Gravina R, Caliciuri G, Fortino G, Liotta A (2018) An edge-based architecture to support efficient applications for healthcare industry 4.0. *IEEE Transactions on Industrial Informatics* 15 (1):481–489.

35. Abdellatif AA, Mohamed A, Chiasserini CF, Tlili M, Erbad A (2019) Edge computing for smart health: Context-aware approaches, opportunities, and challenges. *IEEE Network* 33 (3):196–203.

36. Shuwandy ML, Zaidan B, Zaidan A, Albahri AS (2019) Sensor-based mHealth authentication for real-time remote healthcare monitoring system: A multilayer systematic review. *Journal of Medical Systems* 43 (2):33.

37. Shuhaiber A, Mashal I (2019) Understanding users' acceptance of smart homes. *Technology in Society* 58:101110.

38. Nawaz A, Gia TN, Queralta JP, Westerlund T (2019) Edge AI and blockchain for privacy-critical and data-sensitive applications. In: *2019 Twelfth International Conference on Mobile Computing and Ubiquitous Network (ICMU)*. IEEE, pp. 1–2.

39. Shukla AK, Janmaijaya M, Abraham A, Muhuri PK (2019) Engineering applications of artificial intelligence: A bibliometric analysis of 30 years (1988–2018). *Engineering Applications of Artificial Intelligence* 85:517–532.

40. Cob-Parro AC, Losada-Gutiérrez C, Marrón-Romera M, Gardel-Vicente A, Bravo-Muñoz I (2021) Smart video surveillance system based on edge computing. *Sensors* 21 (9):2958.

41. Khan MA, Khan SF (2018) IoT-based framework for vehicle over-speed detection. In: *2018 1st International Conference on Computer Applications & Information Security (ICCAIS)*. IEEE, pp. 1–4.

42. Jia M, Cao J, Liang W (2015) Optimal cloudlet placement and user to cloudlet allocation in wireless metropolitan area networks. *IEEE Transactions on Cloud Computing* 5 (4):725–737.

43. Capra M, Peloso R, Masera G, Ruo Roch M, Martina M (2019) Edge computing: A survey on the hardware requirements in the internet of things world. *Future Internet* 11 (4):100.

44. Anawar MR, Wang S, Azam Zia M, Jadoon AK, Akram U, Raza S (2018) Fog computing: An overview of big IoT data analytics. *Wireless Communications and Mobile Computing* 2018.

45. Bansal N, Gautam R, Tiwari R, Thapa S, Singh A (2021) Economic load dispatch using intelligent particle swarm optimization. In: *Proceedings of International Conference on Intelligent Computing, Information and Control Systems*. Springer, pp. 93–105.
46. Keutzer K, Malik S, Newton AR (2002) From ASIC to ASIP: The next design discontinuity. In: *Proceedings of IEEE International Conference on Computer Design: VLSI in Computers and Processors*. IEEE, pp. 84–90.
47. Portal J-M, Bocquet M, Moreau M, Aziza H, Deleruyelle D, Zhang Y, Kang W, Klein J-O, Zhang Y, Chappert C (2014) An overview of non-volatile flip-flops based on emerging memory technologies. *Journal of Electronic Science and Technology* 12 (2):173–181.
48. Sodhro AH, Pirbhulal S, De Albuquerque VHC (2019) Artificial intelligence-driven mechanism for edge computing-based industrial applications. *IEEE Transactions on Industrial Informatics* 15 (7):4235–4243.
49. Zhao J, Mortier R, Crowcroft J, Wang L (2018) Privacy-preserving machine learning based data analytics on edge devices. In: *Proceedings of the 2018 AAAI/ACM Conference on AI, Ethics, and Society*, ACM Digital Library, pp. 341–346.
50. Lujic I, Maio VD, Pollhammer K, Bodrozic I, Lasic J, Brandic I (2021) Increasing traffic safety with real-time edge analytics and 5G. In: *Proceedings of the 4th International Workshop on Edge Systems, Analytics, and Networking*. International Workshop on Edge Systems, Analytics and Networking (EdgeSys 2021). pp. 19–24.
51. Shi W, Cao J, Zhang Q, Li Y, Xu L (2016) Edge computing: Vision and challenges. *IEEE Internet of Things Journal* 3 (5):637–646.
52. Adhikari, S., Thapa, S., Naseem, U., Singh, P., Huo, H., Bharathy, G., & Prasad, M. (2022). Exploiting linguistic information from Nepali transcripts for early detection of Alzheimer's disease using natural language processing and machine learning techniques. *International Journal of Human-Computer Studies* 160:102761.

10 Power System Load Research Tool for Energy Supply Industry with Data Analytics and Visualizations

Julius Namwandi and KS Sastry Musti
Namibia University of Science and
Technology, Windhoek, Namibia

CONTENTS

DOI: 10.1201/9781003330875-10

10.1 INTRODUCTION

A modern power grid is truly a composite system with different types of generating facilities connected to it. Loads are located in different regions and continuously changing in real-time. Load demand and energy consumption studies are of significant interest, as they influence overall finances and system operation. Since the underlying objective is to feed the loads in an economical and realizable manner, it is important to match the generation levels with the load. For this, load data and associated research form the basis for both real-time and future improvement studies. Load research is required in analyzing the energy consumptions in various regions, managing the grid better and also in planning generation scheduling. Load research takes into account how consumers are using the energy and calculates the total energy being consumed in KWh, MWh, or GWh (or as Load (MW)) over a year, month, week, or day, or over a season. Load research forms the very basis of planning and designing the system, and then also plays a significant role in real-time operation and control, and other aspects of system management. This study presents a versatile tool that can be used for various planning and operational tasks that require load data, information, and visualizations. Thus, various stake holders such as policy makers, planning engineers, grid operators can look into possibilities of using this framework, if not the actual developed tool itself. The framework supports data analysis and wide-ranging computations besides customization. Essentially, our chapter presents a load research tool to provide an overview of smart grid networks and perform load demand analysis. In doing so, this chapter first provides foundation for data-driven load research, analytics and visualizations for smart grid through literature review. Then key inferences are derived from the literature to provide foundation and rationale for the objectives and wider discussion. The next section provides design and development process along with key variables and visualizations. The later sections provide the results, look and feel of the tool, conclusions drawn, and recommendations for further work.

10.2 LITERATURE REVIEW

To say load research and/or load analysis does not fall under the data science and data analytics domain is an understatement. It is essential to use the standard scientific and statistical methods to interpret the vast amount of data, and to generate visualizations that can be easily understood by the average human to make insightful decisions for businesses and organizations or the society at large. Similarly, with load research there is always a need for information to be interpreted (Puckett et al., 2020). Godin and Puckett (2014) clearly state that load research is the act of using data obtained through measurements. These measurements can be done through various means like conventional electricity meters or high performance, and new tech-based smart meters. Regardless of how data is obtained, it is raw and does not hold any useful information until it goes under processes defined by scientific methods to create useful information that will have an impact.

10.2.1 SIGNIFICANCE OF LOAD RESEARCH

As stated earlier, it is important for utility companies to recognize and acknowledge the behavior of their end-users. This aspect is well aligned with load research in any ESI. The insights gained from load research and/or analysis are used to help with power system stability. Venugopal (2020) has suggested that monitoring residential and industrial usage of electricity is crucial to saving energy usage and cutting down all possible costs. She added that this is in all attempts to stabilize the power system, which is a great challenge recently due to the high energy demand that comes with the increase in population and new technologies. It is a known fact that the main mission of load research is not only to help utility companies operate the grid efficiently and meet all the societal energy demands without any compromises, but also how does the utility company use the insights obtained from load research to make informed decisions?

The load research cycle can bring clarity to that question. The load research cycle is the steps that a typical engineer or the researcher is expected to follow to safely say they have conducted extensive research and analysis (Puckett et al., 2020). The first step in load research is always the need for information, as mentioned earlier. The key steps are: population sampling and data acquisition, data processing, data analysis, modeling, and generation of results (Puckett et al., 2020). All these stages will be discussed in the later sections. The tools, technologies, and methods used to conduct the study are important, as they outline different approaches that are effective and will give the best results for every researcher. The tools and technologies are the equipment used to obtain the data. A few questions that normally arise are: Is the data collected through conventional metering or smart metering? What software platforms can be used? and a few more. A recent study (Yang et al., 2017) has done load analysis and load forecasting using the Apache Spark software based on program-generated data sets. Bhattarai et al. (2019) reviewed and pointed the use of MS-Excel, MATLAB and R platforms for load research.

Load research is important during power system analysis and studies, the main aim or objective is to get information that will help determine whether the power system will be able to handle future strains with emerging technologies, and what techniques to be used to obtain this information. Apart from the mentioned aims and objectives of load research, it is also important to mention that load research is used to make crucial calculations in power system analysis and studies such as, load forecasting, visualization of load curves, load duration curves, and the calculation of load factor. Over the past decade, engineers, researchers, and technicians have looked at how to study the power network and the behavior of its end users with various approaches. Load research is one of those techniques. Various approaches have been used and implemented by different authors before, and they are going to be discussed in this section.

10.2.2 DATA POPULATION AND SAMPLING

Load research deals with huge amounts of data that will take time to process. Before data is collected, the researcher needs to identify the population that the data is being collected from. In this case, the population can mean the total number of customers on the system, a specific city, region, or province. It is the job of the load researcher to create an appropriate population frame (Puckett et al., 2020). The population frame needs to be well-secured and created, as it will represent the entire population. Population information can be obtained from billing information and/or metering information from the past. According to Puckett et al. (2020),

> For classical load research, this comes in the form of the population billing data known for all customers on the system. The customers are typically segmented by rate class or other domains of interest.

The population information is used by load researchers to classify consumers by measures of electricity usage. The information obtained from the population data is then used as the focus of the research. Considering the whole population means dealing with big data; the load researcher should create a subset of the chosen population frame by selecting the minimum number of customers that will represent the entire population (Puckett et al., 2020). Load researchers have to make sure that the sample design has the ability and power to perform estimates of a population-level measure. The next step to take is when sample designing is stratifying the sampled data. Stratification is the arrangement or classification of something into different groups. According to Puckett et al. (2020), stratification includes identifying the variables to use, such as: weekday data, weekend data, seasonal data, etc. It is fascinating that such methods and strategies have been used by past researchers and are still being used today. Garg et al. (2010) used a method known as stratified random sampling to get the target sample size across cities and towns in Gujarat (State in India). In a study conducted recently (Heunis et al., 2014), the researchers used the demographic details corresponding to the ones acknowledged by the sample design to find the load research site. This means that before data can be collected or any other stage of the load research cycle commences, it is of much importance that the focused population is appropriately secured and created.

Population sampling is a crucial aspect of load research for two reasons. Firstly, sampling prevents the researcher from dealing with large amounts of data that have a high possibility of containing errors, and missing segments that take time to clean and later process. The second reason why sampling is important is that it has the potential to allow a researcher to paint a much more complete picture and greatly reduces the guesswork (Yuan et al., 2020).

10.2.3 DATA ACQUISITION

Data collection/acquisition is the act of obtaining data of electricity energy usage from different types of consumers, be it residential, commercial, municipal, or industrial. This act can be achieved by measurements through load monitoring (Yuan et al., 2020). Data collection mainly should be done on sites, where meters are going to be installed to record and monitor the energy usage. It is of much importance to acquire data at sites that correspond with the sample design, as mentioned in the previous subsections. Load researchers have used different approaches and tools for collecting data, and they are going to be discussed here.

Metering has been and is the most common method of acquiring data in ESI. Data collection can include determining an appropriate collection strategy, such as, handheld devices, modems, or a fixed network (Puckett et al., 2020). All these strategies depend on the load research approach. In a recent study (Yuan et al., 2020), the researchers looked at monitoring the electrical energy usage of households by connecting voltage and current sensors at the main electrical feed to measure the energy consumption of the whole house. The study further states that the electrical energy usage data was later sent to a central data server from sensors, or processed by the local data processing unit and then sent to the central data server. This shows an example of an advanced method of data collection that is network related. In the past, the data collection process can take up to 18–24 months, and, due to the high cost of equipment, load researchers have adopted a method of recording and measuring at intervals that can be minutes, hourly, daily, monthly, and yearly (Puckett et al., 2020). With the fast emergence of technology and the introduction of new metering device systems, such as the Advanced Metering Infrastructure (AMI), which gave birth to the smart meters and network-oriented metering systems, it has brought solutions to the conventional methods. Even though these new technologies brought ease, challenges are still being faced, According to Puckett et al. (2020),

> Sample data present several unique challenges, such as storage and how to conduct validation, editing, and estimation (VEE). Added to the challenge of storage is the communication bandwidth needed to transmit interval data from the field. Utilities often find the need to compromise load-interval granularity (5 min, 15 min, hourly, and daily) to ensure that they have the capacity to reliably transmit data while maintaining bandwidth for other operational priorities

There are a lot of contributing variables to as why the quality of data might be compromised and they must be taken into consideration. The introduction of the AMI concept has given researchers the freedom to explore more data collection approaches than before. In a recent study (Venugopal, 2020), the researcher conducted load analysis and energy management on residential loads using a smart meter. The smart meter was designed using voltage and current sensors. In another study, the researchers used an Open Data Kit (ODK) (Heunis et al., 2014), which they claim was a replacement for the paper-based process of collecting data. According to them, the Open Data Kit is an open-source set of tools that help with the organization and collection of data.

Thus, the collection of data is an essential step in load research. A lot of factors such as the accuracy of data collected, data attributes, and the time required to obtain the data have to be considered. However, it is safe to assume that the data is generated and/or collected from the Supervisory Control and Data Acquisition (SCADA) apparatus, since it has the standard set of variables, and most transmission level networks are equipped with real-time SCADA systems. Many load researchers consider population as an important factor during load research, since it gives information on how many customers utility companies are dealing with. Such insights help in the initial stage of load research. Our work does not take population into consideration, as it out of scope, since aggregated load models are used for the majority technical studies in any ESI.

10.2.4 Data Processing

The stage of data processing depends mostly on the preceding stages and how appropriately they were conducted. The data processing stage is a must, because it is a standard for data analysis-type projects and related work. Data processing includes cleaning/cleansing data. Data cleaning is the process of detecting and correcting corrupt or inaccurate records from a record set. Often, we seek perfection in a world rigged that there is no ounce of perfection, the quality of data collected will never be perfect, and mostly there will be some missing and corrupted. If this data is fed to an analysis model without being processed, it is going to affect the accuracy of the results obtained. Data processing is very important and crucial to load research. According to Yuan et al. (2020),

> Cleansing is necessary for data pre-processing, which deals with the noise and missing/bad data from raw measurements.

The researchers went on to use the term bad data, which in their case refers to the information that can be misleading. This data is then removed from the data set before feeding it into a model for analysis and presentation. There are numerous methods to remove bad data from a collected data set. Yuan et al. (2020) outline a number of them; the study mentions that filters can be used to remove noise from the data set. Just like any other stage of load research, the data processing stage comes with its challenges and difficulties too. The nature of residential energy use is mostly irregular and random, and this brings a challenge to cleanse the data even when it comes to automation processes where algorithms play an important role in the detection of bad data. Most approaches to bad data detection are only suitable for commercial and industrial end-users (Yuan et al., 2020). Apart from data cleaning/cleansing, data labeling is also an important step in data processing says (Yuan et al., 2020). The data processing stage in load research must be carefully done to meet the wide-ranging requirements of the users. The sample design/population data needs to be cleansed, and the researcher must ensure that are no corrupted records within the data set. A data set with no bad data ensures a high level of accuracy of results, which means good and useful insights for the business and society at large.

10.2.5 Data Modeling, Analysis and Results

The end goal of data analysis is to produce useful information through a series of computations, verifications, comparisons, etc., and using appropriate computing, graphical, and interactive environments. Though researchers use various tools to achieve their goals, load research in ESI will have its own specific goals and requirements. The useful information obtained from data analysis is used in writing new reports on a new concept for society or the interest of the business. The graphical environment usually involves data tables, graphs, and charts of all sorts (bar graphs, pie charts, and line graphs) for the graphical representation of the data. This subsection describes load data analysis and how authors have approached it earlier.

Yang et al. (2017) used Apache Spark for data analysis, starting with importing map data using GIS Technology. The map has shown information about load statistics at each area where data was collected from. Furthermore, the data was then used to forecast load demand on typical dates using line graphs. This proves the importance of load research. Morch et al. (2013) used a top-down method to analyze the total hourly demand of consumers. In other cases, where data can be collected over a year or analyzed on a daily, weekly, monthly, and yearly basis, it may be usually the case that data can also be considered for different seasons. One can analyze data and observe, as the trends change monthly or as the seasons change from wet to dry seasons. This also involves the trends by day types such as holidays, weekends, and weekdays.

Puckett et al. (2020) have organized a survey wherein the respondents were asked to rank the importance that load research plays in servicing several utility business functions. The following were the answers: load forecasting, special studies, demand–response planning and evaluation, marketing studies, transmission, and distribution planning, distributed energy resource planning, renewables integration, smart grid initiatives, etc. For all these studies, load data analysis forms the basis, and existing literature clearly points to the prominent role played by load research. The importance of load research is usually noticed when the data life cycle is about to come to an end. Usually, it is in the final stages that data is analyzed and interpreted to generate information. The potential application of load research can be grouped into four main aspects: energy usage feedback, demand response (dr), load forecasting, and home automation (Yuan et al., 2020). For these insights to be produced, there are steps to follow when doing data analysis. The first step is for the load researcher to know that the data is in the correct format and arrangement. Tabular formats and arrangements are a common way of storing data, because the structure creates ease for reading and interpretation for humans and other tools (Software). Wang et al. (2017) and Madeira and Christensen (2016) introduced the hierarchical clustering method, then choose typical park users to get the daily load curve, and use this method to do a cluster with a typical daily load curve. Since the focus of this chapter is about data and information analysis, it is important to understand how earlier authors have approached and specifically how the data was presented. Wang et al. (2017) have presented the data of three different commercial consumers, such as a shopping mall, an office building, and then a hotel. Data is represented in a tabular format with type of load class (electrical load, cooling load, etc.) and energy consumed for every hour. In simple words, hourly data related to electrical and non-electrical loads is captured and presented in a tabular format. Qi et al. (2015) presented statistical values of active and reactive powers (in MW and MVAR) that were measured in a substation. They also used tabular formats to present the data. From these two works, detailed information about the load in terms of the type, time stamp, quantification, and units, etc., are of significant interest (Qi et al., 2015). This shows the importance of modeling the load based on the type, so that different tariff structures can be developed for processing and analyzing the raw data. Some of the tasks that need processed information are: load factor calculation, energy maximum demand calculation, load forecasting, electrical energy efficiency, visualization of load curves and load duration curves, energy demand, and supply ratios, etc. Blume et al. (2019) presented the importance of load factor and other parameters in relation to various studies. The average load and maximum demand can be obtained from the data in tabular formats. They also can be used to create line graphs representing the load curves and load duration curves. Line graphs and the trends can later be used for forecasting and any other insights that might be useful. Most researchers produced graphical representations of the usage of electrical energy against time to understand the patterns of consumer behaviors. Waveforms were created (Venugopal, 2020) to show the electricity usage of electric appliances against time. The study clearly shows the graphs illustrating the voltage, and current being used and drawn by the different electric appliances. However, waveforms are more suited for real-time information to capture events, such as the network switching and relay operations (Mks, 2005) and thus not entirely suitable load research studies. Wang et al. (2017) produced load curves of different types of loads to represent energy consumption in a shopping mall, office building, and a hotel. The purpose was to identify the variations in the electricity usage of different loads, mostly using tools such as MATLAB, MS-Excel, Power-BI, and Apache Spark. MS-Excel is used by a majority due to its simplicity and popularity. At the same time, a standard data framework for load data and/or load research is not available. Stephan et al. (2017) stated that "While the literature gives insights into demand response programs, none of them are based on real data and, to sum up, the conclusions drawn are just estimates." Then, Dao Viet et al. (2012) expressed the view that visualization aspect is not yet well utilized in smart grids, and then illustrated various visualization methodologies and how they can be applied to smart grids. However, their contribution is focused on drawing line diagrams of power networks and two- and three-dimensional plots, and did not focus on data and information. This points to the need of creating a framework with a data repository and visualizations to satisfy the needs of ESI.

10.2.6   Energy Policies

In addition to the aforementioned, precise load data is required for other important energy policy-related issues including capacity scheduling and demand side management (DSM).Interestingly, load data is obtained from two different ways: direct measurements and forecasting studies. Load forecast studies provide forecasted (and/or estimated) load data. Forecasted load data is typically used for additional capacity planning. On the other hand, the actual load data can be directly measured using the SCADA system. Load data is very critical when it comes to capacity planning and determining the type of energy resource, its size. Load forecast studies depend mainly on historical data, which is typically collected from SCADA or DSM studies from the past (Musti et al., 2020). Normally environment friendly solar power energy is preferred due to its lower levelized costs. However, excess solar energy leads to duck curve phenomenon where in the additional energy from the solar plant cannot be utilized (Pitra and Musti, 2021), as solar plants are peak plants and do not follow the load. On the other hand, demand profile (or the load curve) influences the type of energy (Musti, 2020). Urban feeders with energy peaks during the noon and with another peak during late hours may warrant DSM) to minimize the supply–demand gap (Musti et al., 2020). Generally, DSM policies influence consumers to install solar water heaters (Musti and Kapali, 2021; Blume et al., 2019). Though capacity planning and DSM coexist in the same energy market, surprisingly they act opposite to each other (Elisa and Vittorio, 2019). Capacity planning results in the adding an additional energy plant, where as DSM is a policy intervention to influence consumers to reduce the consumption or change their energy consumption patterns. Addition of energy plants in microgrids or even independent/isolated smart grids needs to be done strategically so that neither the investor (typically the independent power producer (IPP)) nor the utility are at financial risk. Network topology with protective relaying status is also the key so that extent of operation can be determined (Mks, 2005). However, such information is not entirely related to the load data. Ideally, IPPs set up the plants close to the main power grid to avoid transmission and distribution losses. For that scientific studies need the help of GIS-based power system data that provides information about the network topology with location details (Sastry and Sahadeo, 2015).

DSM is adopted almost in every country for various reasons, but mostly to apply charges on equitable basis. Load data with intrinsic details is important for policy makers to determine the charges. For this, load needs to be represented in the form of several parameters and characteristics. Parameters mostly include demand factor, load factor, diversity factor, peak load, and average load, etc. On the other hand, variation of the load itself is represented by two important characteristics: load curve and the load duration curve. Another aspect in determining the electricity tariff structure is that the information about commercial, industrial, domestic, and municipal loads with the parameters and characteristics. It is well understood that time of use (ToU) tariffs are applied on industrial and commercial loads, and telescopic tariffs based on energy slabs are applied to domestic loads. This requires load information for every 30 minutes so that determination of tariff structure can be done properly. Since seasons play their own natural role in energy usage, different energy prices are applied over different seasons. This requires load data to be collected for every 15- or 30-minute interval, throughout the day, throughout the year. However, such a quantity of data can be huge, if not leading to big data. The data over a specific period, let us say 5 years, will have all the qualities and attributes of normal load variations and features.

From the above, it is clear that load data, parameters, and characteristics are of significant interest to utilities and policy makers. Presently, there are no studies that provide historical data, parameters, and characteristics, along with visualizations. Several authors have discussed various issues connected to load data and/or load research; however, criteria for visualizations have not been identified very well. Even when the visualizations are discussed, historical data is not provided either. It should be noted that historical data is important for almost all studies such as the load forecasting, DSM, tariff structuring, and capacity planning. Policy makers and planning engineers need to simulate several cases on load data, so that in-depth comparative analysis can be done.

From the above discussion and the literature, a few aspects are evident that load research:

- involves big data and thus requires application of the data sciences;
- is required for several studies in ESI;
- provides insights into types of loads, variations over the time, etc.;
- requires both historical data and real-time data; and
- can be done using the popular platforms such as MATLAB, EXCEL, etc.

Keeping the above challenges in view, the following specific objectives are identified:

- Design and development of a data repository for electrical power system load;
- Incorporation of features to support major load parameters, characteristics, and computations;
- Requirement identification for load data visualization;
- Develop a Microsoft Excel tool that can be used for Load Analysis/Research.

At the outset, the tool itself can be downloaded free of cost from the standard Mendeley data repository, at the URL: https://data.mendeley.com/datasets/k5wm-3sw5k5/ (Musti, 2022).

10.3   DESIGN AND DEVELOPMENT OF THE MS-EXCEL TOOL

10.3.1   ASSUMPTIONS

At the outset, a few assumptions have been made. Initial data points are assumed for simplicity, and subsequent values are determined with standard step sizes and random components. A time frame of 5 years and four types of load categories—domestic/residential, commercial, industrial, and municipal are considered. The Daily load data is collected in hourly intervals, and the day is split into four parts, which are: Early Hours, Morning, Afternoon, and Evening, and the day type being a weekend or a weekday. Namibian ESI is considered for this study, since incorporation of locations of load centers and various geographical regions is required for load research.

10.3.2   KEY VARIABLES

Load research involves large data that one needs to be dealing with. This data needs to be classified and structured in a manner that is understood. The load data variables being used are shown in Table 10.1.

The data variables shown in Table 10.1 are used to generate the data. This can be considered as the value of the load at the consumer front or at an aggregated/metered point on the feeder. This involves the specific date on which the recorded information took place, and what day of the week it was. It generally gives a classification—total load of a certain type of consumer in a given city, which is the aggregated information. The Namibian cities—Windhoek, Oshakati, Tsumeb, Swakopmund, Gobabis, and Otjiwarongo—from six different regions are used. The type of consumers that are included in the data that is collected is domestic, commercial, and municipal loads for each city. This means there

TABLE 10.1
Load Data Variables

Load Data Variables	Daily Load Data Variables
Date	Date
Number of the day	Time (specific hour)
Day of the week	Time of the day
Day type (weekend/weekday)	Region
Country	City
Region	Consumer type
City	Load (MW)
Postal code	
Consumer type	
Energy consumption (MWh)	
Reactive power consumption	

would be 24 entries per day. The period for which the collected data is going to cover is from the 1st of April, 2017 to the 29th of September, 2022—a timeframe over 5 years. The design framework can accommodate the real data, if available, since the modeling is done based on standard set of variables from the SCADA. This tool holds the raw data and also aggregates into information in relation to a city or region with the country. The Daily load data is a simple data table that serves a purpose of illustrating load data and how energy is being consumed by customers daily. Further, it will show load demands in hourly intervals for 7 days (23 September 2022–29 September 2022) for all consumer types, and gives results on the total daily energy consumption, maximum demand, average load, and load factor. Since the two data sources are recognized as load data sources, yet they are different; there is a need for clarification.

As seen, the two load data sources as explained above are load data, which involves all the data variables on the right side of Table 10.1, and the Daily load data, which involves all the data variables on the left side of Table 10.1. The Daily Load Data is an impression of how the data in the load data can be obtained. Since the load data only shows the total energy consumption in MWh, this was done to prevent a lot of data entries. It is important to differentiate between measured data and state of the device, as both are different. Protective relays keep operating in real time for various reasons, and this results dynamic changes in the status of the device (Mks, 2005). Such device information is not related to the load data itself.

10.3.3 GENERATION DATA VARIABLES

Though energy generation does not form a part of load research, data is required to test the efficacy of the load research against mismatches. Data from a solar farm and wind farm is included to represent the intermittency effects. Data variables for generation facilities are shown in Table 10.2. Specifications are shown in Table 10.3, and cities and regions are shown in Table 10.3.

Algorithms have been implemented in MS-Excel, using the built-in Visual Basic for Applications (VBA) platform, and thus random energy consumption patterns

TABLE 10.2

Generation Data Variables

Solar Farm Generation Data Variables	Wind Farm Generation Data Variables
Date	Date
Number of the day	Number of the day
Day of the week	Day of the week
Day type (weekend/weekday)	Day type (weekend/weekday)
Generation (MWh)	Generation (MWh)
Generation (MVARh)	Reactive power generation

TABLE 10.3

Generation Power Plant Specifications

Generation Center	
Power Plant	Installed Capacity
Solar farm	5 MW
Wind farm	10 MW
Total installed capacity	15 MW

were generated; computations for all six towns and their respective consumers were carried out. Each town is divided into four consumer types, which are

- Domestic/Residential Consumer
- Commercial Consumer
- Industrial Consumer
- Municipal Consumer

Consumers are grouped in that manner based on their energy usage. Tables 10.4 and 10.5 illustrate the range of energy consumption for every consumer type. This implies that users of the tool can change the ranges to produce different data sets, if required, thus showing that the tool is customizable, which is an important feature.

The design at hand was created in such a way that it is simple and easy to understand to prove the concept being discussed at hand. The design follows the basic structure of a typical ESI Power Plants and Load Centers. Since the data is prepared for over 5 years, it will include a lot of rows up to tens of thousands, and it will be easier if it was generated easily in excel with a press of a button rather than inputting the data manually. This naturally eliminates human errors and yet provides the transparency, as users can always check the data if required.

10.3.4 DESCRIPTION OF THE TOOL

The objectives of this study were clearly outlined in the earlier sections of this chapter, and they are presented in this section in a form of results. The MS-Excel tool

TABLE 10.4
Load Center Details

Regions	City/Town
Khomas region	Windhoek
Oshana region	Oshakati
Otjozondjupa region	Otjiwarongo
Erongo region	Swakopmund
Oshikoto region	Tsumeb
Omaheke region	Gobabis

TABLE 10.5
Consumer Type Energy Consumption Range

Consumer Energy Consumption	
Consumer Type	Energy Consumption Range (MWh)
Domestic/residential	20–30
Commercial	35–45
Industrial	35–50
Municipal	5–8

(Musti, 2022) was built to serve as a data analysis tool for Load research. The tool consists of four major data source tables which are

- Load data Table
- Solar Farm Generation Data Table
- Wind Farm Generation Data Table
- Daily load data Table

A brief description of various tables is provided here in this section for deeper understanding.

- **Load data table:** It consists of the Energy Consumption in Megawatts-Hour (MWh) information, and the Reactive Power Consumption in Megavolt-ampere-reactive-hour (MVarh) of all the Consumer Types for all six regions and cities for each day for over 5 years.
- **Solar farm generation data table:** It consists of the Energy Generation Information in Megawatts-Hour for each day.
- **Wind farm generation data table:** It consists of the generated energies in MW-hour and in MVAR-hour for each day.
- **Daily load data table:** It consists of the load information of all the consumer types for each region and city, as it serves as a prototype in demonstrating the hourly load data. This data set is also used in the computations of average load and the load factor.

The four data sources mentioned earlier have been used to create data models through relationships. Relationships were created through the load data Table, Solar Farm, and Wind Farm Generation Data Table. The relationship was made through two common columns holding similar data for all the three tables, which are;

- Date Column
- Day-Type Column

These relationships resulted in data normalization, and, thus, additional features such as connections to different data models and custom information filtering, etc. can be realized.

10.3.5 VISUALIZATIONS

Simple and user-friendly visualizations are developed to provide insights into the information generated by the tool. The MS-Excel tool was modeled more to give final results in a form of a dashboard. The dashboard has the function of compiling data in one go and displaying them all at once. In this case, two dashboards were designed:

1. Daily Load Visualization Dashboard.
2. Energy Dashboard.

Daily load visualization dashboard holds key graphical elements with useful insights obtained from the daily load data table. On the other hand, the Energy Dashboard holds the key graphical elements with useful insights obtained from the other load and generation tables.

The dashboards are the last step in the MS-Excel tool modeling and that means all the summarized (and detailed) results are available through computations. Dashboards have been used to present the visualizations in line with the contemporary practices. Various built-in features of MS-Excel that have been used to model our tool include pivot tables, macros (VBA), data models, and relationships. Then, from the above components, visualizations are produced using the standard data presentation models (or composite dashboards)—Slicers, Column Graphs, Bar Graphs, Line graphs, Pie Charts, etc.

10.4 RESULTS AND ANALYSIS

With the data sets presented in the MS-Excel tool, the following results were obtained for various tables. Since it is a software product that aggregates raw data through various techniques, the output is more of data visualizations and the overall trends.

10.4.1 MAIN PAGE AND LOOK-AND-FEEL

Figure 10.1 shows the main page that provides the composite dashboard with visualizations showing various aspects.

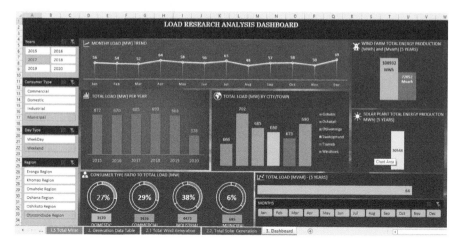

FIGURE 10.1   Load research dashboard first look and feel.

10.4.2   DAILY LOAD DATA TABLE

The daily load data table was structured in hourly intervals for a whole day. The day was then divided into parts illustrated in Table 10.6.

Calculations made from the following data set are as follows:

1. **Daily load consumption:**

$$\text{Daily Energy Consumption (MWh)} = \Sigma \, \text{Load (MW)} \times \text{Time (h)}$$

Load measured in Megawatts (MW) is the Total Load demand at a given point time in a day. Time measured in hours is a given period of a day on which the Load (MW) should be evaluated in. Since the Daily load data Table has hourly data, the energy in one hour will be equal to the numerical value of the load itself, since it will be multiplied by unity.

2. **The Maximum and the minimum demand, and their occurrence points:** The maximum demand is the greatest demand of load required by a customer during a specific length of time, while the minimum demand is the least demand of load required by a customer during a specific length of time. Occurrence points specify at which hour the maximum and/or the minimum demand occur.

3. **Average load:**

$$\text{Average Load (MW)} = \frac{\text{Daily Load Consumption (MWh)}}{\text{Time (h)}}$$

Average load is the mean load of the system for a specific period and, in our study, daily averages (over 24 hours) are computed.

TABLE 10.6
Time of the Day

Time Range	Time of the Day
00:00–06:00	Early hours
06:00–12:00	Morning
12:00–18:00	Afternoon
18:00–00:00	Evening

4. **Load factor:**

$$\text{Load Factor} = \frac{\text{Average Load (MW)}}{\text{Maximum Demand (MW)}}$$

Load factor is the ratio of the average power or actual peak power to the maximum demand of consumers.

Figure 10.2 illustrates the dashboard that shows an overview of all metrics and results obtained from the Daily load data Table. The dashboard itself has its functionality, such as being responsive to filters in the form of slicers to filter through all data types.

10.4.3   LOAD DATA, SOLAR FARM, AND WIND FARM GENERATION DATA TABLES

Key parameters are computed based on the data sets using appropriate formulae as illustrated below.

10.4.3.1   Total Energy Consumption

$$\text{Total Energy Consumption (MWh)} = \Sigma \, \text{Daily Energy Consumption (MWh)}$$

Total energy consumption is the total energy consumed by end-users in a certain period, and this can be calculated for a day, a month, or a quarter of a year.

1. **Reactive energy:**

$$\text{Total Reactive Energy (Mvarh)} = \Sigma \, \text{Daily Reactive Energy (Mvar)}$$

Total reactive energy simply is the sum of daily readings.
2. **Maximum and minimum energy consumption, and their occurrence points:** The maximum energy consumption is the highest consumption of energy by end-users on the system during a specific period, while the minimum demand is the least consumption during the same specific period. Occurrence points for these values are also shown.
3. **Total energy generation:** Total energy generation is the aggregated amount of generations from both the solar and wind farms in a specific period.

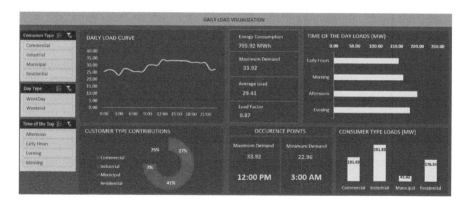

FIGURE 10.2 Daily load visualizations.

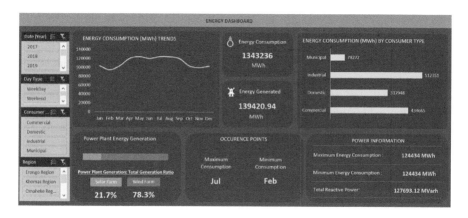

FIGURE 10.3 Energy dashboard.

Figure 10.3 illustrates the insights from the load data Table and two generation data tables.

It can be seen from Figures 10.2 and 10.3 that the information illustrated agrees greatly with the literature and the objectives achieved by past researchers. In Figure 10.2, The Daily Load visualization dashboard shows the load curve with a line graph to demonstrate the trends in hourly intervals. In addition, the dashboard visualizes the calculations obtained from the data sets. Load research illustrates a global relationship between three different data sources and represents visuals of these data in a manner that can be understood with ease.

10.5 RECOMMENDATIONS FOR FURTHER WORK

Load research is a promising strand within the electrical engineering field. With the ever-growing population, technologies are constantly evolving at a faster rate than ever in response to the ever-increasing societal demands. From the literature review and from the tool presented in this chapter, it can be seen that the load research helps the utilities in managing the modern smart grids where data can be collected. Therefore, tools such as this and versatile energy dashboards are of much importance for modern smart cities that utilize fourth or fifth industrial revolution aspects. Load research studies offer several opportunities for further research with deep mathematical, statistical, and computing concepts and approaches to gain exceptional insights into the load consumption patterns. Such insights can be used in tandem with home automation systems, and smart grid systems, etc., for efficient operation of the system. Since load research is used for various studies, algorithms need to be developed based on the data and information provided by the tool. Thus, this work also provides excellent opportunities to further improve the tool, to suit the varying requirements of ESI stakeholders.

10.6 CONCLUSION

The study focused on carrying out data analysis of electrical loads. Foundation and rationale for this study are provided through in-depth literature review, as relevant to big data-based data processing and information generation. Further, data processing aspects related to ESI are considered from the literature to generate information out of computations and visualization. Based on the identified requirements and objectives, a versatile dashboard is generated using the standard MS-Excel platform. Key features such as the data generation, processing, and information generation, etc. have been demonstrated. The tool provides insights that will help grid operators and utility companies predict future demands and energy consumption.

REFERENCES

Bhattarai, B., Paudyal, S., Luo, Y., Mohanpurkar, M., Cheung, K., Tonkoski, R., Hovsapian, R., Myers, K., Zhang, R., Zhao, P., Manic, M., Zhang, S., & Zhang, X. (2019). Big data analytics in smart grids: State-of-the-art, challenges, opportunities, and future directions. *IET Smart Grid*, 2, 141–154.

Blume, S., Herrmann, C., Thiede, S., Flick, D., & Dehning, P. (2019). Load profile analysis for reducing energy demands of production systems in non-production times. *Applied Energy*, 237, 117–130.

Dao Viet, N., Ong Hang, S., Do Nguyet, Q., Chee Yung, X., & Lai Lee, C. (2012), Visualization techniques in smart grid. *Smartgrid and Renewable Energy*, 3, 175–185.

Elisa, G., & Vittorio, V. (2019), Demand response and other demand side management techniques for district heating: A review. *Energy*, 219.

Garg, A., Maheshwari, J., & Upadhyay, J. (2010). *Load Research for Residential and Commercial Establishments in Gujarat*. Available online, https://www.beeindia.gov.in/sites/default/files/ctools/Load research Report for Gujarat-1024.pdf

Godin, C., & Puckett, C. (2014). Load research in the smart grid era: Analytics for harvesting customer insights. *IEEE Power and Energy Society General Meeting*, 2014, 1–19.

Heunis, S., Dekenah, M., & Setlhogo, L. (2014). Domestic load research data collection using Open Data Kit. *2014 International Conference on the Domestic Use of Energy (DUE)*. Proceedings of the 22nd Conference on the Domestic Use of Energy, DUE.

Kaur, D., Bath, S. K., & Sidhu, D. S. (2014). Short circuit fault analysis of electrical power system. *MATLAB*. 9(2), 89–100.

Madeira, C., & Christensen, T. H. (2016), Cluster analysis of residential heat load profiles and the role of technical and household characteristics. *Energy and Buildings*, 125, 171–180.

Mks, S. (2005), Simplified algorithm to determine break point realys & relay coordination based on network topology [for relays read relays]. *2005 IEEE International Symposium on Circuits and Systems (ISCAS)*, Proceedings - IEEE International Symposium on Circuits and Systems, pp. 772–775.

Morch, A. Z., Feilberg, N., Sæle, H., & Lindberg, K. B. (2013). Method for development and segmentation of load profiles for different final customers and appliances. *ECEEE Summer Study Proceedings*, pp. 1927–1933.

Musti, K. S. S. (2020). Quantification of demand response in smart grids. *IEEE International Conference INDISCON*, 2020 IEEE India Council International Subsections Conference (INDISCON), Visakhapatnam, pp. 278–282. doi: 10.1109/INDISCON50162.2020.00063

Musti, K. S. S. (2022). Power system load research tool with energy dashboard. *Mendeley Data*, Available online https://data.mendeley.com/datasets/k5wm3sw5k5/ (accessed November 2022).

Musti, K. S. S., Iileka, H., Shidhika, F. (2020). Industry 4.0-based enterprise information system for demand-side management and energy efficiency. In N. Prakash & D. Prakash (Eds.), *Novel Approaches to Information Systems Design* (pp. 137–163). IGI Global. https://doi.org/10.4018/978-1-7998-2975-1.ch007

Musti, K. S. S., & Kapali, D. (2021). Digital transformation of SMEs in the energy sector to survive in a post-COVID-19 era. In N. Baporikar (Ed.), *Handbook of Research on Strategies and Interventions to Mitigate COVID-19 Impact on SMEs* (pp. 186–207). IGI Global.

Pitra, G. M., & Musti, K. S. S. (2021). Duck curve with renewable energies and storage technologies. *13th International Conference on Computational Intelligence and Communication Networks (CICN)*, Lima, pp. 66–71. doi: 10.1109/CICN51697.2021.9574671

Puckett, C., Williamson, C., Godin, C., Gifford, W., Farland, J., Laing, T., & Hong, T. (2020). Utility load research: The future of load research is now. *IEEE Power and Energy Magazine*, 18(3), 61–70.

Qi, Y., Jun, Y., Bing, Z., Liping, L., & Yong, T. (2015). Deepen research on electric load modelling. *2015 5th International Conference on Electric Utility Deregulation and Restructuring and Power Technologies (DRPT)*, Changsha, pp. 334–339. doi: 10.1109/DRPT.2015.7432253

Sastry, M. K. S., & Sahadeo, A. (2015). Distributed cloud computing based GIS solution for electrical power utility asset management. *2015 International Conference on Computational Intelligence and Communication Networks (CICN)*, Jabalpur, pp. 832–838. doi: 10.1109/CICN.2015.169

Stefan, M., Lopez, J. G., Andreasen, M. H., & Olsen, R. L. (2017), Visualization techniques for electrical grid smart metering data: A survey. *IEEE Third International Conference on Big Data Computing Service and Applications (BigDataService)*, San Francisco, CA, pp. 165–171.

Syed, D., Zainab, A., Ghrayeb, S. S. Refaat, S. S. Abu-Rub, H., & Bouhali, O. (2021). Smart grid big data analytics: Survey of technologies, techniques, and applications. *IEEE Access*, 9, 59564–59585.

Venugopal, C., Govender, T., & Thangavel, B. (2020). Load analysis and energy management for residential system using smart meter. *2020 2nd International Conference on Electrical, Control and Instrumentation Engineering (ICECIE)*, Kuala Lumpur, pp. 1–8. doi: 10.1109/ICECIE50279.2020.9309554

Wang, X.-J., Chen, L., & Tao, W. -Q. (2017). Research on load classification based on user's typical daily load curve. *2017 IEEE Conference on Energy Internet and Energy System Integration (EI2)*, Beijing, pp. 1–4. doi: 10.1109/EI2.2017.8245469

Yang, L., Wei, W., & Noradin, G. (2017). Electricity load forecasting by an improved forecast engine for building level consumers. *Energy*, 139, 150.

Yuan, X., Han, P., Duan, Y., Alden, R. E., Rallabandi, V., & Ionel, D. M. (2020). Residential electrical load monitoring and modeling: State of the art and future trends for smart homes and grids. *Electric Power Components and Systems*, 48(11), 1125–1143.

Zhu, J., Shen, Y., Song, Z., Zhou, D., Zhang, Z. (2019). Data-driven building load profiling and energy management. *Sustainable Cities and Society*, 49, 101587.

11 Data Analytics *Vis-à-Vis* Agricultural Development
International Scenario and Indian Potentialities—A Techno and Managerial Context

P. K. Paul

Department of CIS, Information Scientist (Offg.), Raiganj University, Raiganj, India

CONTENTS

11.1   INTRODUCTION

'Global village' has become possible with the support from the information technology and similar systems. The world is changing by the rapid applications of the information technology. In developing social sector, another subject is considered as important, i.e. Information Science, which is also closed to Information Technology [1–3]. Information Science is also called as Informatics and is emerging worldwide. But Information Science is wider than IT and dedicated in the information activities, *viz.* information solutions, society-centric services, etc. There have been many domain-centric Information Sciences/Informatics gained and developed in the recent

DOI: 10.1201/9781003330875-11

past, *viz.* Geo-Informatics/Geo Information Science, Health Informatics/Information Science, Bio-Informatics, etc. and Agricultural Informatics has also emerged and gained popularity like such subjects. This is responsible in building and developing modern agricultural systems and dedicated in the Collection, Selection, Organisation, Processing, Management and Dissemination. Further in related works of the agriculture and horticulture, Agricultural Informatics is being used. Here, it takes the help of various components of Information Technologies and Computing, in addition to Management Principles and Social Science. Engineering is worthy in the development of various products and services, and, therefore, Engineering degrees is also available with the subjects of Agricultural Informatics; here Data Science and Analytics can be used as a specialisations in allied programs. However, huge potentialities are in Agricultural Data Analytics, and Agricultural Data Science exists as a specialisation in various information-/computing-related degrees and also in agricultural sciences.

11.2   OBJECTIVE

This work entitled 'Data Analytics & Science Vis-à-Vis Agricultural Development: International Scenario & Indian Potentialities—*A Techno & Managerial Context*' is theoretical and conceptual, and focused with following aims and objectives:

- To get an idea on Agricultural Informatics with reference to the evolution and origin of stakeholders.
- To learn about the basic and emerging features of Agricultural Information Science, especially Agricultural Informatics and allied subjects.
- To find out the increasing role of smart and digital agricultural systems using technologies with reference to the Data Science and Analytics.
- To gather knowledge regarding degrees in the field of Agricultural Informatics, including various nomenclature.
- To get a concise preview of education, training and educational programs on Agricultural Informatics with reference to the specialisation of Data Science and Analytics.
- To propose the possible programs on Agricultural Informatics, with special reference to computing and agriculture with Data Science.

11.3   METHODS

The current work is a policy based with the title 'Data Analytics & Science Vis-à-Vis Agricultural Development: International Scenario & Indian Potentialities—*A Techno & Managerial Context*' and, therefore, the work is interdisciplinary and various secondary works in the areas of Informatics and IT, Agriculture, Development Studies and Education, etc. have been consulted to prepare the work. Since the work is policy based and also is a kind of trend report highlighting importance of Data Science, various government reports on education, agricultural development, engineering education, etc. are considered as important and vital. Further, the companies of Agricultural Informatics also studied with their current portfolio to get a current scenario of the field. Furthermore, various search strategies are also being used to get a contemporary knowledge.

11.4 AGRICULTURAL INFORMATICS AND DATA SCIENCES: THE EVOLUTIONS

Informatics is an information and technology-centric subject, and this is considered as an alternative subject in many countries. Informatics is a kind of interdisciplinary subject dedicated in scientific, proper and technological information solution, and it is useful in various areas and zones, *viz.* society, business, education and training, commerce, agriculture, healthcare, transportation and tourism, government and so on [4–6]. There are various domain-specific nomenclatures that have been developed *in the initial age and periods* of Informatics, *viz.*

- Bio-Informatics
- Health Informatics
- Geo-Informatics.

However, gradually other areas of Informatics have become popular as a branch of study, field and programs, *viz.*

- Quantum Informatics
- Chem-Informatics
- Social Informatics
- Community Informatics
- Rural Informatics
- Urban Informatics
- Irrigation and Water Informatics
- Design Informatics
- Diversity and Eco-Informatics
- Environmental Informatics, etc. [7–9].

However, among these subjects some are considered as a practicing field, and some are considered as an independent subject, and even degrees are also been offered [10–12]. Agricultural Informatics is being offered with the Bachelor of Science, Master of Science, Bachelor of Technology and Master of Technology degrees. Some of the possible and emerging nomenclatures in this regard include agricultural information systems, Agricultural Information Technology, Smart & Digital Agriculture, etc. The basic Information Technology components are also being used, which is depicted in Figure 11.1.

Agricultural Informatics is a field study and practice with interdisciplinary facets associated with various subjects, which helps in fulfilment of the agenda and objective of the Agricultural Informatics:

- Management
- Commerce and Economics
- Social Science
- Policy Studies and Management

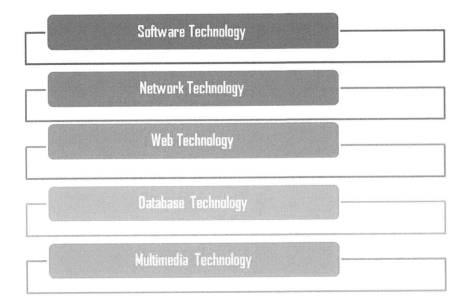

FIGURE 11.1 Basics IT components that are prerequisite for agricultural systems.

- Biological and Mathematical Sciences
- Environmental Science and Management, etc. [13–15].

And due to interdisciplinary nature, this trend is growing rapidly worldwide.

11.5 DIGITAL AGRICULTURE POWERED BY AGRICULTURAL INFORMATICS

Due to its multidisciplinary nature, it is not only regarded as an investigation but also as a practice, hence it has the following characteristics:

- It is merged with the Agricultural Sciences and Information Sciences, surrounded by various tools, techniques as well as technologies that help in information processing. Further, here management science components also played an important role.
- In many allied areas, such as botany, horticulture, environment, veterinary sciences, sustainable development, anthropology, etc., agricultural informatics is also considered as vital and worthy.
- The advanced and smart agricultural system becomes easily developed with the field of Agricultural Informatics. Therefore, this is considered as important and effective in developing digital agriculture [3,16,17].
- The basic and emerging technologies of database, networking, web systems, multimedia systems, etc. are considered important, apart from the software engineering/technologies as well.

- The areas like Computer Science, Computer Engineering, Information Studies, Information Management, etc. are considered as vital in respect of allied field of Agricultural Informatics [18–20].
- Environmental Informatics, Geo-Informatics and Ecological Informatics are also considered as important in proper utilisation of Agricultural Informatics [21–23].

Agriculture is important for everyone, and this has become a popular field in many developing nations; here different efforts are noted by the government agencies for complete and healthy agricultural development. Therefore, developed nations, including developing, are considered as important and vital in proper development of ICT-enabled agricultural systems too [24–26]. It is important to note that many professionals depend on agricultural systems, but there is a lack of knowledge in advanced cultivation methods. But for healthy and wider benefits of the technology, Agricultural Informatics or ICT can be considered as important and vital, including their uses for the purpose of heating, extreme cold, flood, higher drought, insect and pest infestations, disease identification, weather, etc. This field is also partially required for managing food habits, including nutritional requirements, ecological systems. Using proper strategies, Agricultural Informatics can gift us following:

- Impactful agricultural systems and management.
- Proper and healthy output systems of the agriculture.
- To the enhanced and integrated agro-related systems and products.
- To develop agro systems with proper post-production activities.
- In managing proper and healthy food security.
- fective in agricultural and environmental systems.
- Value-chain systems' designing and development.
- In developing and managing healthy climate systems.
- In proper supply chain management systems, Agricultural Informatics can be an important tool [27–29].

In enhancing *Efficiency*, including in monitoring of cultivation with agro products management, the Agricultural Informatics is very important and required.

Expansion of traditional agricultural systems with proper cleaning and purity of agricultural systems in managing pesticides and fertilisers, Speedy and Quicker Agricultural Systems and *also* Agricultural Informatics. The technologies and emerging systems of Cloud, Internet of Things (IoT), Big Data, robotics, analytics, etc. are considered as important in proper and healthy agricultural systems' development (refer Figure 11.2).

Therefore, *Quantity of Production of Agricultural Systems* powered by proper pre-production management, Livestock Management, Supply Chain Management and Agro Business promotion becomes healthy with Agricultural Informatics' practices. With respect to enhancing quality of the foods, Agricultural Informatics helps in:

- Sustainable Agriculture
- Advanced Agriculture
- Digital Agricultural Systems.

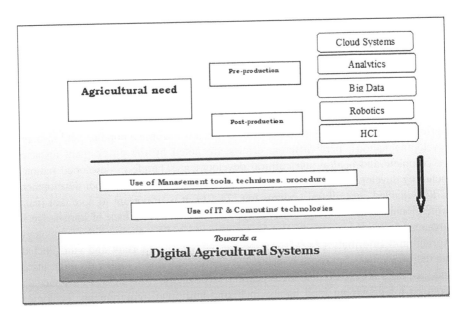

FIGURE 11.2   An overview of sample smarter agricultural systems.

The proper education and training program in this area is the need of hour regarding proper delivery and management of agricultural systems in many ways [16,30,31].

11.6   DATA SCIENCE AND ANALYTICS: OVERVIEW

Data is one of the important aspects and components for the day-to-day activities in our lives. It is required and applicable in different sectors, such as healthcare, government and administration, business and organisation, agriculture, transportation, management, education, research and training, etc. For the proper management of such data, here emerging Big Data is applicable and effective with managing large and complex data. Management is required and powered by different analytical tools to come a conclusion and here Data Analytics (or simply Analytics) is considered as worthy. The applications of the analytics in various areas reveal other analytics areas such as:

- Business Analytics, which is simply the application of analytics in business, industries and organisations [32–34].
- Healthcare and Medical Analytics is the application of Big Data in medical and healthcare systems.
- Marketing/Retail Analytics is a gift of Big Data/Analytics application in marketing as well as retail.
- Learning analytics is simply Big Data applications in education, teaching and learning.

Though it is worthy to note that Big Data applications initially emerged in the 1990s, major applications were noted in different organisations internationally in the recent past. It is also worthy to note that Teradata Corporation had coined the term in 1984, and further 'Teradata' is being used in several structured and unstructured data management [1,23,35].

Data Science is, therefore, a field of study that deals with the Big Data and Data Analytics-related issues and concerns. It is further an interdisciplinary field of study that requires and processes healthy and scientific methods, and algorithms related to the Data. It is dedicated in extracting knowledge and insights of data in structured and unstructured ways. Therefore, Data Science is the combination of Data Mining, Data Warehousing, Data Analytics, Big Data, AI and Machine Learning, etc. It is, therefore, engaged in statistics, mathematical sciences, data analysis and their relationships properly. Big Data is gaining as an important tool for the development, and it is worthy in almost all the sectors and industries. It is worthy to note that data-related businesses touched $1.2 trillion collectively in 2020, and then $333 billion in the year 2015. Big data is useful in information and data management, and here Data Science experts played role in creating software and algorithms. Big data continues to be important in major impact on the world, and therefore, it is the thrust area and importance in many segments [7,31,36].

11.7 DATA ANALYTICS AND SCIENCE IN AGRICULTURAL SECTOR WITH REFERENCE TO INDIA

Data Science is the most promising system and technology in agricultural systems internationally in many developed countries. This is considered as the backbone in Indian and other developed economies. In India, about 70% of the population lives in rural settings, and most of rural Indians depend on agriculture. Furthermore, 40% of the nations' workforce is based on agriculture and similar industries. Instead of developing stage of nation, there are many examples of using technology-based agricultural systems (refer Figure 11.3 for further knowledge).

But still it is worthy to note that Agriculture in India needs proper support and attention to the farmers, agricultural professionals in respect of basic financial support, welfare schemes, disaster management, technological adoption and management [6,11]. There are many other basic issues of implementing proper agricultural systems, such as groundwater levels, rural development, climate change, unpredictable monsoon droughts, floods, migration of farmers for better jobs, and others.

Internationally, many countries have implemented information technologies into agricultural systems, and even in India too. Big Data and Analytics is applicable in Indian context too in the areas of agricultural firms, organisations and sectors. In the recent past, investors and market players play a leading role in uses of Big Data in agricultural sector and systems.

In big agricultural organisations and ventures, such applications are well noted and emerging. There are many big and small startups engaged in technological implementation in agricultural systems, *viz.* SatSure (a small startups) with contemporary Big Data and Analytical solutions in healthcare. It is also noted that emerging technologies of the following play an important role in proper Big Data Analytics into Agricultural Systems, *viz.*

FIGURE 11.3 Technology and data science integrated agricultural systems.

- IoT (Internet of Things)
- Cloud Computing and Virtualisation
- Virtualisation and Fog Computing
- Robotics
- Machine Learning and Deep Learning, etc.

It is well noted that Indian farmers are many ways unable to know about the soil health and crop growth due to non-use of proper systems and technology, and here immensely uses Big Data in this context, and Machine Learning may be considered as important and worthy. Further Indian agricultural sector is very disorganised and traditional; even here, very less utilisations of electronics transactions were noted. The finance is an important obstacle in proper agricultural implementation, and finance insurance is also needed in light of healthy and proper agricultural systems; here Big Data and Analytics is required regarding settlement of higher management and risk assessment and loss of the crops; moreover, it offers proper analysis of current and historical satellite images.

The population of the world is growing, and it is estimated that within this century itself the world population will cross 10 billion, and proper agricultural products are urgent to serve this amount of population and humanity. Here, smart farming, precision faming is considered as important and urgent in healthy and sustainable food, including feed and fibre. Proper systems and techniques should be considered as important and vital in healthy Data Science and Analytics applications in agricultural and environmental solutions, *viz.*

- For the purpose of app-based data generation as well as extraction
- Storage of the agro and allied contents on the cloud
- Satellite observation and monitoring
- Regarding data visualisation in real-time manner and machine learning [21,37].

In addition to the previously described technologies, field-related tasks are also important in properly anticipating production, managing risk, maximising quality and quantity, etc. Therefore, Data Science and Analytics is needed in proper banking and financial institutions solutions, solutions in insurance companies and farming enterprises, proper and healthy seed manufacturing; and so on.

Some of the facilities of Agricultural Informatics supported with the Data Science is helpful in satellite monitoring, embedded sensors systems, prediction analysis for the purpose of wind direction, to know about the need of fertiliser, pest management and infestations, GPS-based tracing systems, automatic water cycling management, and automatic and intelligent business solutions. Therefore, Big Data and Analytics helps to the agriculturist, farmers for the data-based decisions, including proper health analysis of soil, availability of the water, and predictions on rainfall and precipitation. There are potentialities of technologies such as:

- Virtualisation and Cloud Computing
- Machine Learning and Deep Learning
- IoT (Internet of Things) and Fog Computing
- HCI (Human Computer Interaction) and User Experience Systems, etc.

Consequently, in a nutshell, data science and analytics give a healthy output ratio cost, reduce input consumption optimization, higher and enhanced yields, and necessary data/information in a timely way [2,34]. Therefore, in short, Data Science and Analytics is helpful in:

- Smart Farming/Agriculture
- Precision Agriculture

Smart Farming lies in a different kind of science and technology in the areas of agriculture, and in this regard, applications and utilisations of some technologies such as Big Data, Data Analytics, Internet of Things (IoT), virtualisation and cloud computing, Deep Learning &Machine Learning, etc. are helpful in making healthy agricultural systems with better and informed decision on farming practices. Smart living depends on various kinds of technologies and applications of Analytics and Big Data with applications of supply chain, offering predictive insights, regarding redesign business models, real-time decisions. Smart farming is composed with many components are mainly considered as (MIS and Devices & Technologies).

MIS or Management of Information Systems is the organisational systems for information and data with proper techniques, tools, procedure and ways. MIS also helps in getting data from multiple sensors for gathering, storing, analysing and

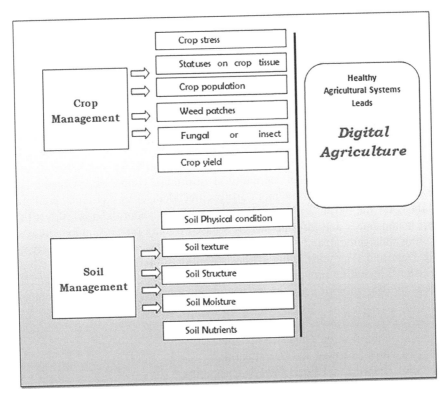

FIGURE 11.4   Data science utilisations in crop and soil management.

retrieving for various activities. MIS is an optimised system and deals the benefits (mentioned in Figure 11.4) in respect of crops and soils.

Further, as far as climate is concerned, Data Science and Analytics is considered as vital and important and required in following:

- Humidity Prediction
- Prediction of Rainfall
- Proper and Healthy Wind speed
- Prediction of the Temperature.

Devices and Technologies are considered as vital in smart farming as well, such as:

- Global positioning systems: It is required to find out healthy and proper accuracy.
- Geographical information systems: It is needed for better monitoring and management.
- Remote sensing: It is helpful to liaison with data transmitters, drones, cameras, etc.

- IoT: It is helpful in getting proper crop status, understanding and managing water conditions and levels, moisture content, crop yield and so on.
- Machine Learning and Deep Learning is also an important technology in Data Analytics, which is required in designing of healthy process and further activities [4,38].

Precision Agriculture is a kind of specific Crop Management System, and it basically depends on proper observation, measurement of the agricultural fields; and here Data Science and Analytics is an important tool. It helps in finding better inbound and outbound requirements in agricultural fields. *Precision Agriculture* is based on optimising revenue of income, and also allows farmers for the optimised and informed decisions based on generated data. Precision agriculture helps in healthy environmental management with zero-down precise locations and improves in:

- Water level and availability
- Topography identification
- Organic matter in respect to soil fertility
- Moisture content including nitrogen level
- Magnesium and its presence
- Potassium and other ingredients in agricultural systems.

In Precision Agricultural Systems, the Global Positioning Systems devices as well as sensors are also even able to measuring chlorophyll levels. Drones and satellite imagery are also helpful for the farmers to also get the treasure chest of information.

11.8 ISSUES AND CHALLENGES OF INDIAN AGRICULTURAL SYSTEMS WITH ANALYTICS AND TECHNOLOGIES: HR AND MANPOWER CONCERNS

India is the biggest country with lots of opportunities and issues. As far as agriculture is concerned, there are many issues and concerns. Totally 14%–15% of the GDP basically comes from the Agriculture sector, as far as India is concerned. Agriculture offers about 40-45% of total employment in India. There are different areas and sectors in India, and the data science and allied technologies are helpful in landscape, grain demand, insights of the crops and soil systems. With the help of technology, agricultural-enabled systems helps in decision making regarding the crop selection, soil management and planning logistics, etc.

It is estimated that world population will rise to 10 billion by 2050, and in this regard, agricultural sector may face approximately 56% gap between food demand and supply. Here, in making of productive agro products, Data Science and Technology can definitely help in making informed, *viz.* situation predication, task recommendation and automation, etc.

It is worthy to note that though there is healthy potentiality in Agricultural Informatics practice including Data Science and Analytics integration, but it has also various issues and concerns, *viz*.

- There is the need to educate farmers and associates on the benefits of Agricultural Informatics with reference to the Data Science and allied technologies, and this is required in mitigation of risk and potential upsides probable with the use of data.
- There is the need to educate farmers and associates on the issues of risk mitigation and probable potential upsides, including the use of data.
- nderstanding and managing fundamental data usage, sophisticated device applications, and electronic device troubleshooting is important for successful agricultural data management.
- Proper internet, basic internet connectivity, and deployment of the technology are always a concern.
- Financial support is also an important issue in developing agricultural systems in effective manner.
- Technological integration with manual system is an important concern in Agricultural Data Science practice.
- Integrating newer technologies with the existing technologies are considered as important and vital concern.

Agricultural Informatics, including Agricultural Data Science, is considered as important and vital concern and interdisciplinary. As an interdisciplinary field, it also incorporated with the subjects of IT, Computing, chemistry, physics, mathematical science, biological sciences, and economics and management. Therefore, it is having the potentiality of jobs from the diverse educated and qualified. Here, Figure 11.5 shows some of the existing academic degree programs on Agricultural Informatics (and allied fields) being offered in India [12,37].

Figure 11.6 illustrates a potential programme in the Indian setting that would follow worldwide trends in higher education by specialising in data science and analytics.

The possible programs here are depicted as Science, Engineering/Technology only; however, such programs also can be offered with the Management, Commerce stream with proper educational policy adaptation. Similarly, Agricultural Informatics

Universities/ Institutes	Programs
Tamil Nadu Agricultural University, Coimbatore, Tamil Nadu, India	BTech Agricultural Information Technology
Centre for Agricultural Informatics and E Governance Research Studies Shobhit University, Meerut, UP, India	MTech Agricultural Informatics
Anand Agricultural University, Gujarat, India	MTech Agricultural Information Technology

FIGURE 11.5   Few agro informatics few institutes from India.

Agricultural Informatics allied possible nomenclature
BSc-Information Science (Agricultural Data Analytics)
MSc-Information Science (Agricultural Data Analytics)
MTech/ME-Information Science (Agricultural Data Analytics)
PhD (Science/ Technology)-
Information Science (Agricultural Data Analytics)

FIGURE 11.6   Possible agricultural informatics information science concentration.

Agricultural Informatics allied possible nomenclature
BSc- Agricultural Data Analytics/ Agricultural Data Science
MSc- Agricultural Data Analytics/ Agricultural Data Science
MTech/ME- Agricultural Data Analytics/ Agricultural Data Science
PhD (Science/ Technology)-
Information Science (Agricultural Data Analytics)

FIGURE 11.7   Possible agricultural informatics information science concentration.

can be started as a full-fledged subject or degree, instead of any specialisation within IT or Information Science, as depicted in Figure 11.7.

There is an urgent need of developing manpower in Data Science, Analytics and Big Data. The role and importance of a data scientist in agricultural sector is important and required in allied areas, *viz.* environment and ecology, plant and allied science, plant biotechnology, animal science and soil science, etc. to make more sense of data. And, therefore,

- **Data capture:** Data Scientist and Data Science professionals are being involved with the IoT-based sensors, biometric sensing, reciprocal data and other ways in capturing data.
- **Data storage:** Building cloud-based platforms and solutions using data science and analytics systems and tools is also viable. In addition, a variety of hybrid hybrid storage options, comprising load balancing, are now definitely feasible.
- **Data transfer:** Data Science professionals are also involved with the cloud-based wireless platforms, information transfer cycles and so on.
- **Data transformation:** Data scientists and other data science professionals work on processes and projects involving normalisation, machine learning algorithms, ontology-based DSS and MIS, and other related tasks that are necessary for planting instructions, yield models, marketing strategies, and other related tasks.
- **Data marketing:** Data scientists and professionals are engaged in the Digital Data Marketing, and this is helpful in proper and healthy Agricultural Data Marketing.

Therefore, Agricultural Data Science and Analytics is the need of hour and can be offered not only as a specialisation/major but also as a full-fledged degree to gear-up the role of Data Science in agricultural field and to enhance job-related issues

Agricultural Informatics allied possible nomenclature
BSc (by Research)- Agricultural Data Analytics/ Agricultural Data Science
MSc(by Research)- Agricultural Data Analytics/ Agricultural Data Science
MTech/ME(by Research)- Agricultural Data Analytics/ Agricultural Data Science

FIGURE 11.8 Agricultural informatics and allied programs in information science concentration.

perfectly. The probable research mode for a Bachelor's or Master's degree in agricultural computing or related subjects is shown in Figure 11.8.

Apart from such proposed and depicted degrees and academic programs, there is also potentiality in developing the following programs to enhance the sector and skill development:

- Certificate
- Advanced Certificate
- Diploma
- Advanced Certificate
- Advanced Diploma
- Post-Graduate Certificate
- Post-Graduate Diploma, etc. [39,40].

11.9   SUGGESTIONS WITH CONCLUDING MARKS

Today Agricultural Informatics is required in different areas, and here Agricultural Data Science and Analytics play a leading role for complete agricultural development systems. As far as agricultural applications of analytics are concerned, it is essential in the activities, *viz.* pre-production and post-production. In many developed countries, lots of initiatives have taken in proper and smarter agricultural development. However, it is worthy to note that not only developed nations but even many countries that belong to the developing and undeveloped 'tags' have started scientific agricultural informatics practice with the latest technologies and components of IT. Agricultural Informatics is offered as Science and Engineering degrees, but for healthy and smart agricultural systems' development, it may be offered with emerging areas like Data Analytics in the engineering colleges and universities. Moreover, here agricultural programs may also be offered with the Agricultural Data Science/Agro Data Analytics as a specialisation. The adoption of such educational strategies can led to the proper agricultural development, leading to a proper knowledge economy.

REFERENCES

[1] Abbasi, A. Z., Islam, N., & Shaikh, Z. A. 2014. A review of wireless sensors and networks' applications in agriculture. *Computer Standards & Interfaces*, *36*:263–270.

[2] Balamurugan, S., Divyabharathi, N., Jayashruthi, K., Bowiya, M., Shermy, R. P., & Shanker, R. 2016. Internet of agriculture: Applying IoT to improve food and farming technology. *International Research Journal of Engineering and Technology (IRJET)*, *3*:713–719.

[3] Paul, P. K., Ghosh, M., & Chaterjee, D. 2014. Information systems & networks (ISN): Emphasizing agricultural information networks with a case study of AGRIS. *Scholars Journal of Agriculture and Veterinary Sciences, 1*:81.

[4] Channe, H., Kothari, S., & Kadam, D. 2015. Multidisciplinary model for smart agriculture using internet-of-things (IoT), sensors, cloud-computing, mobile-computing & big-data analysis. *International Journal of Computer Technology & Applications,* 6:374–382.

[5] Othman, M. F., & Shazali, K. 2012. Wireless sensor network applications: A study in environment monitoring system. *Procedia Engineering, 41*:1204–1210.

[6] Paul, P. K. 2015. Agricultural problems in india requiring solution through agricultural information systems: Problems and prospects in developing countries. *International Journal of Information Science and Computing, 2*:33–40

[7] Ahmad, T., Ahmad, S., & Jamshed, M. 2015, October. A knowledge based Indian agriculture: With cloud ERP arrangement. In *2015 International Conference on Green Computing and Internet of Things (ICGCIoT)* 333–340. IEEE.

[8] Aubert, B. A., Schroeder, A., & Grimaudo, J. 2012. IT as enabler of sustainable farming: An empirical analysis of farmers' adoption decision of precision agriculture technology. *Decision support systems, 54*:510–520.

[9] Paul, P. K., Sinha, R. R., Bhuimalli, A., Baby, P., Saavedra, R., & Aremu, B. 2020. Agricultural informatics with reference to its possibilities and potentialities in management, commerce and allied branches. *World Academic Journal of Management,* 8:35–43.

[10] Gill, S. S., Chana, I., & Buyya, R. 2017. IoT based agriculture as a cloud and big data service: the beginning of digital India. *Journal of Organizational and End User Computing (JOEUC), 29*:1–23.

[11] Kajol, R., & Akshay, K. K. 2018. Automated agricultural field analysis and monitoring system using IOT. *International Journal of Information Engineering and Electronic Business, 11*:17.

[12] Paul, P., Ripu, R. S., Aithal, P. S., Saavedra M, R., & Aremu, P. S. B. 2020. Agro informatics emphasizing its potentiality as a full-fledged degree programs: International context & Indian potentialities. *Asian Journal of Computer Science and Technology,* 9:19–26.

[13] Adetunji, K. E., & Joseph, M. K. 2018, August. Development of a cloud-based monitoring system using duino: Applications in agriculture. In *2018 International Conference on Advances in Big Data, Computing and Data Communication Systems (icABCD)* 4849–4854. IEEE.

[14] Guardo, E., Di Stefano, A., La Corte, A., Sapienza, M., & Scatà, M. 2018. A fog computing-based IoT framework for precision agriculture. *Journal of Internet Technology, 19*:1401–1411.

[15] Paul, P.K., Saavedra M, R., Aithal, P. S., Ripu Ranjan Sinha, R. R. S., & Aremu, P. S. B. 2020. Agro informatics vis-à-vis internet of things (IoT) integration & potentialities: An analysis. *Agro Economist: An International Journal, 7,*13–20.

[16] Gómez-Chabla, R., Real-Avilés, K., Morán, C., Grijalva, P., & Recalde, T. 2019, January. IoT applications in agriculture: A systematic literature review. In *2nd International Conference on ICTs in Agronomy and Environment* 68–76. Springer.

[17] Goraya, M. S., & Kaur, H. 2015. Cloud computing in agriculture. *HCTL Open International Journal of Technology Innovations and Research (IJTIR), 16*:2321–1814.

[18] Babu, S. M., Lakshmi, A. J., & Rao, B. T. 2015, April. A study on cloud based Internet of Things: CloudIoT. In *2015 Global Conference on Communication Technologies (GCCT)* 60–65. IEEE.

[19] Kamble, S. S., Gunasekaran, A., & Gawankar, S. A. 2020. Achieving sustainable performance in a data-driven agriculture supply chain: A review for research and applications. *International Journal of Production Economics, 219*:179–194.

[20] Zamora-Izquierdo, M. A., Santa, J., Martínez, J. A., Martínez, V., & Skarmeta, A. F. 2019. Smart farming IoT platform based on edge and cloud computing. *Biosystems Engineering*, *177*:4–17.

[21] Khattab, A., Abdelgawad, A., & Yelmarthi, K. (2016, December). Design and implementation of a cloud-based IoT scheme for precision agriculture. In *2016 28th International Conference on Microelectronics (ICM)* 201–204. IEEE.

[22] Manos, B., Polman, N., & Viaggi, D. 2011. *Agricultural and Environmental Informatics Governance and Management: Emerging Research Applications*. IGI Global.

[23] Paul, P. K. 2016. Cloud computing and virtualization in agricultural space: A knowledge survey. *Palgo Journal of Agriculture*, *4*:202–206

[24] Muangprathub, J., Boonnam, N., Kajornkasirat, S., Lekbangpong, N., Wanichsombat, A., & Nillaor, P. 2019. IoT and agriculture data analysis for smart farm. *Computers and Electronics in Agriculture*, *156*:467–474.

[25] Nayyar, A., & Puri, V. 2016. Smart farming: IoT based smart sensors agriculture stick for live temperature and moisture monitoring using Arduino, cloud computing & solar technology. In *Communication and Computing Systems - Proceedings of the International Conference on Communication and Computing Systems, ICCCS 2016*, 673–680. https://doi.org/10.1201/9781315364094-121.

[26] Tsekouropoulos, G., Andreopoulou, Z., Koliouska, C., Koutroumanidis, T., & Batzios, C. 2013. Internet functions in marketing: Multicriteria ranking of agricultural SMEs websites in Greece. *Agrárinformatika/Journal of Agricultural Informatics*, *4*:22–36.

[27] Na, A., & Isaac, W. 2016, January. Developing a human-centric agricultural model in the IoT environment. In *2016 International Conference on Internet of Things and Applications (IOTA)* 292–297. IEEE.

[28] Adão, T., Hruška, J., Pádua, L., Bessa, J., Peres, E., Morais, R., & Sousa, J. J. 2017. Hyperspectral imaging: A review on UAV-based sensors, data processing and applications for agriculture and forestry. *Remote Sensing*, *9*:1110.

[29] TongKe, F. 2013. Smart agriculture based on cloud computing and IOT. *Journal of Convergence Information Technology*, *8*:130–145.

[30] Nandyala, C. S., & Kim, H. K. 2016. Green IoT agriculture and healthcare application (GAHA). *International Journal of Smart Home*, *10*:289–300.

[31] Paul, P. K. 2013.Information and knowledge requirement for farming and agriculture domain. *International Journal of Soft Computing Bio Informatics*, *4*:80–84

[32] Bauckhage, C., & Kersting, K. 2013. Data mining and pattern recognition in agriculture. *KI-Künstliche Intelligenz*, *27*:313–324.

[33] Liu, S., Guo, L., Webb, H., Ya, X., & Chang, X. 2019. Internet of things monitoring system of modern eco-agriculture based on cloud computing. *IEEE Access*, *7*:37050–37058.

[34] Paul, P. K., Bhuimali, A., Sinha, R. R., Aithal, P. S., Saavedra, R., & Aremu, B. 2020. Artifcial intelligence and robotics in agriculture and allied areas: A study. *International Journal of Bioinformatics and Biological Sciences*, *8*:1–5.

[35] Ojha, T., Misra, S., & Raghuwanshi, N. S. 2015. Wireless sensor networks for agriculture: The state-of-the-art in practice and future challenges. *Computers and Electronics in Agriculture*, *118*:66–84.

[36] Paul, P. K. 2015. Information and communication technology and information: Their role in tea cultivation and marketing in the context of developing countries—A theoretical approach. *Current Trends in Biotechnology and Chemical Research*, *5*:155–161.

[37] Paul, P. K., Bhuimali, A., Sinha, R. R., Tiwary, K. S., Baby, P., & Deka, G. C. 2020. Agricultural informatics: The emerging field with references to potentiality as post doctoral certificate programs. *International Journal of Information Science and Computing*, *7*:01–13.

[38] Rezník, T., Charvát, K., Lukas, V., Charvát Jr, K., Horáková, Š., & Kepka, M. 2015, September. Open data model for (precision) agriculture applications and agricultural pollution monitoring. In *Environmental Information and ICT for Sustainability 2015*. Atlantis Press.

[39] Ozdogan, B., Gacar, A., & Aktas, H. 2017. Digital agriculture practices in the context of agriculture 4.0. *Journal of Economics Finance and Accounting*, 4:186–193.

[40] Paul, P. K., Sinha, R. R., Aithal, P. S., Saavedra, R., & Aremu, B. 2020. Agro informatics with reference to features, functions and emergence as a discipline in agricultural sciences: An analysis. *Asian Journal of Information Science & Technology (AJIST)*, *10*:110–120.

12 IoT and Big Data Analytics-Based Smart System for Precision Agriculture

*Sangini Miharia, Shelly Garg, and
Sudhanshu Srivastava*
University of Petroleum & Energy Studies

CONTENTS

DOI: 10.1201/9781003330875-12

12.1 INTRODUCTION

12.1.1 OVERVIEW

Agricultural growth is necessary to develop the economic conditions of the country. As per 2011 Agricultural Census of India, out of 1300 million Indian population, 61.5% population is sub-urban and dependent on agriculture to a large extent. There are 159.6 million faring households in India. Majority out of this are small-scale farmers and have very small capital investment. Often they fail to obtain the expected outcome. This happens either due to extensive pest and insect attack, or due to misjudgment of the soil conditions or climate. Thus, the close and accurate monitoring of factors, such as moisture on land, humidity, temperature of the area, and even the pH of the soil becomes necessary for the production of best-quality lands. Integrating automation and computer-based algorithms into the system can benefit the farmers, as they provide information at real time about the condition of their land and crops at their fingertips. This information can help the farmer to understand if their field needs irrigation, or whether their crops are under the risk of being affected by a disease. This project discusses the development of such a model at an affordable price, so that it may come to the benefit of the small-scale planters [1].

12.1.2 OBJECTIVE

1. To design a system capable of analysing the factors of soil that affects the cultivation of crops.
2. Design a system that helps the farmers to gain more profit.
3. Capture and convert solar energy to electric current that can be utilised by the system and supply surplus energy to the grid.
4. Enhancement of plant health and soil quality through automation.
5. Accurate prediction of plant diseases.
6. Promote and provide novel methods of sustainable agriculture.

12.1.3 Need of the Project

The paramount interest of this project is to promote agriculture through ways that was unfamiliar before. It helps planters and farmers to obtain multilevel income. It also aims at increasing the production of a farm through accurate measurement of different factors that affect the crop. It also helps in prediction of diseases that could possible affect the crops at a very early stage. Thus, this model helps to improve the production quantitatively and qualitatively [2].

Our aim is to obtain values of parameters such as, moisture in the soil, atmospheric temperature and humidity and pH, which will influence the plant growth. The system analyses the data and triggers action like controlling irrigation system, provide warnings for the farmers, etc. By controlling these factors, the effects of seasonal changes on plant health can be controlled [3].

12.1.4 Work Flow (Figure 12.1)

12.1.5 Proposed System

This project puts forward a proposal to develop a device that can monitor various environmental conditions crucial for the plant, such as soil moisture, humidity, temperature, pH value, and also keep an eye on the its growth. Successful integration of sensors and its communication helps the device to perform various actions, such as run a pump and activate the irrigation system when the value of the moisture content of the soil falls below the threshold level or maintain the soil moisture at a particular level, the system can be modified and integrated into a poly-house, and thus it can perform automatic control of temperature, the system when placed in a field can monitor its surrounding and keep a check on the safety of the crops by scanning for rodents or other animals that might be detrimental to the crops and sound alarms to notify the user. The system ultimately needs power to activate the irrigation system and keep the system active. As a solution for this problem, the design we are suggesting depends on energy from the sun, and thus it can keep running and perform its function. Solar cells that are ideally installed on the device result in a structure that resembles the branches of a tree. The energy produced by the cells can be stored on a battery and can even be utilised later when the sunlight cannot alone sustain the system and also to power the circuit. The excess power, if generated, can be always transferred to the grid. A Raspberry Pi will be used as a central system to gather as well as process all the information, so the sensors as well as actuators have been connected to the pi. All of the operations will be carried out and controlled through a smart IoT-based device remotely or a computer [3].

12.1.6 Existing System

For over a century, we have been seeking an alternate source of energy. The conventional forms of energy are non-renewable and not ecofriendly. In the modern era, solar energy is proved to be efficient, ecofriendly and abundant availability. But the only challenge faced by solar energy is a method of harnessing it [4].

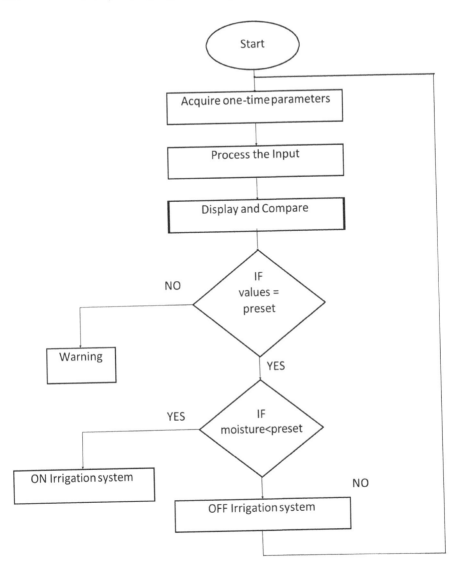

FIGURE 12.1 Work flow.

After years of research and development, solar energy has been feasible on a large scale of electronic appliances, such as street lights, traffic lights, vaporisers, heat treatment, etc. Since solar energy is abundantly available, it can be incorporated with modern day agriculture. Indian agriculture faces so many challenges like erratic power supply, scarcity of water, un-monitored irrigation, etc. Using solar energy would provide a solution for the crisis faced by the farmers. In the year 1998, a scientist named Gleisdorf from Austria, designed a 7KW solar tree. A bunch of solar panels were arranged on a tree-inspired model. These solar trees were powered at various locations like schools, museums, public parks, etc. Over the years, these solar trees have evolved in their design and methodology. In the year 2013, a study was conducted on a solar tree that used nano-wired photovoltaic cells. The results showed that it was five times more efficient than the conventional ones [5].

These solar trees were also used in assisting agriculture by powering an automatic irrigation system. This system included a moisture sensor that monitored the moisture level of the soil. The sensor was connected to a water pump. The pump would function based on the readings of the sensor. This system solved the issue of erratic power supply and irrigation [6].

12.1.7 MOTIVATION

There are already many proposed models in the market, but to a common man, it's not available at a rate that is available to him. Many farmers suicide due to the lack of income or due to the failure of a successful yield, which is left unnoticed among the city dwellers who know very little about the process and the pain farmers go through to develop one handful of rice grains. And about people who would like to cultivate but have very less agricultural land have the option of carrying out terrace farming, which can also be automated if at all they are busy with some work and forget to water the field; the system would automatically sense the water level in the soil, calculate if the level of water is low, and accordingly will irrigate the soil. It also has a warning system; let us consider paddy fields, and the enemy of every rice cultivator are crayfish. Sensors also help to detect these unwanted creatures [7]. So, this project aims to be able to provide the farmer with power, soil and crop monitoring systems, and also a method to earn more for those who want to begin cultivation on their own. Many may think that, if the project is powered by solar energy, why don't we convert the entire farmer's land into a solar farm by paying the farmer an amount as a rental for his land. But this would destroy the fertile agricultural land [8]. So, to preserve the agricultural land as well as to earn more money and to keep have an extra lookout, it would be useful to farmers if they install this setup in their lands at various positions based on the location of cultivation and also keeping in mind the path of the sun. About the extra income that the farmer receives, if he is generating a certain amount of electricity and is excess after all his consumption, he has the option to let it into the grid where the electricity board would pay him for the units that are fed into the grid [9].

12.1.8 ADVANTAGES AND DISADVANTAGES

12.1.8.1 Advantages [10]
- Sustainable energy source.
- Reduces manpower and labour cost.
- Helps in producing high yield.
- Enhances plant health.
- Predicts diseases that might affect the plant.
- Automation.

12.1.8.2 Disadvantages [11]

- Higher initial cost.
- Requires multiple module installations.
- Limitations due to corrosion of components.
- Requires sunlight.
- Installation besides tall trees would be a challenge.

12.2 LITERATURE REVIEW

12.2.1 RELATED TO HARNESSING SOLAR ENERGY

12.2.1.1 Why Solar Energy?

Farhan Hyder, K Sudhakar and Rizalman Mamat did a study on the merits of harnessing solar energy. They have made an attempt to review the required components and its design. The research paper all the more caters the challenges related with this technology and promotes future directions in research [12].

12.2.1.2 Nanowire Solar Cells Design

R. and C. Bhuvaneswari mentioned this in their article *Idea to Design a Solar Tree Using Nanowire Solar Cells*. Rajeshwari noted that 'Nanoparticles exhibit a number of distinctive features relative to bulk material'. These nanowire solar cells solar tree model can be used in our project design. A single nanowire concentrates the sunlight up to 15 times more than the typical sunlight intensity [13].

12.2.1.3 Achieving Maximum Efficiency in Harnessing Solar Energy

Kishore Gaikwad and Smitha Lokhande have discussed about a method to increase efficiency. They have us an algorithm called as 'Novel Maximum Power Point Tracking'. The control system constantly monitors temperature and irradiance. The paper covers various topics, such as design, simulation and practical implementation of MPPT algorithm using DC–DC Converter [14].

12.2.2 RELATED TO MOISTURE SENSOR NETWORK

12.2.2.1 Smart Irrigation System

S. Harishankar and R. Sathish Kumar in their research paper titled *Smart Solar Powered Irrigation System* have developed a water flow control that was automated using moisture sensor, which is powered by solar energy. It is a proposed solution for the ongoing energy crisis faced by Indian farmers [15].

12.2.2.2 Moisture Monitor Network

To demonstrate the responsiveness, robustness and longevity of a moisture monitor network, Rachel Cardell-Oliver, Mark Kramer, Keith Smettem and Kevin Mayer conducted field testing. Their article analyses the effectiveness of a reactive network, and details how it was designed and implemented for environmental soil moisture monitoring [16].

12.2.3 RELATED TO HUMIDITY AND TEMPERATURE MEASUREMENT

12.2.3.1 Why Use DHT11 for this Project?

Ni Tianlong (Microcontrollers and Embedded Systems 6, 026, 2010) has discussed the merits of using DHT11 humidity and temperature sensor for monitoring humidity and temperature. He has also described an efficient application in the DHT11 temperature and humidity control system [17].

12.3 PROJECT IMPLEMENTATION

12.3.1 HARDWARE (TABLE 12.1)

12.3.1.1 Raspberry Pi 3 Model B [1]

Obtaining the data, processing the raw data obtained and giving instructions to the actuators are the main functions that cannot be avoided. These important jobs are performed by one single component that makes the central controlling unit—the Raspberry Pi. It is a compact size of computer with a 1.2GHz Broadcom processor. The sensors are connected to various pins of the device and is programmed using python codes. Even though there are many models of the system that are available, the one used for this project is Pi 3 Model B [18].

12.3.1.2 FC-28 Soil Moisture Sensor [2]

The moisture in the soil has to be monitored, so as to determine when the irrigation system has to be switched on and off. As for some cultivations maintaining the moisture content is of cardinal importance, its presence is measured using sensors of these kind. LM393 is a probe-type sensor capable of obtaining information regarding the soil moisture by performing comparative operations with preset values. It gives output either as a high or low signal [19]. The sensor has four pins, namely Vcc, Digital output, Analog output and GN. The sensor works on the capacitance to measure the amount of water content of the soil that can be otherwise explained as dielectric permittivity. By putting the sensor under the soil, the data about the percentage of water that is there in the soil can be reported [20] (Table 12.2).

TABLE 12.1
List of Electronic Components

S. No.	Name	Quantity
1	Raspberry PI 3B	1
2	FC-28 soil moisture sensor	1
3	MCP3008 ADC	1
4	DHT11 humidity sensor	1
5	PH sensor probe type	1
6	HCSR501 PIR sensor	1
7	Relays 5V single channel	3

TABLE 12.2
Specifications of FC-28 Soil Moisture Sensor

S. No.	Parameter	Specification
1	Input voltage	3.3–5 V
2	Output voltage	0–4.2 V
3	Input current	35 mA
4	Output signal type	Both analog and digital
5	Working temperature	10–30°C

12.3.1.3   MCP3008 [3]

To solve the problem with analogue pins, an analogue-to-digital converter called the 10-bit, 8-channel MCP3008 IC is employed. SPI bus protocol is used to accept analogue input values from the Raspberry Pi. Four Raspberry Pi along with eight analogue inputs are used, rather than the power and ground pins. It produces output values in the range of 0 and 1023 (0 stands for OV and 1023 for 3.3V) [21].

12.3.1.4   Humidity Sensor DHT-11 [4]

Temperature and humidity are other factors of the climate that directly affect the cultivation. Continuous monitoring of these factors enables the user to keep track of the changes in the weather conditions and take necessary actions before the changes have a harsh effect on the crop. The sensor that measures these factors in this design is DHT11. This employs a unique method of digital signal capture, together with temperature- and humidity-measuring equipment [22] (Table 12.3).

12.3.1.5   pH Sensor [5]

Adapting scientific methods of agriculture will benefit the farmers in ways that otherwise cannot be obtained. One such method is controlled and measured administration of fertilisers. However, it cannot be possible if information regarding the chemical properties of the soil are not available to the farmer. One such factor is the soil's pH [23]. Maintaining the pH of the soil ensures that the perfect quality of the products are maintained. The pH sensor is available in various configurations; the one used in this project is a probe type [24]. A glass membrane at the sensor's tip permits hydrogen ions to diffuse into the outer layer. The bulky ions are still present in the solution, though, and the difference in concentration results in the generation of a very weak current that can be measured and standardised [25] (Table 12.4).

12.3.1.6   HC-SR501 Pir Motion Detector [6]

Rodents and other animals sometimes make things harder for the farmers. Sometimes people even will have to stay awake and watch their farms 24 hours a day. With this in mind, we have integrated a 'Passive Infrared Sensor' into the system [26]. The module that we are using is HC-SR501. It uses the infrared technology; it detects motion based on the infrared heat signatures present around an object. This feature of the device makes it the most suitable choice for detecting intruders [27] (Table 12.5).

TABLE 12.3
Specifications of Humidity Sensor DHT-11

S. No.	Parameter	Specification
1	Operating voltage	3–5.5 V
2	Current supply	0.5–2.5 mA
3	Output signal type	Serial
4	Temperature range	0–50°C
5	Humidity range	20%–90%
6	Accuracy	±1°C and ±1%

TABLE 12.4
Specifications of pH Sensor

S. No.	Parameter	Specification
1	Module power	5 V
2	Sensitivity	0.02 pH
3	Range	0–14 pH
4	Resolution	±0.001
5	Accuracy	±0.002
6	Working temperature	5–99°C

TABLE 12.5
Specifications of HC-SR501 PIR Motion Detector

S. No.	Parameter	Specification
1	Operating voltage	5–20 V
2	Quiescent current	<50 uA
3	Angle sensor	<110° cone angle
5	Sensing range	<120°, 0–7 m
6	Working temperature	15–70°C

12.3.1.7   DC Pump [7]

This type of pump can be used when the system has to be submerged in water. It provides considerable output without drawing huge amount of current. This has been used to demonstrate the working of automatic irrigation system in our project [28].

12.3.1.8   Micro-Sprinkler Irrigation

Just letting the water flow would actually have an adverse effect than positive effects. Thus, it is important to distribute the water uniformly. For this purpose, a micro-sprinkler is used. It uses a dancer that rotates when water comes and fills the inlet tube. This is nowadays used in almost all types of agriculture [29].

12.3.1.9   Solar Panel

Photovoltaic (PV) module is the scientific name for solar panels. In an aluminium (lightweight) framework, multiple photovoltaic cells are assembled to form a photovoltaic module. To generate direct-current electricity, the photovoltaic cells use the sun as its energy source. These photovoltaic cells are either connected in parallel or series electrically to produce higher voltages, higher currents and higher power levels [30]. Multiple photovoltaic cells are sealed in a laminate, which is environmentally protective, which forms the basic building block of a photovoltaic system, which in turn forms a module. Photovoltaic modules consist of multiple photovoltaic panels put together as a single pre-wired, field-installable unit.

A solar array is a system to generate power, which is made up of several photovoltaic modules and panels. In all the photovoltaic modules, the photovoltaic effect is used to produce energy from solar photons. The load-bearing component of photovoltaic modules is typically a wafer-based crystalline silicon (c-Si) cell; however, thin-film cells are occasionally used as well. Every solar panel has a photovoltaic junction on the back that serves as an output interface and is connected externally using MC4 connectors for simple weatherproofing [31].

Standards generally used in photovoltaic modules:

- IEC 61215 (crystalline silicon performance)
- IEC 61646 (thin-film performance)
- IEC 61730 (all modules, safety)
- ISO 9488 Solar energy
- UL 1703 from Underwriters Laboratories
- UL 1741 from Underwriters Laboratories
- UL 2703 from Underwriters Laboratories
- CE mark
- Electrical Safety Tester (EST) Series (EST-460, EST-22V, EST-22H, EST-110).

The maximum DC power output (watts) of photovoltaic modules and arrays is commonly used to evaluate their performance under STC. Standard test conditions consist of an air mass 1.5 spectral distribution, $1000\,W/m^2$ of incident solar radiation and a 25°C (77°F) operating temperature for the module. Since these settings are not usually representative of how photovoltaic modules and arrays operate in the field, the majority of the modules has a projected lifespan of 20–30 years, and actual performance is often 85%–90% of the STC rating. Typical modules will have ratings ranging from 75 W to 350 W and will be as large as $1\,m \times 2\,m$ (3 ft by 7 ft). When exposed to sunlight, a PV array produces electricity, but other components are required to conduct, control, convert, distribute and store the energy the array produces. Depending on the system's functional and operational requirements, the precise components required may comprise core components such as DC–AC power inverter, battery bank, system and battery controller, auxiliary energy sources and occasionally the prescribed electrical load (appliances). Hardware for various balance of system (BOS) components, including wiring, over-current, surge protection, disconnect and other power processing tools, is also included. When needed (during the night or during times of cloudy weather), batteries are frequently employed in PV systems to store energy generated by the PV array during the day and to provide it to electrical loads. Most of the solar panel options currently available in the market are:

- Mono-crystalline
- Poly-crystalline (multicrystalline)
- Thin film

The above-said three categories vary in manufacturing process, appearance, costs and installations. Each type has its own unique pros and cons, which should be considered while purchasing, keeping in mind factors like geographical location, application of the system, environment in which the panels are going to be installed, etc.

- Mono-crystalline panels
- Pros:
- High efficiency and performance
- Aesthetics
- Cons:
- Expensive
- Poly-crystalline panels
- Pros:
- Less expensive when compared to mono-crystalline panels
- Cons:
- Lower efficiency compared to mono-crystalline panels
- Thin-film panels
- Pros:
- Portable and flexible
- Aesthetics
- Light weight
- Cons:
- The lowest efficiency of the lot

12.3.1.10.1 *Efficiency*

Mono-crystalline panels are the most efficient panels and power capacities of all kinds of panel. Generally, most poly-crystalline solar panels have efficiencies between 15% and 17%, while the majority of mono-crystalline solar panels frequently achieve efficiencies higher than 20%. Due to their efficiency and availability in larger wattage modules, mono-crystalline solar panels have a tendency to produce more energy than other types of panels. Many mono-crystalline solar panels have power capacities greater than 300 W, with some exceeding 350 W. Contrary, poly-crystalline solar panels often have lower wattages. This need not imply that mono-crystalline and poly-crystalline solar panels aren't the same size in terms of their physical dimensions; in actuality, of various kinds of solar panels, each basically consists of 60 silicon cells; but for large-scale installation, these panels can vary, having 72 or 96 cells. However, mono-crystalline panels can generate more electricity even with the same number of cells. While the efficiency of thin-film solar panels is often closer to 11%.

The functional and operational requirements, component configurations, connections to other power sources and electrical load requirements are frequently used to categorise photovoltaic power systems. Stand-alone systems and grid-connected or utility-interactive systems are two of the main classifications. In addition to operating independently or being connected to the utility grid and supplying Direct-Current and/or Alternate-Current electricity, photovoltaic systems can be coupled to other energy sources and energy storage systems. Grid-connected or utility-interactive PV systems are designed to function alongside and in addition to the electrical utility grid. The inverter, which is frequently referred to as a power conditioning device, is crucial in grid-connected PV systems (PCU). The PCU transforms the DC power produced by the PV array into AC electricity, while adhering to the utility's criteria for voltage and power quality. When it is not in use, the utility grid quickly stops supplying power to the grid. In many cases, at an on-site distribution panel or service door, the AC output circuits of the PV system are interfaced with the electrical utility network in both the directions. When the output of the PV system exceeds the demand from the on-site load, the AC power produced by the PV system can be used to either back-feed the grid or to satisfy on-site electrical needs.

When compared to conventional power-generating technologies, photovoltaic systems provide a number of advantages. PV systems can be used for either distributed or centralised power generation, and they can be configured to meet a wide range of operational requirements and applications. PV systems are portable in some circumstances, easily expandable and modular. Additionally, they lack any moving parts. The PV system has several compelling features, including energy independence and environmental friendliness. PV systems operate silently and without emitting any noise or pollution because to their free fuel—sunlight. Well-designed and installed PV systems frequently require little maintenance and have extended service lives. The largest barrier to the current technology is the high cost of PV modules and equipment (in comparison to other energy sources). As a result, the economic return on investment for PV systems is slow. In some circumstances, the surface area requirements for PV arrays may be a limiting constraint.

The output of each panel is calculated by:

(The Wattage of the Solar Panel) × (Average Hours of Sun Light) × 75% = Daily Watt hours

Let us consider that we have a 300-watt panel, and the place of installation receives about 6 hours of sunlight, and then

300 × 6 × 75% = 1350 watt-hours 1350/1000 = 1.35 kilowatt hours for a panel

12.4 MECHANICAL DESIGN

12.4.1 Prototype Design (Figure 12.2)

12.4.2 Concept Design (Figure 12.3)

12.4.3 Material

One of the most often used building materials, mild steel is exceptionally robust and can be produced from easily available natural resources. Due to its comparatively

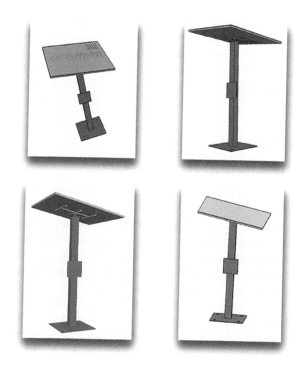

FIGURE 12.2 Prototype design.

FIGURE 12.3 Concept design.

low carbon content, it is referred to as mild steel. Because there is so little carbon in mild steel, it is extremely robust and has a great resistance to breaking. Strength is a challenging concept in materials science. Mild steel has a high tensile and impact strength, because it is fairly pliable, especially when cold, in contrast to higher carbon steels, which typically shatters or breaks under stress; and only pressure causes it to flex or distort.

12.4.4 BLOCK DIAGRAM (FIGURE 12.4)

12.5 CONCLUSION AND FUTURE SCOPE

The study seeks to answer the research question: how can solar energy be harnessed for a smarter agriculture? Solar energy makes the system self-sufficient; it also might quench the energy needs of a small-scale farmer. While designing the system, one of the factors that we gave utmost important is its affordability. However, rigorous tests have to be performed in order to ensure that it satisfies the demands that the user might have. The younger generation is not benevolent to agriculture. This could be because the conditions of work are far more austere and not as comfortable as other fields, or maybe because obtaining a harvest that is equivalent to the salary that they might be offered otherwise is a task so difficult. This project would also address such social issues and would definitely involve people into smart modern farming. Solar TREE has many applications in the future, like setting up EV charging stations that

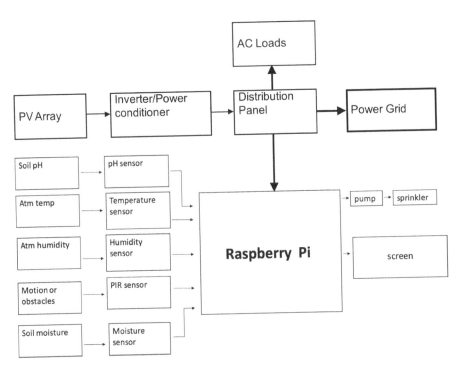

FIGURE 12.4 Block diagram.

are powered completely by a tree nearby or above it. In the case of agriculture Smart Solar TREE, the up-coming generations don't have any idea of how various pulses, grains, etc. are cultivated, and the preservation of fertile land is necessary for their learning. It can be used for greenhouse farming where space below the tree is utilised. Already many farmers use solar-powered pumps for irrigation purposes with only the knowledge that a solar panel can be used only for the generation of electricity and to power only the motor. It fulfils the energy demand of the people, therefore, decreasing the frequent power cuts in starving areas.

We have no idea if we are letting in the right amount of water for irrigating the land and if the amount of fertilisers is right or not; we don't know all this until all the yield has been lost or until we send the soil to a lab for testing. This Smart Solar TREE can be the solution to decrease the deaths of many farmers, and also with the increasing technology and using data analytics the system can determine if there is going to be rain, and based on that the fields can be watered. It aims at the management of spatial and temporal variability to increase the returns based on the inputs and reduction of environmental impact. In the future, the whole farm can be managed by Decision Support Systems (DSS), which aims at optimisation of the returns on the inputs yet preserving the resources. Widespread use of GPS, GNSS and aerial imaging by drones allowed the creation of a schematic of the entire farm, and it also would help in key variables like crop yield, terrain features, pH content, moisture levels, organic matter level, etc.

REFERENCES

1. Gondchawar, N., & Kawitkar, R. S. (2016). IoT based smart agriculture. *International Journal of advanced research in Computer and Communication Engineering*, 5(6), 838–842.
2. N. Suma, S. R. Samson, S. Saranya, G. Shanmugapriya, R. Subhashri, "IOT based smart agriculture monitoring system", *International Journal on Recent and Innovation Trends in Computing and Communication*, vol. 9, 2015.
3. K. Lakshmisudha, S. Hegde, N. Kale, S. Iyer, 'Smart precision based agriculture using sensors', *International Journal of Computer Applications*, vol. 11, 2011.
4. V. Vidya Devi, G. Meena Kumari, "Real-time automation and monitoring system for modernized agriculture", *International Journal of Review and Research in Applied Sciences and Engineering*, vol. 7, 2013.
5. M. Chetan Dwarkani, R. Ganesh Ram, S. Jagannathan, R. Priyatharshini, "Smart farming system using sensors for agricultural task automation", *IEEE International Conference on Technological Innovations in ICT for Agriculture and Rural Development* (TIAR), pp. 49–53, 2015. doi: 10.1109/TIAR.2015.7358530
6. S. R. Nandurkar, V. R. Thool, R. C. Thool, "Design and development of precision agriculture system using wireless sensor network", *IEEE International Conference on Automation, Control, Energy and Systems (ACES)*, Adisaptagram, pp. 1–6, 2014. doi: 10.1109/ACES.2014.6808017
7. J. Gutiérrez, J. F. Villa-Medina, A. Nieto-Garibay, M. Á. Porta-Gándara, "Automated irrigation system using a wireless sensor network and GPRS module", *IEEE Transactions on Instrumentation and Measurements*, vol. 63, no. 1, pp. 166–176, 2013. doi: 10.1109/TIM.2013.2276487
8. M. Jhuria, A. Kumar, R. Borse, "Image processing for smart farming: Detection of disease and fruit grading", *IEEE Second International Conference on Image Information Processing (ICIIP)*, Shimla, pp. 521–526, 2013. doi: 10.1109/ICIIP.2013.6707647

9. S. A. Jaishetty, R. Patil, "IoT sensor networkbased approach for agricultural field monitoring and control", *IJRET: International Journal of Research in Engineering and Technology*, vol. 5, no. 06, pp. 45–48, 2016.

10. N. Suma, S. R. Samson, S. Saranya, G. Shanmugapriya, R. Subhashri, "IOT based smart agriculture monitoring system", *International Journal on Recent and Innovation Trends in computing and communication*, vol. 5, no. 2, pp. 177–181, 2017.

11. C. Cambra, S. Sendra, J. Lloret, L. Garcia, "An IoT service-oriented system for agriculture monitoring", *2017 IEEE International Conference on Communications (ICC)*, Paris, pp. 1–6, 2017. doi: 10.1109/ICC.2017.7996640

12. F. Karim, "Monitoring system using web of things in precision agriculture", *Procedia Computer Science*, vol. 110, pp. 402–409, 2017.

13. A. Khattab, A. Abdelgawad, & K. Yelmarthi, "Design and implementation of a cloud-based IoT scheme for precision agriculture", *2016 28th International Conference on Microelectronics (ICM)*, Giza, pp. 201–204, 2016, December. doi: 10.1109/ICM.2016.7847850

14. I. Mat, M. R. M. Kassim, A. N. Harun, & I. M. Yusoff, "IoT in precision agriculture applications using wireless moisture sensor network", *2016 IEEE Conference on Open Systems (ICOS)*, Langkawi, pp. 24–29, 2016, October. doi: 10.1109/ICOS.2016.7881983

15. S. R. Prathibha, A. Hongal, & M. P. Jyothi, "IOT Based monitoring system in smart agriculture", *2017 International Conference on Recent Advances in Electronics and Communication Technology (ICRAECT)*, Bangalore, pp. 81–84, 2017, March. doi: 10.1109/ICRAECT.2017.52

16. H. Channe, S. Kothari, & D. Kadam, "Multidisciplinary model for smart agriculture using internet-of-things (IoT) sensors cloud-computing mobile-computing & big-data analysis", *Int. J. Computer Technology & Applications*, vol. 6, no. 3, pp. 374–382, 2015.

17. C. Yoon, M. Huh, S. G. Kang, J. Park, & C. Lee, "Implement smart farm with IoT technology", *2018 20th International Conference on Advanced Communication Technology (ICACT)*, Chuncheon, pp. 749–752, 2018, February. doi: 10.23919/ICACT.2018.8323908

18. N. Gondchawar, & R. S. Kawitkar, "IoT based smart agriculture", *International Journal of advanced research in Computer and Communication Engineering*, vol. 5, no. 6, pp. 838–842, 2016.

19. K. A. Patil, & N. R. Kale, "A model for smart agriculture using IoT", *2016 International Conference on Global Trends in Signal Processing Information Computing and Communication (ICGTSPICC)*, Jalgaon, pp. 543–545, 2016, December. doi: 10.1109/ICGTSPICC.2016.7955360

20. M. K. Gayatri, J. Jayasakthi, G. A. Mala, "Providing smart agricultural solutions to farmers for better yielding using IoT", *2015 IEEE Technological Innovation in ICT for Agriculture and Rural Development (TIAR)*, Chennai, pp. 40–43, July 2015. doi: 10.1109/TIAR.2015.7358528

21. L. Yuanguai, W. N. Long, W. U. Jiang, "Application of zigbee wireless sensor network in precision agriculture [J]", *Journal of Qiongzhou University*, vol. 5, pp. 32–34, 2009.

22. C. Verdouw, S. Wolfert, B. Tekinerdogan, "Internet of things in agriculture", *CAB Reviews: Perspectives in Agriculture Veterinary Science Nutrition and Natural Resources*, vol. 11, no. 35, pp. 1–12, 2016.

23. S. Veenadhari, B. Misra, C. D. Singh, "Machine learning approach for forecasting crop yield based on climatic parameters", *2014 International Conference on Computer Communication and Informatics*, Coimbatore, pp. 1–5, 2014, January. doi: 10.1109/ICCCI.2014.6921718

24. N. Khera, D. Shukla, P. Sharma, I. G. Dar, "Development of microcontroller based lemon ripening condition monitoring system", *2017 6th International Conference on Reliability Infocom Technologies and Optimization (Trends and Future Directions) (ICRITO)*, Noida, pp. 591–593, 2017, September. doi: 10.1109/ICRITO.2017.8342496

25. M. Jhuria, A. Kumar, R. Borse, "Image processing for smart farming: Detection of disease and fruit grading", *2013 IEEE Second International Conference on Image Information Processing (ICIIP-2013)*, Shimla, pp. 521–526, 2013, December. doi: 10.1109/ICIIP.2013.6707647

26. J. Gutiérrez, J. F. Villa-Medina, A. Nieto-Garibay and M. Á. Porta-Gándara, "Automated irrigation system using a wireless sensor network and GPRS module", *IEEE transactions on instrumentation and measurement*, vol. 63, no. 1, pp. 166–176, 2013.

27. I. Mohanraj, K. Ashokumar, J. Naren, "Field monitoring and automation using IOT in agriculture domain", *Procedia Computer Science*, vol. 93, pp. 931–939, 2016.

28. S. R. Nandurkar, V. R. Thool, R. C. Thool, "Design and development of precision agriculture system using wireless sensor network", *2014 First International Conference on Automation Control Energy and Systems (ACES)*, Adisaptagram, pp. 1–6, 2014, February. doi: 10.1109/ACES.2014.6808017

29. S. A. Nikolidakis, D. Kandris, D. D. Vergados, C. Douligeris, "Energy efficient automated control of irrigation in agriculture by using wireless sensor networks", *Computers and Electronics in Agriculture*, vol. 113, pp. 154–163, 2015.

30. S. Roy, R. Ray, A. Roy, S. Sinha, G. Mukherjee, S. Pyne, "IoT big data science & analytics cloud computing and mobile app based hybrid system for smart agriculture", *2017 8th Annual Industrial Automation and Electromechanical Engineering Conference (IEMECON)*, Bangkok, pp. 303–304, 2017, August. doi: 10.1109/IEMECON.2017.8079610

31. S. Namani and B. Gonen, "Smart Agriculture Based on IoT and Cloud Computing," *2020 3rd International Conference on Information and Computer Technologies (ICICT)*, San Jose, CA, 2020, pp. 553–556, doi: 10.1109/ICICT50521.2020.00094.

Index

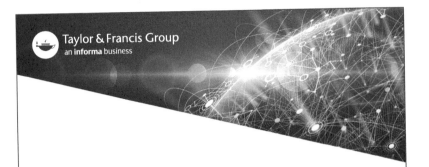